LORD CHANGE ME

JAMES MACDONALD

MOODY PUBLISHERS
CHICAGO

Edited by Neil Wilson
Interior design: Smartt Guys Design
Cover design: Walk in the Word

Library of Congress Cataloging-in-Publication Data

MacDonald, James
    Lord Change Me / by James MacDonald.
        p. cm.
    ISBN: 978-0-8024-0526-5
    1. Christian life. 2. Spiritual life—Christianity. 3. Change—Religious life—Christianity.
I. Title.

BV4501.2 .M22744 2000
248.4—dc21

99-058539

We hope you enjoy this book from Moody Publishers. Our goal is to provide high-quality, thought-provoking books and products that connect truth to your real needs and challenges. For more information on other books and products written and produced from a biblical perspective, go to www.moodypublishers.com or write to:

Moody Publishers
820 N. LaSalle Boulevard
Chicago, IL 60610

3 5 7 9 10 8 6 4

Printed in the United States of America

About the Author

JAMES MACDONALD is the founding and senior pastor of Harvest Bible Chapel in Rolling Meadows, Illinois. Pastor MacDonald has written many books, including *Lord, Change My Attitude, When Life is Hard,* and *Gripped by the Greatness of God.* Pastor MacDonald's teaching can be heard on Walk in the Word, a daily radio program heard on outlets across North America. Pastor MacDonald and his wife, Kathy, have three children and reside in the northwest suburbs of Chicago.

To Kathy,
my lifetime partner in love and service and change,
an exhorter, an encourager,
and an example

CONTENTS

AN INVITATION

H i! Thanks for picking up this copy of *Lord Change Me*. I know you're very busy and there are a lot of different books to choose from. This book is not for everyone, so please let me show respect for your time by helping you decide if this book is really for you.

The following explanations should help you settle quickly whether you need a book like this. Read each explanation and then answer the question that follows it.

First, this is a book to help people actually change. This is not for people who want to debate different strategies for change. It is not a book to argue about how to do it best and why the "other guys" are doing it wrong. It's not for the professor or pastor or counselor who wants to debate how change happens. It's for people who desperately want to change. In other words, this is a practical "how-to" manual, not a philosophical discussion of how people can change.

1. *Do* you want to change? Yes or No (circle one)

Second, this is a book about you *changing, not others.* It's about personal transformation. It's not intended to give you ammunition against the character flaws of those around you. It is a manual for a kind of do-it-yourself surgery. *Lord Change Me* is about locating and removing the "tumors" in your own life that are keeping you from the joy and happiness that your Creator longs to give you.

2. Do *you* want to change? Yes or No (circle one)

Third, this is a book about change, not growth. Growth is like a ship on a voyage: slow, steady progress toward the distant land of maturity. Change is much more radical. It's like the captain shouting: "Quick, start bailing; we're taking on water and if we don't fix the gash in the boat we're gonna go down!" Growth deals with increasing the strengths of who we already are, improving who I already am. Change is about becoming different—radically different as soon as possible!

Change requires the elimination of character traits and patterns of behavior that are doing damage to my life and those around me. Growth is about health and happiness and someday and steady. Change is about critical, now, I have to be different or the fallout will be big. Growth is about reformation; change is about transformation.

3. Do you want to *change*? Yes Or No (circle one)

Fourth, this book is about change according to God's Word, the Bible, not about personal reformation. With truckloads of self-help books and articles published calling for personal transformation, there is hardly a person among us who does not know the pain of trying and failing with a self-help methodology. If changing ourselves were possible, everyone would be doing it. Fact is, only God can change us! This is a book that explores God's pattern for people changing as found in the Bible, and excludes all other man-made plans. So much of so-called self-help is really just surface adjustment, a "makeover" that leaves the heart unchanged. **"Man looks on the outward appearance, but the LORD looks on the heart"** (1 Samuel 16:7).

4. Do you want to change *God's way*? Yes or No (circle one)

Finally, this is a book about "how" to change; it spends little time on "what" you must change or "why." If you have a hard time locating anything in yourself that really needs transformation, this book is not for you. If you know something is wrong, but you're not sure what, there are other books to help you locate the problem. This is a book for people who know what they need to change and are willing to do whatever it takes. They truly want to change.

5. Do you *want* to change? Yes or No (circle one)

If you're still reading, there is at least a big part of you that really wants to change. Maybe right now you're feeling the weight of your own character deficiencies. Maybe there is a sin that seems to keep coming back, that you think you have defeated, only to see it reappear in your life. Maybe your marriage is in trouble. Maybe you are enslaved to a habit and feeling the pain of falling flat on your face after you vowed (and really meant) you would never do "it" again. Maybe you're deeply wounding those you love and want to stop. Maybe you have a way of relating to people that pushes them away and causes you both much hurt. Maybe your life is turning out far different than you had thought and you want to get it going in a better direction before it is too late.

Whatever the specifics, if you believe there is a God and you are open to considering what the Bible says about how to change, *this book is for you!* If you picked this book up with your own problems in mind and really want to see a breakthrough for personal transformation, *this book is for you!*

I invite you to join me in discovering the areas in your life that need change, the biblical process for change, and the power behind lasting change. Change is *possible*. It's God's plan for our lives.

If you can say with sincerity, "Lord Change Me" this book is definitely for *you!* Read on.

JAMES MACDONALD

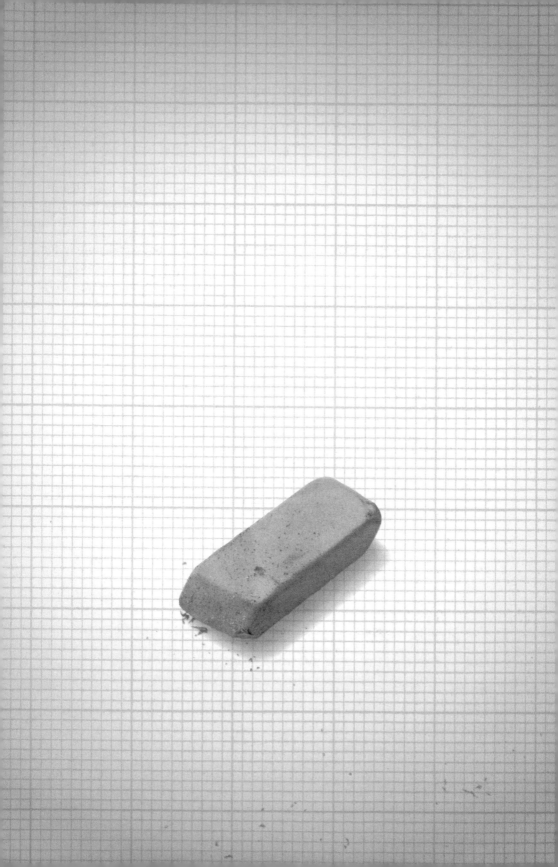

HOW TO MAKE THE MOST OF THIS BOOK

C hange is not easy. It is always difficult and sometimes painful. The results of change are phenomenally rewarding and fulfilling, but the process can be excruciating. For that reason, I am not going to pull any punches with you. This is not a book to curl up by the fire with, and you won't find any warm fuzzies in these pages. What you will find is the kind of truth that Jesus promised will **"set you free"** (John 8:32).

This book has three parts on the path to lasting change:

1. "The Preparation for Change." Three chapters will get you ready to change. You will learn to choose the right method, partner with God, and select the specific areas that need change first.

2. "The Process of Change." The next four chapters will describe the biblical method for saying no to sinful patterns and yes to the good things God desires for you.

3. "The Power to Change." We cannot change ourselves. Without God's help, our efforts to change will always fail. The book concludes with three chapters explaining how to experience the power of God personally and continuously.

Each chapter has five helpful tools to assist you in the journey toward change. The tools will help you understand key concepts and apply them in your life. Use each tool consistently and watch biblical change occur. The five are:

• "Say It in a Sentence." Each chapter begins with a summary of the truth of that chapter. Read it and you'll know where we are headed.

- A study of the Scriptures. Did you know that God wrote a book? With millions of copies sold every year and as many lives transformed by its truth, the Bible should be taken seriously by anyone who is serious about change. The Bible is the only book on change that carries the 100 percent endorsement of the Creator of the universe. Each chapter contains several sections, which detail a portion of God's pattern for change from the Bible.

- Study questions. Most, if not all, of the personal, behavioral problems we face in this world are the result of ignorance, rebellion, or discouragement. We don't know how to live—that's ignorance—or we know but are unwilling to conform to what we know—that's rebellion. Or perhaps we know and are willing to conform but have failed in our attempts and become discouraged. Those are three very different problems. The end of each chapter includes three kinds of questions designed to probe your life according to your greatest need. "Teacher Questions" will aim at your mind and seek to improve your understanding of a specific matter related to personal change, a sort of "quiz" to see if you are really getting it. In biblical times, prophets were generally pretty aggressive guys who went after sin in people's lives. "Prophet Questions" are designed to confront with direct, concise language. They might make you squirm a bit, but the goal is to challenge your will with truth you may have known but rebelled against. For some, the primary issue is not ignorance or rebellion; for you we have "Shepherd Questions." The goal of these questions is to promote hope. If you are struggling to find the strength to implement God's plan for change, honestly answering these questions should help. Answer all the questions honestly, and great things are going to happen in your life.

- "Let's Get to Work." The end of each chapter also includes a specific exercise to help you implement what you are learning. It is essential that you complete the exercise before moving on. At times it will be hard or embarrassing or awkward. If change were easy, everyone would be doing it. Let your passion to be different carry you through the "hard work" of change, and you will see results.

- "Look Up!" Once you have the truth downloaded to your life and experience, you need to go directly to God with it. Each chapter will close with a prayer that will help you verbalize what you are learning and connect with the only One who can give you the power to change.

Except for chapter 5, the study questions, exercises, and prayers that con-clude each chapter are in the same order. However, you may want to vary the order in which you complete them from chapter to chapter, depending on how the Lord is leading you. Feel free to do so. Also, several of the assignments will require a little writing. You may want to use a notebook or journal to record your progress.

Remember, this is not a book to help you "talk a better game," nor is it de-signed to fill your head with information. This book is about a different you. After much prayer and reflection, I believe I can promise you with 100 percent assurance that if you apply to your heart and life the biblical principles in this book, you will be changed!

And now a personal note. Please do not hear the directness of my commu-nication as coldness or indifference to the hurt that comes with your need to change. When I began in pastoral ministry over twenty-five years ago, I was out to change the world, but quickly and painfully learned that God was more inter-ested in changing me. The truths in this book are stained with my own tears of trying and failing and trying again to be the man God wants me to be (more on that later). Too much of the Christian writings in our day amuse and tickle with-out dispensing the transforming truth of the gospel. I will try to avoid that error. I am writing with the urgency of a loving heart for you and your situation.

You say, "You don't know my situation!" and you are right. But in the count-less hours I have spent praying and writing and preaching this material, I have probably thought of a situation similar to yours. I do care for you and want you to believe that change is possible. Your life can be much different than it is now. Yes—it can! *God loves you and wants to pour His transforming power into your life.*

In fact, that is the subject of the first chapter. So we are ready to begin. Let me take a moment just before we do and pray with you. My desire is that your heart and mind be ready for this message, and so here is a prayer on your behalf (one I have prayed in slightly different form during the development and writing of this book). Let's "Look Up" together, praying for the effectiveness of the message that follows.

LOOK UP!

Dear Father in heaven:

Thank You for loving us so faithfully. Thank You that Your love is not dependent on our performance. Thanks that You love us when we do what is wrong as much as when we do what is right. Please forgive us for using that truth as an excuse to keep on sinning.

Lord, I pray for the one holding this book right now, so precious to You, known so perfectly by You, yet loved so completely and eternally.

Lord, would You begin to create a hope in their heart that You will use these truths to change their lives? May they sense just now a growing hunger to discover what You have for them here.

May they have concentration as they read and diligence as they go to work in applying these truths. May Your Word bring light and Your Spirit bring hope. I ask for true life change and for the lasting joy You promised to those who obey Your Word. I am asking all this so that many more will come to know the transforming power of Jesus Christ and spread the fame of His name alone. Amen.

THE
PREPARATION
FOR
CHANGE

Personal change is kind of like building a home. Before you can begin, you have to prepare. You will need a builder, a blueprint, and materials if you hope to be successful. In the first three chapters I want to acquaint you with your Builder and Maker, who is God (see Hebrews 11:10), and help you pull together the basic materials for transformation.

Please don't be impatient with this part and rush to the process for change. Without preparing to change, you will never achieve your goal.

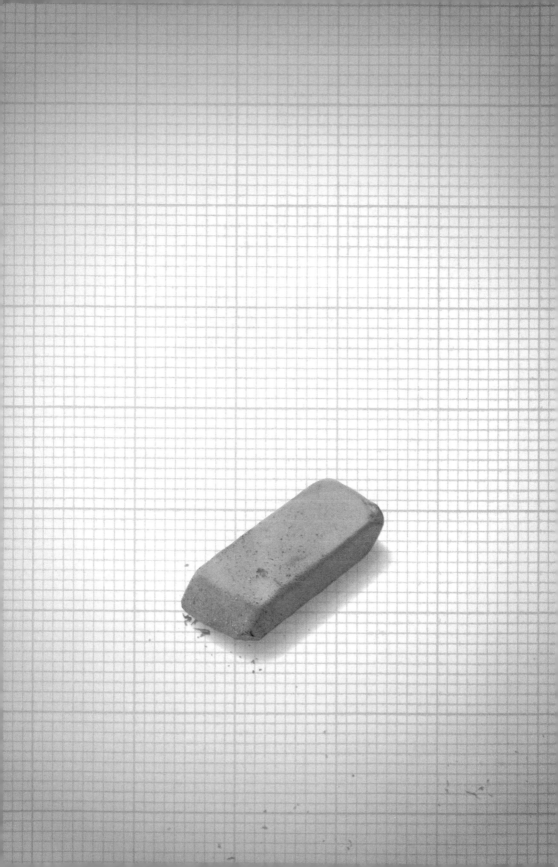

1

TAKE OUT THE GARBAGE

SAY IT IN A SENTENCE:
*True life change comes only through partnership with God
and begins by rejecting all self-centered change methods.*

I love to tell stories of change—dramatic, detailed accounts of the transforming power of almighty God. When I was writing the first edition of *Lord Change Me*, the curtain was coming down on the 20th century. The frenzy of the moment was Y2K and the fear that the end of computerized civilization was near. Among the retrospectives on the century, I don't remember much attention given to some of the remarkable people who became Christians during the previous 100 years. People like G. K. Chesterton, C. S. Lewis, Dorothy Sayers, A. W. Tozer, Billy Graham, and many other notables came to faith in Christ. All except the last one I listed have been dead for a while. The testimony of their lives is finished and sealed. They joined the race, kept the faith, and crossed the finish line. Other people came to faith in such unusual circumstances that their conversions were met with derision. Frankly, celebrity conversions are usually put in the same category with foxhole conversions and aren't expected to create lasting change. But some people change and their conversion stands the test of time. One remarkable story of God's grace features Chuck Colson. Now there's a guy who got changed! He was on President Richard Nixon's political team. He was the most brutal, ruthless, get-out-of-my-way-or-I'll-kill-you kind of guy. As a gung-ho presidential aide, he once said, "I would walk over my grandmother if necessary to assure the president's reelection."

In the early 1970s, however, Colson's whole world came crashing down. He pleaded guilty to obstruction of justice in the Watergate case and served seven months at Maxwell Federal Prison in Georgia. He was shamed before the whole world.

In the midst of that, Chuck Colson found a personal relationship with Jesus Christ. As he went into prison and began to articulate and grow in his faith, many people thought, "Yeah, right. Chuckie's got religion. What a joke. It'll never last." But you know what? It did. Chuck is no longer the celebrity he was in the 1970s but for believers, his story of change remains compelling.

Colson said, "I don't just want to be saved. I don't just want to be forgiven. I want to be changed." He has been changed and has emerged as one of the greatest Christian leaders in our world today. He is a powerful force. His life touches hundreds of thousands of men and women in prison every year through a ministry he began called Prison Fellowship. He's an author, writer, and leader who is tireless in his effort to get out the good news about Jesus. Colson has received many awards for his impact upon our world.

Chuck Colson went from ruthless political hatchet man to loving selfless minister of the gospel of Jesus Christ. Transformed! And you can be too!

TAKING OUT THE GARBAGE

"Take out the garbage!" It was never a gentle command at my house growing up. Instead, it was a harsh order, barked at high volume, designed to produce an action that everyone loathed. Amazingly, in a family of four boys, each child usually remembered somehow having taken his turn at the dreaded task just the previous week. To this day I loathe taking out the garbage. Why? Simply because nothing was in those bags that I wanted to save, just gross food remains and wrappers and things that . . . well, garbage.

In this chapter we have to take out some garbage, and you may not like it. It's going to be somewhat negative. The reason for the negativity is really quite simple: I believe and have observed that the number one reason we don't change is because at some time in the past we have attempted to change, then failed, and in the process have been deeply hurt. After trying that a few times, we give up. We conclude that the only pain worse than needing to change is trying to change and failing.

Now I need to let you know: When we pursue God's plan for change, it *always* works. If you've tried to change and failed, it's because you've tried to change according to an unbiblical method. That's the garbage we need to take out: faulty change methods! We need to uncover the faulty change methods, and then we need to sweep them off the table and into the trash so that we can once-and-for-all focus exclusively on God's program for change. It's ugly work, but it's gotta get done if we're gonna change.

I've heard someone say, "If I keep doing what I've always done, I'm going to keep getting what I've always gotten." That's right, isn't it? We're going to look at three faulty psychological methods for change and three faulty spiritual methods for change—the things we've always done. We'll see how they're just trash, worthless. Are you with me? Let's do it together. Let's take out the trash!

Faulty Method #1: Environmental Change

Environmental change is an approach made popular by John Watson and later by B. F. Skinner. You might recognize this concept as *behaviorism*, which is a popular—but faulty—approach to change. Behaviorism is the idea that the environment conditions a person to behave in certain ways, that you are the result of the environment that you have come from. Therefore, change the environment and you will change.

Skinner and Watson relied heavily upon the findings of an experiment conducted by a Russian psychologist named Pavlov. You may have heard of the experiment or of Pavlov himself. He was the dude with the slobbering dogs. Pavlov would put food in front of a dog and the dog would begin to salivate. Then Pavlov rang a bell just seconds before the food appeared. After countless repetitions of hearing the bell followed by getting tasty food, the dog would salivate simply upon hearing the bell, even when no food was laid out. Pavlov concluded that the dog had been changed by his environment and called it conditioning.

From these findings, Pavlov, and later Skinner and Watson, concluded that most, if not all, human behavior is the result of conditioning.

As with most psychological theory, there is some validity here. Certainly behavior is influenced by patterns of thinking formed over a long period of time. The problem with behaviorism is twofold:

1. A cause/effect relationship does not necessarily exist between environment and change. In fact, studies have been done on identical twins from the exact same environment. You would expect them to grow into very similar adults but often they turn out as different as day and night. Though it may be a factor in who you become, environment is not the determining cause in character formation or in transformation.

2. Changing the environment does not automatically change the person. A perfect environment does not lead to a perfect person. Wasn't that the original setting? Adam and Eve had a pretty good environment in Eden, a beautiful and bountiful garden setting. God Almighty Himself said that it was perfect (see Genesis 1:31), and yet Adam and Eve sinned! So environment does not control who I become.

Consider the story of the prodigal son in Luke 15. Now there was a guy who said, "You know what? I'm going to change my environment. I'm not really liking my dad these days. I'm so tired of working on this stupid farm. My brother's getting on my nerves. And their lifestyle is way too restrictive for me. I'm blowing outta here." (I'm paraphrasing now.)

You can read the story yourself in Luke 15:

"There was a man who had two sons. And the younger of them said to his father, 'Father, give me the share of property that is coming to me.' And he divided his property between them. Not many days later, the younger son gathered all he had and took a journey into a far country, and there he squandered his property in reckless living. And when he had spent everything, a severe famine arose in that country, and he began to be in need" (verses 11–14).

He finally found a job at a farm. There he ended up feeding pigs and wanting to eat what the pigs were eating. **"But when he came to himself,"** verses 17 and 18 report, **"he said, 'How many of my father's hired servants have more than enough bread, but I perish here with hunger! I will arise and go to my father, and I will say to him, "Father, I have sinned against heaven and before you.""'**

Now here's the point: He originally thought the problem was his environment: his family, the way he had been brought up, the lifestyle that he had been given. So he took off and got a new environment. The Bible says, **"When he came to himself"** he figured out that *he* was the problem, not his environment. Maybe you have been struggling to change and tempted by the notion that a change of environment will change the way you're feeling. A new job or a new city or a new spouse. "Out with the old and in with the new and then I will be happy." It's a lie!

The depth of the lie that external fixes are the answer can be seen in the human wreckage recorded almost daily in the tabloids. A recent tragic example is the life of Amy Winehouse, a British musical star who was found dead in her apartment at the age of twenty-seven. Her ten-year career was a mix of musical successes and troubled personal life, punctuated by drug and alcohol abuse. She is probably best known for her hit single "Rehab," in which she made public her refusal to get help with her obvious substance problems. She represents the countless millions who deal with their inner longing for meaningful change by trying to inoculate themselves with alcohol and drugs. For Amy and so many, the environmental change offered through rehab centers is a failure highlighted by the revolving door effect of the experience. Celebrities often seem to arrange "frequent visitor" passes with rehab locations, hoping one of the stays is going to "take." Perhaps Amy realized at some level that no amount of rehab would help her—she needed change that wouldn't happen by going somewhere for treatment. In the end, success and the adulation of millions couldn't overcome the struggle Amy faced and she apparently settled for an escalation of destructive behavior that led to her alcohol-related death. Her tragic end is a warning to all of us of the destructive ends of sin if it is never resolved by the Redeemer.

Our problem is inside us, not around us. We are the ones who need to change, not our environment. Behaviorism is deceptive window dressing; it does not work. That's going in the trash.

Faulty Method #2: Change By Digging Up My Past

A popular notion today is "I am the way I am because of my past." The psychological theory that seeks to remedy our problems from the past is *psychoanalysis*. An Austrian physician named Sigmund Freud developed it well over a hundred years ago. Freud taught that human behavior is determined by painful memories that are buried in our subconscious mind. Freud believed that we force from our conscious mind any awareness of thoughts, needs, or experiences that are unacceptable to us or to others and try to bury them deep inside ourselves. What psychoanalysis says is this: "There's something back there. You're not aware of it, but it's back there and it's very dark. You may not remember it, but it's controlling you. It's your past. It's your parents. It's some painful experience. And it's making you fearful. It's making you angry. It's making you depressed."

Psychoanalysis teaches, "You've got to dig it up and spill your guts! Figure out what that thing is and get it out. And until you do, you will never really change."

The problem with all of this is that you are continually cast in the victim role. But you do not have to accept that role. You are *not* a victim. Awful things may have happened to you, but they do not control you! You may *let* them control, but they don't have that power in themselves. Romans 8:1 says, **"There is therefore now no condemnation for those who are in Christ Jesus."** Once you are in Christ, nothing can condemn you, knock you down, or grind you under its heel. You are a son or a daughter of the Living God! You are not a victim. Romans 8:31 says, **"If God is for us, who can be against us?"** The answer is: No one can. God is for you!

Romans 8:37 says, **"In all these things we are more than conquerors through Him who loved us."** *Nothing* has happened or will happen that, by God's grace, you can't climb on top of and rule over and, in the power of the Holy Spirit, be set free from. But first we've got to dump faulty plans for change that don't work, like constant digging in the past.

Instead of endless trips down painful memory lane, the biblical message is quite the opposite. Here's God's message:

THE KEY TO CHANGE IS FORGETTING,
NOT REMEMBERING.

What does that mean? It means facing what you *do* remember, forgiving it, and forgetting it. And that's the order that it happens: face, forgive, and forget. Don't try to forget without forgiving. Don't try to forgive without facing. But after you face it, by God's grace you forgive it. And then you forget it. And don't waste time wondering about what you can't remember—let God take care of that!

Consider the life of Joseph. If anyone was a candidate for ten years of therapy because of a painful past, it was Joseph. This guy was coddled by his father and pampered as the favorite to the point that even though he developed faith in God at an early age, he was so socially awkward that he offended his brothers. Jacob's unwise preferential treatment was evident in his gift to Joseph of a coat that was the envy of his older siblings, who ridiculed and ultimately rejected him. His efforts to tell his family what God was showing him in dreams came across to them as prideful to the point that even Jacob wondered what was going on with Joseph. Finally, when they caught him alone one day, Joseph's ten brothers stripped him naked, threw him into a pit to die, then hauled him out and sold him as a slave in Egypt. They decided a living death in slavery was a more fitting vengeance on their little brother than leaving him to die in a hole. Now would that mess with your mind?

Then Joseph got a job in Egypt; he was working hard and trying to build a life for himself. He was living for God and providing good service to his owner. Soon he was managing that household with incredible efficiency. But when his boss's wife tried to seduce him, Joseph responded with words that give us a glimpse into his character: **"How then can I do this great wickedness and sin against God?"** (Genesis 39:9). She flipped out and falsely accused him of trying to rape her. Unable to defend himself, Joseph was chained up in some rat-infested prison and completely forgotten for several years.

Now you would think that Joseph would be messed up for life or certainly would need endless hours of therapy to process all that pain. Yet the Bible teaches something quite different. In all of it, Joseph saw a sovereign God who was at work. Was Joseph devastated at times? Yes, but he was not destroyed. Were there pain and loneliness and heartache and, at times, despair? Yes, but Joseph found a better way to deal with his pain. He would forget the injustice, trust a wise and sovereign God, and move ahead with his life. He gained the trust of his jailer and was soon managing the prison as he had managed the house of Potiphar. God gave him favor. Instead of fighting his situations, he trusted God to help him advance through even the most difficult circumstances. His was not an easy journey by any means, but he ended up right where God wanted him.

Imagine the day the Pharaoh sent a limousine to the prison to transport Joseph to the palace. In one sense it was the biggest test Joseph had ever faced—put on the spot to interpret the king's dream. In another sense it was the moment God had been preparing Joseph for to display His glory. He stood before Pharaoh without missing a beat and said, **"It is not in me; God will give Pharaoh a favorable answer"** (Genesis 41:16). As tempting as it may have been to "work" the change opportunity, Joseph never took an ounce of credit for the news he delivered to the king. **"The dreams of Pharaoh are one; God has revealed to Pharaoh what he is about to do"** (Genesis 41:25).

Later, when the famine struck and even the sons of Jacob found themselves traveling all the way to Egypt to look for food, Joseph did not take advantage of the "turned tables" to take vengeance on his brothers. In Genesis 45:8, Joseph looked into the eyes of the brothers who did so much to hurt him and said, **"It was not you who sent me here, but God. He has made me a father to Pharaoh, and lord of all his house, and ruler over all the land of Egypt."**

Just to make sure the point is made, the Scripture quotes Joseph affirming that message once more in Genesis 50:20a. **"As for you, you meant evil against**

me, but God meant it for good." Did they sin against him? Yes! Was it evil? Yes! But did God use it for Joseph's good? Yes! God did. As a confirmation that Joseph found healing by forgetting his past, he named his first son Manasseh, which means "the Lord made me forget." Between thinking about the pain of the past and thinking about the delight of his relationship with God, Joseph chose God. The only time he even mentioned the past was when his brothers revealed their own load of guilt and kept bringing it up. Joseph lived free from his past because he let God take care of that part of his life.

There's a lesson on change right there: asking God for the grace to forget my past. This digging-up-the-past thing is a worldly and faulty method of change. Transformation is not about remembering, and it's not about digging up things that may or may not have even happened! It's about forgiving and forgetting. It's about trusting a sovereign God. It's about focusing in on my own need to change and saying with the apostle Paul, **"forgetting what lies behind"** (Philippians 3:13).

Is it important to deal with your past? Absolutely! God doesn't want us to pretend. He wants us to face our past and to deal with it by focusing on forgiveness, and putting it behind us. Many people do find it helpful to sit with a wise Christian counselor who will prayerfully listen and offer biblical answers and counsel from the Lord. But the answer is not in the past, and no process of examining our past will lead to the change our heart desires. Have you been seeking personal transformation by digging up your past? Find a big green plastic bag and put that approach to change where it belongs—at the curb.

Faulty Method #3: Change Through Self-Discovery

Even psychologists themselves began more recently to criticize behaviorism and psychoanalysis, realizing that it was not helping people. (Research shows that those who get into this kind of therapy have a statistically worse chance of seeing personal transformation than if they did nothing at all.) Around 1960, Abraham Maslow and Carl Rogers proposed a third faulty method for helping people called *humanistic psychology*. While behaviorism focuses on environmental conditioning and psychoanalysis drills for something dark and hidden in your past, humanistic psychology teaches that people are controlled by their own values and choices. The goal of this approach to change is to have people clarify their values to achieve their own potential. That's the key word: *potential*. It's in you. Tap into that and you can change into anything you desire!

In North America, this is the most popular faulty method for change. We see this message every day in many forms, from TV infomercials to the Internet: "The answer is within you. Find yourself. Love yourself. Help yourself. You have the answer. Pump it up, baby! Find it inside. You're okay. Be all that you can be." And on and on.

I began to wonder just how pervasive this concept was, so I logged on to Amazon.com, the number one Internet bookseller, and typed into their search engine the word *self-help*. There are at least 234,000 self-help published materials on Amazon. Crazy titles like:

- *Get Out of Your Way: Overcoming Self-Defeating Behaviors*
- *When Am I Going to Be Happy?*
- *The Power of Self-Helping*

Of course the idea here is just positive self-talk. "I'm a good person." "I'm going to buy myself something because I'm a nice guy and I deserve it." When I did the same search a decade ago for the first edition of this book, there were 12,223 book titles on self-help, at the time a larger category than "God" or "marriage." Self-help is definitely an expanding market.

I suppose I understand why people who don't know any better might think that they have the power to change themselves. What troubles me, however, is to see people who claim to believe in the power of almighty God turning to pagan philosophies and ignoring the transforming ministry of the Holy Spirit, which is available to every one of us who comes to God and asks in faith.

The biggest problem with promoting self-esteem as the road to personal growth and fulfillment is that it doesn't work. I was watching Chicago TV news the other day and heard a statistical report on how the self-esteem movement has affected public education. The reporter announced that after spending multiplied millions of dollars and man-hours on building kids' self-esteem at school, "Self-esteem scores have never been higher and educational test scores have never been lower." Or, to put it another way, "The better I feel about myself, the worse I do." Chicago area public schoolteachers observed that students who feel really good about themselves have little or no interest in learning anything or improving in any way at all! High self-esteem makes me want to change less, not more. C. S. Lewis said, "Look for yourself and you will find in the long run only hatred, loneliness and despair."

Many do not recognize that the Christian self-esteem movement is at its core blasphemous. It fails to account for the biblical view of fallen man. **"The heart**

is deceitful above all things, and desperately sick; who can understand it?" (Jeremiah 17:9). If you understand even a fraction of the depravity in your own heart, you know it's that very depravity that makes you want to believe that you *are* good enough. The motivation behind self-esteem self-talk is the result of depravity. We want to deny what we know to be true about ourselves. We can't lift ourselves or talk ourselves out of our fallen nature. The fact that God loves you and me is wonderfully comforting, but it says absolutely nothing about your and my "worth." The fact that God loves us and is committed to us does not reveal anything about us; it reveals something extraordinary about God. It's called grace!

In my office is a book on self-esteem written by a Christian counselor I know. When he gave it to me, he wrote in the front cover, "James, I hope that you will experience the wonderful truth that you are lovable, capable, valuable, and redeemable." How sad. To attempt to draw a line and say that "Because God loves me . . . because Christ died for me . . . because I am eternally a child of God, therefore I am . . ." is to pump myself up through the nature of God. That is blasphemy and a thorough degradation of the glorious grace of God.

In 2 Timothy 3:1–2, Paul described the characteristics of apostasy in the last days: **"But know this, that in the last days perilous times will come: For men will be lovers of themselves . . . blasphemers"** (NKJV). Was that a compliment? Was he saying, "Man! I can't wait for those last days to come. We're finally going to figure out how important it is to love ourselves!" No! He has listed it as a characteristic of extreme unrighteousness.

Again, psychology has an element of wisdom. When people hate themselves and think they're just trash, that is a problem. *I can't do anything. I can't change . . . I'm just nothing* are destructive thoughts. Psychology does observe a legitimate problem in low self-esteem, but psychologists act like the Keystone cops running in circles when they prescribe high self-esteem as the solution to low self-esteem. The Bible says we think too highly of ourselves (see Romans 12:3).

THE ANSWER TO LOW SELF-ESTEEM
IS NOT HIGH SELF-ESTEEM.

Yes, you read that right. The answer to low self-esteem is not high self-esteem. It's no self-esteem. No estimation of self. Jesus said, **". . . whoever loses his life for My sake will find it"** (Matthew 10:39b).

Humanistic psychology says, "Find yourself; the answer is in you!" And

Jesus says, "Lose yourself; the answer is in *Me*!" **"For whoever would save his life will lose it, but whoever loses his life for My sake will find it"** (Matthew 16:25).

Be honest; those approaches to change are not two shades of the same color. They are opposites. Let's take out the trash and reject change through self-discovery as a faulty method.

Of course, psychology is not the only villain in faulty change methods. Now let's look at three faulty methods of change that some people have tried to prove from the Bible. They are potentially even more destructive than the three I've already mentioned.

Faulty Method #4: Legalistic Change

Legalistic change is the idea of change by the power of rules. In the military it works with orders that better be obeyed. "Shine your boots. Make your bunk. March in formation. Don't talk back. Do this! Shut up! Get in line. Keep moving. Double-time!" Does that produce change? It sure does: It produces *external* change, change on the surface. "Oh, look at you; aren't you a nice soldier! You have your boots so nice and shined and under your bunk there. Wow! You're not like those bad soldiers; you're really on the program!"

Inwardly, though, the soldier may be chafing, doing what he must do, not what he desires to do. Rules may produce external change, but hear this: Rules don't change the heart!

In fact, rules by themselves just make you want to sin more. That's the truth of Romans 7:5, **"For while we were living in the flesh, our sinful passions, aroused by the law, were at work in our members to bear fruit for death."** A couple of verses later Paul asked, **"What then shall we say? That the law is sin?"** (verse 7). He meant, "Are the rules that God laid down bad?" And Paul's reply? **"By no means! Yet if it had not been for the law, I would not have known sin. For I would not have known what it is to covet if the law had not said, "You shall not covet."** Paul was saying that if all we are about is just knowing the rules, it only makes us want to sin more.

I remember when I was a kid and playing in the basement after school. Mom would pop her head in the door and say, "There's cookies on the counter upstairs. They're for dessert. Don't touch them!" I'm down there having a great time. I wasn't even thinking about cookies. Then all of a sudden, I'm thinking, *Hmmm, cookies; that's what I was smelling*? I felt my body being drawn upstairs. *Cookies! I need a cookie; I must have a cookie!*

I remember the same thing when my mom would say, "Your father and I are going to the store; keep on playing in the backyard with your friends like you're doing now. Just stay in the backyard. Don't leave! We'll be back in an hour." I was very content in the backyard until I heard a rule—the rule that I couldn't leave. I saw a friend through the fence with a ball, saying, "C'mon over here and play with me." The fence seemed a hundred feet high, I felt so closed in, and I became desperate to get out of a place that I was content in only moments before. Why? Because the rule pricked my sinful heart, and it made me want what was forbidden. Paul stated the problem this way: **"But sin, seizing an opportunity through the commandment, produced in me all kinds of covetousness. For apart from the law, sin lies dead"** (Romans 7:8). Rules by themselves just amplify our desire to sin.

Perhaps you grew up in a legalistic spiritual environment as I did. With legalism, Christianity is all about conforming to a code of conduct that has been added to the precepts and principles of the Bible and then judging people on the degree to which they conform to the extrabiblical code. "I'm a good Christian because I don't do the 'filthy five' (or the 'dirty dozen')." That kind of legalistic focus produces external conformity, like in the military, but not the kind of true life change we are looking for.

Actually, I believe there's more disobedience to God in the legalistic Christian subculture than anywhere else, because so often there has been no real heart change. Instead, sinful patterns that God wants to change are forced under the surface—a sort of conspiracy of silence. Legalistic Christians are hiding the real truth of who they are from everyone around them. The result? Biblical fellowship is hindered and true life change becomes very difficult. Legalism is a stifling environment where lasting heart change is impossible.

Over the Christmas holidays, my family and I visited a church caught in legalism. I didn't want to go, but I had no choice and so I went. The problem was I forgot about the dress code. I was sort of "dress casual," if you know what I mean. Then we got in the building. Oops! Every single male from three years of age to ninety-nine had a suit on, and those ties sure looked tight. Now to their credit, they were friendly, but even the handshake itself was kind of compassionate. "Oh, poor brother. We hope you'll soon be within the reach of the gospel." You know, that feeling you get when people are judging you because you're not quite like they are.

Anyway, I snuggled up my coat, brought my kids in, and sat down. Being familiar with this approach, I was doing really well until they started a baptismal service where the pastor walked right into the baptistery with his suit on, coat and all. I just wanted to stand up and go, "What are you *thinking*! It's not about rules! Jesus died so we could have a genuine intimacy with Him, not just look the part, or what you think looks the part. Won't you ever learn that rules by themselves don't change us? They just force our sinful natures under the surface and help us hide behind externals and pretend we're closer to God than we really are."

Of course, God is not for or against suits. Dressing up for church when motivated by reverence and not religion can be good. Similarly, dressing down can be irreverent when done for the wrong reason. The key is always to remember that **"the Lord looks on the heart"** (1 Samuel 16:7).

Legalism is a faulty approach to change that has been prescribed within the church of Jesus Christ by sincere people who want to take the Bible seriously. Systems of behavior that try to produce change through external conformity may produce surface change, but they ultimately collapse, because they do not change the heart.

Faulty Method #5: Monastic Change

"Monastic" comes from the Greek word *monas*, which means *alone*. The first Christian monk was a man named St. Anthony of Thebes; he was a desert dweller in AD 271. The goal of monasticism is true holiness by a complete suppression of the will. It was popular during the Middle Ages, as thousands of monasteries dotted Europe and housed men or women who took three vows: a vow of poverty —"I will own nothing"; a vow of chastity—"I will abstain from all sexuality"; and a vow of obedience—"I will be in full submission to all authority."

Monks, men who practice monasticism, took on a very difficult life. They were committed to three main activities: work, prayer, and meditation on the Scriptures. I've always tried to picture a monk on a cold winter night in a monastery: lonely, hungry, battling covetousness or lust, trying to suppress the will to sin and trying to deny his human desires. Then I would imagine the monk reading his Bible and coming upon Romans 7:15–18:

> **For I do not understand my own actions. For I do not do what I want, but I do the very thing I hate. Now if I do what I do not want, I agree**

with the law, that it is good. So now it is no longer I who do it, but sin that dwells within me. For I know that nothing good dwells in me, that is, in my flesh. For I have the desire to do what is right, but not the ability to carry it out.

I could see him bursting out of his little room and running down the stone hall, breaking the silence code (they weren't allowed to talk to each other, either) and then telling his fellow monks: "Guys! Have you checked this out? We can't do this. It doesn't work!" Imagine their frustration to realize that they had been trying to change by a faulty method.

You *cannot* suppress your will and make yourself change. Piles of discarded New Year's resolutions prove you cannot change simply because you purpose to change. In fact, when we say, "I'm not going to do that anymore," not only will we likely do it again, but we may actually want to do it more. When we fail, we feel the waves of regret wash over us, and we promise ourselves, "I'll never do that again." For a while, we really try to be different, but again we fall flat on our face. After repeated failure, there is often a backlash, and we return to our sin with accelerated vigor, thinking, "Well, if I can't change, then I'll just stop trying."

You may be thinking "I'm not a monk and I've never been to a monastery," but how often do we try to live like monks? We try to change by suppressing our will. We try to change without the power of God, using just our own human strength. We experience the frustration of Paul's words in Romans 7:18b, **"For I have the desire to do what is right, but not the ability to carry it out."**

Possibly you are reading this book right now, and you are standing at the end of another week of defeat, wondering to yourself, "Will I ever treat my children the way I want to?" "Will I ever break this awful habit?" "Will I ever go through a week without failing in that secret sin?" "Will I ever walk with God as I purpose to walk?" You may be among the majority of listeners sitting in churches week after week and saying, "I agree with the pastor; I want to be that kind of person," who leave encouraged, only to go right out each week and fail again. No wonder so many people have stopped trying to change; it's a lot less painful than trying and failing.

Monastic change has to go. Take it to the trash; no more trying to change through my own willpower. It will never work. As Jesus said, **"The spirit indeed is willing, but the flesh is weak"** (Matthew 26:41).

Faulty Method #6: Intellectual Change

In Robert Louis Stevenson's classic story *The Strange Case of Dr. Jekyll and Mr. Hyde*, a mild-mannered doctor would drink a potion and change from a sweet innocent bookkeeper-type to a hideous monster. When the potion wore off, Dr. Jekyll would feel very ashamed. He'd say, "I can't believe that was inside me. I just cannot believe that I could live like that and do those things." Even though he was ashamed and recognized his behavior was wrong, he was strangely drawn to drink the potion again. There was this on-and-off craving and Jekyll's thoughts, "I want to do right, but I don't."

Many times we feel like Dr. Jekyll—the back-and-forth struggle of trying to change. We say to ourselves, "Why did I do that? Why did I say that? Why am I like that?" Then we say these three words: "I know better." In our minds, we agree our actions are wrong. Yet somewhere between knowing and doing, it doesn't happen for us. We begin to discover that there's a big gap between knowing what to change and actual heart change.

It takes more than knowing what God wants. It takes more than knowing how I should live. Most of us would agree there is a great gulf between what we know and what we do. Paul put it this way in Romans 7:22–23: **"For I delight in the law of God, in my inner being, but I see in my members another law waging war against the law of my mind** [working against what I've learned], **and making me captive to the law of sin that dwells in my members."** He later added, **"So then, I myself serve the law of God with my mind, but with my flesh I serve the law of sin"** (verse 25). In effect, Paul wrote, "I've come far enough to know what God wants me to do. In my mind, I'm phenomenal. Mentally, I get an A+. But when you look at my actual résumé, there's a lot of failure in my life. There is a big gap between what I know I should be doing and what I am actually doing."

Change cannot begin until we know that knowing is not enough. Are you as good an employee as you know to be? Are you as pure in your thoughts as you know to be? Are you as truthful and loving as you know to be? You say, "No, I'm not." That's right, and neither am I. None of us will be if we keep fooling ourselves into thinking that knowing what to change will bring about change. It won't. Churches and pastors and schools and books that promote change through information alone are really promoting frustration, and it's sad, because there is a better way.

START CHANGING HERE.

It's time to admit that we can't do it ourselves, and to recognize none of these six methods has the answer. So how do we change? Where do we begin?

The answer is simple and has two parts: admit and turn.

WHERE TO BEGIN

1. Admit: I am the problem.

First, admit, "I am the problem." Let's accept once and for all that our problems are not due to other people, our parents, or our past. Let's take total responsibility for who we are going to become and bring our desires before God. When we do that, we have taken the first step in change. To take total responsibility is to admit like Paul did in Romans 7:24, **"Wretched man that I am!"** Are you willing to say that?

The word "wretched" means *distressed or miserable through exhaustion from hard labor.* I believe those words came from Paul's lips because he was exhausted from trying to change himself. He came to a desperateness where he said, "God, I want to be a different person. I'm not going to shield myself from the darkness in my own heart anymore. I really want to be the person You want me to be. I want to be righteous and godly and true. So I'm going to face up to who I really am."

"O wretched man"—or woman—realize that change begins with a genuine, humble, contrite admission: "It's me; I'm the problem."

2. Turn: Only God can change the heart.

Second, turn to God. Realize only He can change your heart. Notice those words in Romans 7:25: **"Thanks be to God through Jesus Christ our Lord!"** Students of Scripture get very frustrated with that because they want Paul to say a lot more. "Can't you break that down for me, Paul? Can't you add any stuff? You have me at this desperate condition and I am so ready for the answer and all you say is 'I thank my God—through Jesus Christ our Lord!' Paul, isn't there more?"

It's so simple that we often miss it. The answer is Jesus Christ. He wants to do a work of change in our hearts. We need to come desperately before Him and ask Him to do what only He can do for us—and *in* us. You ask, "Does God still change people?" Yes, He does! God changes people and He wants to change you.

You say, "I want to be changed." Good! That's what this book is about—change. A key strategy in this change is to complete the activities that conclude each chapter. Do these three things: (1) Answer the questions, (2) do the work, and (3) pray the prayer. Begin below, and then join me in chapter 2.

Teacher Questions

1. Why is it essential that you eliminate faulty change methods?
2. Which of the faulty methods have you tried? What benefit, if any, did you experience?
3. What are you planning to do with what you learned in this chapter?

Prophet Questions

1. What excuses have you used for not changing?
2. What makes you think that this time things will be different?
3. If your answer to question 2 left out Jesus, why?

Shepherd Questions

1. What does your willingness to read this book say about the sincerity of your desire to change?
2. In what ways are you beginning to sense that God wants to help you change?
3. How would you put your heart's desire for change into a one-sentence prayer?

LET'S GET TO WORK

It will not be easy to read this book quickly. Each chapter will take an hour or more to complete, including answering the teacher, prophet, and shepherd questions and doing the "Let's Get to Work" exercise. Take a few moments now and plan a schedule for completing all ten chapters. Mark your dates next to the boxes below. Choose a specific time and place for reading each chapter over the next few days and weeks. Then call a friend and tell them you are reading a book on change and ask them to pray for you during this important time in your life.

☐ Chapter 1   Date: _____   ☐ Chapter 6   Date: _____
☐ Chapter 2   Date: _____   ☐ Chapter 7   Date: _____
☐ Chapter 3   Date: _____   ☐ Chapter 8   Date: _____
☐ Chapter 4   Date: _____   ☐ Chapter 9   Date: _____
☐ Chapter 5   Date: _____   ☐ Chapter 10   Date: _____

Before you begin chapter 2, spend some time alone with the Lord. Kneel down and pray something like:

LOOK UP!

Lord, I admit it. I'm not nearly as much like Jesus Christ as I should be. I'm not and I know it. The problem is me. I'm not thinking about the weaknesses of others anymore; I am asking You to change me. God, You could do so much more in me.

Lord, change me. I know You want to. And I know I need to. I can't do it alone. Please forgive me for blaming others. God, forgive me for trying to change in my own strength and apart from You. I admit the problem is me, and I know I desperately need Your help. I believe that, so help me, God. I do. So please help me, God.

Change me. I'm asking in Jesus' name. Amen.

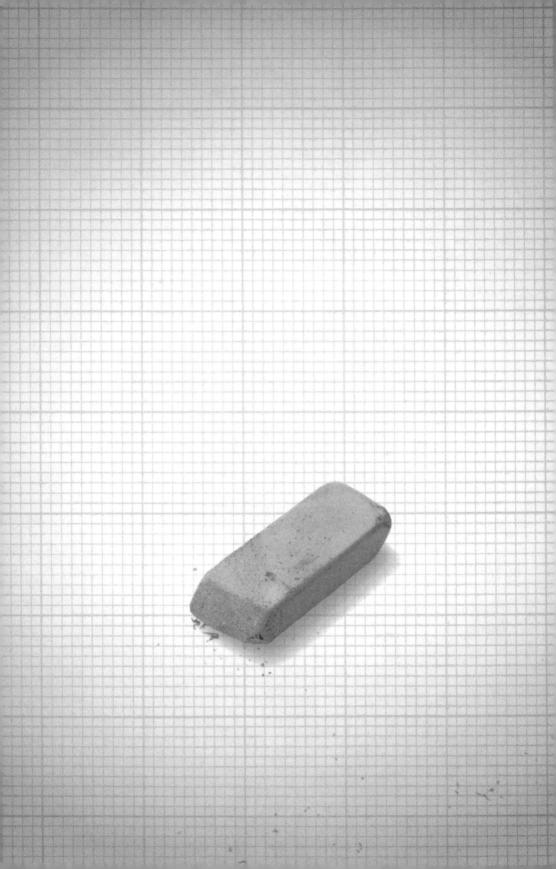

2

SIGN ME UP

SAY IT IN A SENTENCE:
*For life change to happen, we must commit
to full cooperation with God's desire to transform us.*

That's one big sentence! Did you read it critically? I think about careful readers all of the time when I'm writing because I imagine how I would read that sentence. I'd be thinking, "Commit!?! Must!?! Full cooperation!?! I want my whole *life* in God's hands? Give Him everything? Is He going to start driving the car now? Where are we going?" That's the way I think. And in writing that summary sentence I didn't want to assume you are already at the conclusion. The goal in this chapter is to get everyone on board. That's why the title is "Sign Me Up." And I realize you might not be there yet, but I have hopes for you!

One Sunday not so long ago I gave a message in our church about the wisdom of total abstinence from alcohol. I did not teach that the Bible requires abstinence, only that there is wisdom in such a position. Many people in our church left convinced that day that God had spoken to them. The key, however, was not in agreeing mentally but choosing to act on what they understood.

One man, who I'll call Jeff, did. He wrote me a letter; here is an excerpt:

Dear Pastor James:
Because of hearing your message, I asked the Lord to help me with my drinking. I have not had one drink since. . . . I would always come home from work and have a couple of martinis with dinner and a couple of beers throughout the evening. Usually it was four drinks—sometimes more. I am forty-two years old and I have been in this habit for a long time. Lately, though, I

noticed that I was really looking forward to that first drink of the evening.

I've been a Christian for a number of years now and I felt this drinking was not exactly honoring to God. But sinner that I am, I kept right on doing it until the Sunday morning of your message. After I heard it I asked our Lord to help me through the power of the Holy Spirit. Enclosed you will see a rather odd item. This is the last page off of my desk planner last year. It has X's through the days that I've been without alcohol.

On each day of December Jeff had marked a big "X" with the letters WPHS, which his letter explained stood for "with the power of the Holy Spirit." He remains to this day fully transformed by Christ because he chose to cooperate fully with God.

Jeff didn't try to change on his own; he turned to God for help. Have you? This chapter is about making that choice!

GOD HAS A GREAT RÉSUMÉ AS A CHANGE AGENT

Do you have a résumé? I haven't had one for years, but I have seen quite a few. They come in all shapes and sizes. Each one is designed to make an impression. "Look at me; I can do the job." "Take me, I will be the best worker or the best trained or the most trustworthy." I think résumés are a good idea. They help employers know what they are going to get before they sign someone on. They help employees show their qualifications for the job. In this chapter I am going to try to convince you to sign on 100 percent for God's desire to change you, so let's begin with a quick look at His awesome résumé. Believe me, our awesome God can do the job.

Imagine for a moment a book that is filled with the stories of the millions of lives that God has changed. What a book that would be: countless pages telling the stories of every conceivable kind of person from every conceivable walk of life and every area of need. All changed by the transforming power of God. Chuck Colson would be there. So would my friend Jeff.

Wow! Talk about a bestseller. If you could pull together a summary of that book, a book of transformed lives—sort of a résumé of God's very best work— you would never again doubt if you should give God full permission to change you. He's been in the business since time began and has millions of satisfied customers. He's got great product knowledge and there is excellent return on your investment.

Are you ready to sign on? Maybe you'd like to do some reference checks before you completely turn over control of your life to God. No problem: Here's a sampling from God's résumé on changing people. Let's start way back, near the beginning of time, and we'll end up right here at the beginning of the third millennium since Jesus walked the earth.

God's Résumé Reference #1: Moses

Think about the life of Moses, circa 1400 BC. This story is found in the book of Exodus in the Old Testament. But he also shows up repeatedly in Scripture as an example of a life through which God worked. In Acts 7, Stephen is making the case for Jesus as God's best and last word on change, and he uses Moses as a test case. After a brief review of the unusual circumstances of Moses' childhood and early years as an adult, Stephen said, **"When he** (Moses) **was forty years old, it came into his heart to visit his brothers, the children of Israel"** (Acts 7:23). God began to move in Moses' life. Being brought up by Pharaoh's daughter, Moses was pampered, kind of cocky, and self-assured. By the time he was forty, a significant part of his identity was wrapped up in being a prince of Egypt. So, when God first reached out to him and said, "I want you to lead My people," Moses took matters into his hands. He saw an Egyptian beating a Hebrew slave, so he looked both ways and then stepped in and killed the Egyptian, burying him in the sand (see Exodus 2:12). When others discovered the murder, God had to send Moses to the desert for forty years. Forty years of learning that you can't accomplish God's agenda in your own strength.

Finally, at age eighty, Moses saw a burning bush that was not consumed by the fire—God was now reaching out to him again. At that point, you'd think Moses would have it all together, but instead he went from cocky and self-assured to hesitant and lacking in confidence. He went from taking matters into his own hands to refusing to take the ball God was handing to him.

God said, "I want to use you to lead My people."

And Moses was like, "I . . . I . . . I . . . don't talk very good."

"I'll be your mouth," God replied.

"I can't," Moses said. "Get someone else."

But God insisted (see Exodus 3:1–4:17), as He always does, and used Moses as one of the greatest leaders the world has ever known. He led two million people from Egypt to the Promised Land.

How was that possible? Let me tell you . . . God had to change that guy. If you want to look at God's résumé as a change agent, Moses's life shouts: "No matter how old you are, there's always time to change. It's never too late!"

You may have opened this book to read that word today. You're in your forties or in your fifties and your marriage isn't what you wish it was; your career didn't become what you had hoped it would, and you're starting to get into this attitude that thinks, "Well, I'm just going to kind of cruise through because I've missed my chance to change. Maybe God will do something in my kids." Look at Moses. It's not too late for you. Hear this: Even if you would do many things differently—Moses would have said the same thing, but God wasn't done with Moses! And God isn't done with *you*. You can still climb to some of the heights where you will see God use your life in ways you've only dreamed until now. Let God change you, and He will use you in extraordinary ways.

God's Résumé Reference #2: The Woman at the Well

Flip the calendar of human history forward to AD 30 and there is almighty God again, still changing people. This time it's the Samaritan woman at the well of Sychar (John 4:7-26), an ancient version of what we might call "woman at the bar." She was highly immoral—five husbands and now living with a sixth man. How many lovers in between we could only guess. She was looking for change in relationship roulette and it wasn't happening. Words like *loose, easy, cheap* would certainly be accurate, and the fact that she visited the well at midday when she didn't expect to meet anyone hints that she was avoiding potentially humiliating encounters. But there's not a hint of disdain in Jesus' interaction with her.

Jesus, the Son of God, was loving and gracious, so forgiving. Remember her remarkable testimony? **"Come, see a man who told me all that I ever did. Can this be the Christ?"** (v. 29). She didn't try to convince anyone—she just pointed at Christ and said, "He figured me out! He knew exactly what I needed. What do you think?" Her transformation was so powerful that many who observed it chose to believe in Christ also (see John 4:39).

We don't know where her life went from that point on, but we know this woman from Samaria was dramatically transformed because she trusted Christ to do the work.

Do you know what her life says to us? She teaches us that no matter how tragic or filled with failure our past might be, God can reach down into the middle of where we are and absolutely transform us. Don't be afraid of the word *sin*. We feel the suffering that results of our sin. Don't be afraid. We are *all* sinners.

We have all broken God's law. The Scripture says that **We all stumble in many ways** (James 3:2). The question isn't, "Have we sinned?" The question is, have we recognized ourselves as sinners and asked God for forgiveness?

Please don't doubt! If you're holding this book and thinking, "The grace of God can't get to where I am," let me just tell you—you're wrong! There's not a person reading this book who can say "my sin is too great," or "I'm too far gone," and get agreement from God. God has changed people who are so much worse than either of us, and He wants you to be a trophy of His grace too!

Won't you let Him reach into your heart and do that work? God is really, really good at changing people!

God's Résumé Reference #3: Saul/Paul

The apostle Paul began life with the name Saul. (God likes to change the names of the people He's changing. It helps them remember, "I'm not the person I used to be.") Saul was a religious zealot, very educated, very powerful, and very ruthless. Initially, he rejected Christ. In fact, we are told in Acts 7 that when religious people took Stephen—one of the most phenomenal preachers the early church knew—dragged him out of the city and stoned him to death, Saul was standing there holding the murderers' coats (verse 58). Talk about coldhearted! Do you think Saul smiled? Apparently this event created a frenzy of hatred in Saul because he began to persecute every Christian he could get his hands on. He beat them, threw them into prison, and actually murdered some of them.

If you did not know the outcome, you probably would be thinking, "This guy is too far gone; no way can the Lord reach a mass murderer with His power to change." Wrong! One day, while Saul was on the road to Damascus, he had a powerful, transforming experience with Jesus Christ. Years later, when sharing the gospel with King Agrippa, Paul remembers the moment: **"At midday, O king, I saw on the way a light from heaven, brighter than the sun, that shone around me and those who journeyed with me. And when we had all fallen to the ground, I heard a voice saying to me in the Hebrew language, 'Saul, Saul, why are you persecuting Me? It is hard for you to kick against the goads'"** (Acts 26:13-14). Saul recognized in that instant that what he thought was zeal for God was actually struggling against God getting close enough to change his heart. The *goads* were a gauntlet of pointed sticks used to keep an ox going in a certain direction. Any deviation from the path caused immediate pain. Jesus was telling Saul that even with the wickedness that he had done, God had surrounded him in such a way that he could only move in one direction. God was coming after him! God had been closing in on him for a while, and he hadn't been able to move in any direction without feeling the pain of restraint.

That picture may strike you as familiar. You can't sleep because of the guilt—you feel the sharp prods. You can't act normally because of the pain of the things that you've done. The memory weighs on you. And you carry it constantly. And you try to kick against it, but you can't keep it from poking you. You, like Saul, need to find God at the end of your gauntlet. He's waiting to change you.

So dramatic was Saul's conversion that he turned from being a ruthless murderer of Christians to the greatest preacher of the gospel the church has known. He became the great apostle Paul. How did that happen? How could a person go from that far-out to that sold-out for Jesus Christ? God did it; that's how. It's His thing to change people.

GOD'S GREATEST PASSION IS
THE TOTAL TRANSFORMATION OF PEOPLE.

God hasn't changed from Saul's day. Twenty centuries later, He wants to do for you what He did for Saul: total transformation, a complete change. The years between then and now have been filled with generation after generation of notorious characters and little-known people God has changed. The fact that you are reading this book today is a small testimony to the unbroken chain of change that God has managed since the launch of the church. At any point in history we can identify people who experienced the same power to change that God used on Bible people.

God's Résumé Reference #4: Amy Carmichael

Let's move to more recent history, less than two centuries ago, to another life transformed by almighty God. Amy Carmichael was a really neat lady who lived from 1867 to 1951. Her life remains a testimony to those who are tempted to think that change is only for people who have really dark pasts. Maybe you're saying, "I have always been a pretty good person. I mean, I got a few things wrong on my spelling tests and stuff, but I haven't done any of that really dark sinning like some people have." If that's how you feel, then the story of Amy Carmichael is important for you. She was brought up in a spiritual home, obeyed her parents, didn't break any laws. But Amy came to understand that she had never really trusted Jesus Christ. In fact, it was while she was singing the song "Jesus Loves Me" that she realized she had not really opened her heart and loved Him back. She trusted Jesus Christ as her Savior.

Amy went through some pretty significant trials in her life. While still in her teens, her family suffered financial loss and soon after, her beloved father died, leaving her mother with seven children and little income. In her early twenties, Amy moved with her family to the slums of Manchester, England, where her mother had taken a job as a superintendent of a rescue home for women. Ultimately, Amy went as a missionary to Japan and then to India. She lived to be eighty-four years old and wrote more than fifteen books, urging others to live a holy life in Christ.

Have you wrongly assumed that the majority of change God wants to produce in you is about BC stuff; you know, before Christ? That is not true. Salvation is just the beginning. Amy's life also stands as a testimony to the ongoing transforming power of God, because God wants to do far more than just forgive you—He wants to transform you into a witness who shines the glory of who He is to everyone you meet. He did it in Amy and He can do it in you!

God's Résumé Reference #5: Peter Hitchens

You say, "Well, this is all great—all these people from the past—but is God still really changing the lives of people today?" I was reading this week about Peter Hitchens. He's the brother of the late well-known atheist, Christopher Hitchens. Peter reports that during his teenage years and early twenties he lost his faith. He admits, "I rebelled against everything that I've been brought up to believe in."

In his recent book, *The Rage against God*, he describes his journey back to God and the end of a feud with his brother. He vividly remembers a time when he was fifteen years old:

I was on the playing fields of Cambridge. And at a boarding school one bright, windy, spring afternoon, I took my Bible out into a field and I set it on fire.

He *burned* his Bible—that's how much he hated God. He continued,

It would be many years before I would feel a slight shiver of unease about that act of desecration. Did I then have any idea of the forces that I was trifling with? No doubt I should have been ashamed. But it was many years before I could confess that God had brought my heart back.

It was specifically a painting by Rogier van der Weyden from the 15th Century that brought his heart back. That painting is entitled *The Last Judgment*. Peter recalls the event:

> I was studying a guidebook. And I scoffed at the mention of this painting. But when I stood before it, my mouth gaped, hanging open at the naked figures falling toward the pit of hell. These people did not appear remote or from the ancient past. They were my own generation. Because they were naked in the picture, they were not imprisoned by their age or bound by fashion in time. On the contrary, their hair and . . . the set of their faces were entirely in the style of my own time. These people . . . I saw them in the painting falling into hell were me and the people I knew. And I had a sudden, strong surge of faith as being something for the present day, not imprisoned under thick layers of time. Suddenly, my large catalogue of misdeeds replayed rapidly in my head. I had absolutely no doubt that I was among the damned if there were any damned. This began my journey back to faith and the church.

This guy *burned* his Bible and walked away. And God went after him and took hold of him and pulled him back. It's *awesome* what God can do in a person's life.

God's Résumé Reference #6: Everyday People

I thought I would give you just one more example from God's résumé on change. This is actually a composite of amazing stories of life transformation that have occurred among people at Harvest, the church I'm privileged to pastor. These people are not celebrities and they will probably never be famous this side of eternity, but the changes God brought about in their lives are no less remarkable. That's because the stories are really about the Change-agent even more than the person being changed. (The video testimonies of these people are available on our website.)

Take Bob Zielinski as a God-project. This guy is at least eighty years old. He didn't open his heart to God in his forties or in his fifties or in his sixties or in his seventies. When he was eighty, something tragic and awful happened in his family. And he still tears up when he talks about the loss. He ended up living at the YMCA, desperately alone. And a young man—thank God for this guy at our church campus down in Niles—befriended him and began to visit him, and brought him to church. And his life has been gloriously transformed by the power of the gospel in our church! God did that *here* for him.

Then there's the story of Rob Weinsek. This guy was a piece of work! He would attend the Elgin Campus. His wife brought him—not like, "Hey, do you want to go to church with me?" She issued a "you're-coming-with-me-and-no-discussion" kind of an invitation. And he *looked* like he got dragged to church because he'd sit stiffly in his chair with I-don't-want-to-be-here written on his face.

Andy Rozier observed this guy while he was leading worship—his arms folded and leaning back. But he kept coming. And good for him for listening to a loving wife. For a long time his attitude remained, "Yeah, I'm not feeling it; I'm not seeing it; I don't get it." But he showed up every week.

Andy tells the story that eventually he noticed Rob was kind of like, "Okay." His shoulders relaxed and he leaned forward. He even started to sing. I'm sure he heard himself and thought, "HUH?!?!"

Rob now says, "Do you know what? I just found as I sat under God's Word and gathered with believers—Hey! I believe this!" God began to work in his heart. All of his defenses came down. Years of resistance and hurt dissipated. And Jesus Christ penetrated his hard heart with the gospel. And his life has been changed forever!

And then I think of Scott Faulkner, who is one of the neighbors of our camp up in Michigan. Scott *hated* Harvest. He thought we were about to ruin his little corner of paradise! He called the *Daily Herald* newspaper in the Chicago area and got them to write articles about how nasty we are. He lobbied against our camp and publicly attacked our church. I mean, *venomous* is the word that comes to mind to describe his attitude until one day—God just nailed him! Not like Rob—taking over a year to wear him down—God just dropped Scott with a knockout punch!

One day, one of his friends who had known Scott for many years said, "I want to show you a verse in the Bible." Since he didn't want to be rude, he said, "Fine. Show me." And he recited it. Then his friend flipped a few pages and said, "Here, read this one." So Scott grudgingly repeated the words on the page. One of the verses he read was **"God shows His love for us in that while we were still sinners, Christ died for us"** (Romans 5:8).

He later said that by the third or fourth Scripture, he just began to weep. God was speaking to him. He said, "I had to get as low as I could get as fast as I could get. Jesus Christ Himself showed up in that room and He took hold of my life! When I stood up, I said 'I am saved!'" Later he explained, "I didn't see it coming. One minute I was preparing to resist and the next I was overwhelmed by repentance!"

Sometimes God slowly comes up on a person and gently draws them. But other times? He decides, "We're taking this one *down* today!" What He did with Saul on the road to Damascus, He did to Scott and He's done to others. God does what it takes to change people.

A last character God changed is Alex Callaway, a big, tough, rapper. He was brought up to know better, but he rejected the example of his family. "I don't need that! I don't need my parents' thing! I don't want it!" And off he went and got listening to some awful music—awful because of its content: violence; drug addiction; and abuse of women. The vile message began to mess up his mind. He began hanging out with the wrong people. With the wrong people came doing wrong things. He got involved with drugs and then started selling drugs. Eventually, he got caught and arrested.

While in jail during his trial, he was listening to our *Walk In The Word* radio program. And he heard a Scripture that someone else had also shared with him: "**Do you not know that if you present yourselves to anyone as obedient slaves, you are slaves of the one whom you obey, either of sin, which leads to death, or of obedience, which leads to righteousness?**" (Romans 6:16). And he said, "I don't want to be a slave to sin anymore. And I saw that I was." So he gave his heart to Christ.

Did God keep Alex from going to prison? Nope! Off you go. God sent him away for a little captive seminary time. He came out of prison a transformed man—not because he was in prison, but because God was in him! His music is now being used in our church and a lot of other places. We're going to watch this guy. I think God's hand is really on him! But before Christ intersected his life you would have thought that he was too far gone. I bet you his parents looked at his life and said, "He is *never* coming back he's so far gone!" The only person who could get to him was Jesus Christ who transformed his life.

I told you these stories because I want you to know that you can trust God. He's got a great résumé on change. Of course, I could go on for a million pages with stories of people God has changed, but the point is this: God wants to add your greatest areas of defeat and frustration to His record. Here's how. It involves a crisis and a process.

GOD'S PLAN FOR CHANGE BEGINS WITH A CRISIS.

In Matthew 18:3, Jesus said these words, **"Truly, I say to you, unless you turn and become like children, you will never enter the kingdom of heaven."** Little children are so trusting, and Jesus was teaching that we too must learn to trust God for our salvation and stop trying to earn it with our own efforts.

"Unless you turn" (literally "change" or "are converted") . . . **"you will never enter the kingdom of heaven."** Unless you are converted! Now the Bible uses many words to describe this unique change called conversion. A key phrase is "born again." We are all born once physically; we need to be born a second time or born spiritually.

"Unless one is born again he cannot see the kingdom of God" (John 3:3). That's converted! Here are some other biblical words: *saved*, like a drowning man; *justified*, like a person who is condemned but set free; *redeemed*, like a debt that has been canceled; and *converted*, like a blind man who can now see.

GOD'S PLAN FOR CHANGE
1. A Crisis Called Conversion

The Bible calls all people everywhere to a crisis of conversion. The words are important—*saved, justified, redeemed,* and *converted*—but most important is the actual event, an actual conversion. This crisis of conversion means a complete change of direction, what Jesus called "getting off the wide road and getting on the narrow road" (see Matthew 7:13). As in, "At one point in my life, I was going in this direction and I thought, 'There is no God,' or 'Everyone's going to heaven,' or 'You get to heaven by being a good person.' But then one day, I began to hear the truth and I converted. I changed the way I thought; I changed the direction I was heading. Now I believe that the only way to get to heaven is by confessing Jesus Christ as my personal Savior. I believe that Jesus Christ came into the world; that He died on the cross to pay the penalty for my sins; and I have placed my faith and trust in Him as my only hope for God's forgiveness and eternal life."

At this point in the book I want to try to share the gospel with you—the Good News. If you've been reading and praying, "Lord, change me now," you've got to get into partnership with God. Partnership with God begins with this thing called conversion. It's where it has to start.

Let me describe for you the conversion mechanism or the way God enters a person's life. It's called the gospel—what Jesus Christ has done for us. I want to tell it to you by talking about three doors. On one side of the door is God; on the other side of the door is you.

Blank Door

The first door I'm going to call the Blank Door. Or really, we could call this the Dead Door. This is about the life of the person who doesn't know there's a door; doesn't recognize there's a God; and doesn't realize that life has a God-given purpose. They're just clueless—completely unaware of reality. Dead is the picture that comes to mind.

I was walking behind my house yesterday and I found a small bird that flew into our patio door. It didn't look injured, but it was dead. One minute it was soaring, the next it was gone. It was still beautiful to look at and I expected it to wake up and take off any moment—but nothing. Even in death it still bore the indications of being a marvelous creation.

Now the Bible says that we are born into this world like that bird after his encounter with the glass. **"And you were dead in the trespasses and sins"** (Ephesians 2:1). "Fly birdie! Fly!" Why can he not fly? He's dead. We are born into this world just as *dead* to God. We definitely look alive, and we even bear the image of our Creator, but we remain spiritually dead unless God intervenes. A lot of people live their lives behind the Blank Door.

Jesus said, **"No one can come to Me unless the Father who sent Me draws him"** (John 6:44). He also said, **"You did not choose Me, but I chose you"** (John 15:16a). The first thing that happens in anyone's heart who is dead to God is God initiates. This is important. *God* makes the first move. But I have faith to believe that God is making a move toward you as you are reading this. There was a time in your life when you would have confessed, "I was so dead to God. I didn't care. I wasn't interested. It didn't matter to me. I thought I had it all together. I didn't need *any*thing. But then *God* began to stir something in my heart." Suddenly, where there was a blank wall, a door appears. Has that been happening to you? Has God been stirring something in you?

Barrier Door

Once you get past the Blank Door, you find out that there's another door. We're going to call this the Barrier Door because even when your heart starts to become, by God's grace, alive to God, you also become aware that there's a barrier. And the barrier is a thing called sin. Sin blocks the way to God like a sealed door. Isaiah 59:2 says, " **. . . your iniquities have made a separation between you and your God, and your sins have hidden His face from you."**

Sin is a problem. God is holy. There's not going to be any sin in heaven. So sin is a blockage, a barrier. God is on one side of that door; you're on the other. And if the arrangement stays that way, nothing is going to change. How sad if you closed this book right now and thought, "Well, God has been stirring in my heart, but now I realize there's a barrier. I guess that's it for me." The fact of the matter is that God Himself solved the barrier problem; a problem we could not solve ourselves. You can't be good enough to erase that barrier. You can't be faithful enough to get through the door. You can't go to church or love your neighbor enough to open that door. Goodness doesn't erase the sin problem; only God can do that. Until you realize that you are powerless to open the barrier door of sin, you remain on the wrong side, but that's not the end of the story!

Blood Door

Beyond the Blank Door and the Barrier Door, there's this—it's called the Blood Door. And the Blood Door represents the verse that I quoted to you previously: **"But God shows His love for us in that while we were still sinners, Christ died for us"** (Romans 5:8). This is the Good News—the good news that you don't have to go to hell to pay for your sin. You don't have to bear the guilt of your sin every day of your life. God *loves* you. Jesus *died* for you. He died to pay the penalty for your sin. He took the just condemnation of a Holy God and placed it upon Him; on Him almighty judgment fell that would have sunk the world to hell. **"For Christ also suffered once for sins . . . for the unrighteousness** (1 Peter 3:18). The door is unlocked. Christ died for us. He died for *you*. And you have to personalize that. That's what it means to be converted.

Now I'm *on* it, so stick with me. You have to make this personal. You must make it your own. When you get a job, you sign a contract. If you get married, you come to the front of a church and you exchange vows and rings. And if you want to be saved, if you want to be converted, you have to act on the gospel information. You have to make a choice. That knocking you hear in your life is Jesus on the other side of the Blood Door, waiting for you to open to Him.

My dad was converted in 1942, about seventy years ago. He has walked with God his whole life. It's awesome what the Lord has done in him. It began when he went to a little country church and a man was preaching on this verse: Revelation 3:20, where Jesus Christ said, **"Behold, I stand at the door and knock. If**

anyone hears My voice and opens the door, I will come in to him and eat with him, and he with Me." I've heard the story all my life—that story of my dad's conversion and that important verse that my mom would teach on quite frequently. Maybe that's why my favorite painting in all of the world is by Warner Sallman. It's called *Christ at Heart's Door* and is based on Revelation 3:20. It's easy to find online, but you are probably familiar with it. There are some interesting details in this picture.

Notice the heart shape above the door. That entryway is a person's life—you.

Notice that Jesus Christ is knocking. (Knock-knock-knock-knock, knock-knock-knock-knock.) "Behold, I stand at the door and knock! If anyone . . . opens the door, I will come in . . ."

The little window in the door reveals that it's dark inside that room—light and beautiful outside where Jesus Christ is—darkness, guilt, shame, and sin behind the door. How long has Christ been knocking at the door of your heart wanting to truly come in?

There's no latch on the outside of the door. The next move is yours. **"But God shows His love for us in that while we were still sinners, Christ died for us"** (Romans 5:8). That was God's move. Now it's your move.

John 1:12 says, **"But to all who did receive Him, who believed in His name, He gave the right to become children of God."** And so you have to receive Him. You need to open the door.

You say, "How do you do that?"

Receiving Christ involves just these two things: you need to turn from your sin ("I have failed. I have fallen. I have broken God's law. It's only made me miserable. It's only dragging my life down. I don't want that anymore"). Turn from your sin and then you have to embrace Christ by faith for your forgiveness. You have to get off the "Well, I'm going to be a good person; I'll show God; I'm going to earn it somehow." You've got to get off that. And you've got to get on "Jesus died for me. I don't deserve to be forgiven, but I believe that Christ died for me. And I receive that as my assurance of heaven someday."

Those who experience a crisis of conversion often will recall their past and realize that a change has occurred: "There was a time," they will say, "when if someone would have asked me, 'Hey, how do you get to heaven?' or, 'Are you going to heaven?' I would have been like, 'Well, I don't know,' or 'I think so,' or 'I'm going to get to heaven because I'm a good person.' I once thought that. But then I converted; I changed direction."

Please hear me, dear reader: You cannot go on with this book on change until you are sure that you have had the crisis I am talking about. Have you had the crisis—a pivotal point when you converted, turning from self to God alone? Can you look to a time in your life when you changed the road that you were on?

Please understand you cannot fall into this by accident. I'm not pressing you for the exact date and the time, but if you are not absolutely certain that you have converted and become a follower of Jesus Christ, you haven't. You can't merely say, "Oh, you know, I think somewhere, sometime that might have happened." If you don't have a conversion story, you probably don't have a conversion. Let today be your story. In the next eight chapters you will read all about the process of change, but you can't have the process if you've never had the crisis.

Does that make sense to you? If you're not 100 percent sure, why not choose right now? Your story can be: "I was reading this book on change and figured out that I had never really been converted. I knew some things about Jesus, but I didn't know Him personally, so I repented of my sin. I told God how sorry I was, and I thanked Him for sending Jesus to pay for my sin. I invited Christ to come into my life, to forgive me, and begin a new work of transformation in my life." If you stop now and do that from your heart, you can be converted. That's the crisis. That's the beginning. That's where real life change always begins.

Stop! The rest of the book will only make sense to followers of Jesus Christ. If you have not yet made that choice, please review the previous part of this chapter and see the first prayer in "Look Up!" at the end of the chapter. If you have made that choice, you have a lot to look forward to, so read on! (Also, contact the publisher at the address in the front of this book and tell them about your conversion. They'll send you valuable literature to help you begin the Christian walk.)

2. A Process Called Sanctification

Conversion is not the end of something; it's just the beginning! When God forgives you and wipes the slate clean in your life at conversion, He begins a process called *sanctification*.

This is the real work that God wants to do in you; it's the work that conversion was designed to initiate. This is why He forgave us. God's plan for change continues through a process called sanctification.

The apostle Paul described the beginning of the process in 2 Corinthians 5:17: **"Therefore, if anyone is in Christ, he is a new creation. The old has passed away; behold, the new has come."** Paul referred to the process in

1 Thessalonians 4:1: **"Finally, then, brothers, we ask and urge you in the Lord Jesus, that as you received from us how you ought to walk and to please God, just as you are doing, that you do so more and more."** Do you see it in that verse? *More and more* I'm growing and growing in Him. He's changing me *more and more.*

That kind of ongoing change is supposed to take place the rest of our lives—more and more.

When you're a new Christian, you begin with immense uncertainty. You step in stuff all the time and then have to clean up the mess. But eventually you learn, as a follower of Jesus Christ, how to walk, and then you don't have messes as much, and life is so much better. That's the process of sanctification. As Paul explained, **"You ought to walk . . . to please God. . . . For you know what instructions we gave you through the Lord Jesus. For this is the will of God, your sanctification"** (1 Thessalonians 4:1–3).

IS IT REALLY GOD'S WILL TO CHANGE ME?

As a pastor, I often hear questions about God's will. "What does God want me to do?" is the most common, but there are others: "Where does God want me to live?" "Who does God want me to marry?" "What job does God want me to take?" The Bible doesn't spend much time on that stuff. God's focus is on changing the inner you. He says, "If I can change you into the person I want you to be, *you'll know where* you're supposed to go and *you'll know who* you're supposed to marry and *you'll know where* you're supposed to work." God's will is 98 percent about who you are . . . not where you are or who you are with. The Bible teaches that God's will is your sanctification.

The word *sanctification* comes from a root word that means *to sanctify.* (Isn't that helpful?) Specifically, the word *sanctify* means *to make holy.* Ah, now we're getting somewhere. Thus, sanctification is the process by which God takes sinful people and makes them holy. It's not really as churchy as it sounds. *Holy* is a great word; it means *set apart* or *distinct.* It means *different from the sinful world around us.* It means being like God! **"This is the will of God, your sanctification."** That's what God is doing—He's trying to sanctify or change you—more and more.

Choose to believe the truth that God is changing you, and you should clear up a lot of confusion. Next time you wonder about what you are seeing or experiencing and struggle to know what God could be up to, just say to yourself, "He is changing me," and you'll be right. Next time disappointments or heartaches come (maybe you're in the midst of them right now), you might hear yourself asking, "God, what are You doing?" Next time you look over your shoulder in the midst of your pain, try to recognize that God Himself is holding the hammer and chisel.

Try not to ask the silly question, "God, what are You doing?" because the answer is always the same: "I'm changing you!" Don't ask, "What are You doing that for? You're supposed to be making me happy!" or He'll answer, "Who told you that? That's not what I'm trying to do. I'm not trying to make you happy; I'm trying to make you holy!"

Sometimes we respond honestly—but incorrectly—with, "Well, stop. It's hurting." And God's answer would be, "Haven't you read Hebrews 12:6, where I say, **'For the Lord disciplines the one He loves, and chastises every son whom He receives'**?" See! It's all about transformation!

Let's deep-six some wrong ideas about what God is doing in this world:

1. *God's just loving everybody.* Many people believe the whole world is just this big lovefest. The world is like some supernatural, Jesus-oriented, anything goes Woodstock. "We're all together and God is just loving us. Isn't this groovy?" That's not happening. God loves us. Yes, He surely does. Absolutely, but it's not some *pampering* love—it's a *perfecting* love. It's a love that wants our highest and best usefulness for His purposes. And because of that, at times He will need to discipline and correct us.

2. *God is trying to make us healthy, wealthy, and happy.* Incorrect! That kind of teaching could only come from North American preachers and television. If you tried preaching that almost anywhere else in the world the Christians there would laugh you right off the platform. The tragic fact is that many Western Christians have surrounded themselves with teachers who tell them the things they want to hear. Even a casual study of the life of Jesus proves that teaching to be nonsense. The Bible doesn't come even remotely close to teaching that.

3. *God's trying to reach everybody with the gospel.* Is that what God is doing? Is that the bull's-eye on God's heart—evangelism? The Bible does say **"The Lord is . . . not wishing that any should perish, but that all should reach repentance"** (2 Peter 3:9). Yes, God does love the world, and we are commanded to go into all the world and preach the gospel. And yet Jesus taught that **"No one can come to Me unless the Father . . . draws him"**

(John 6:44). God's highest purpose is not to reach the whole world, or the whole world would already be reached. He is partnering with us to get the gospel out, so that everyone can hear. But Christ told us that only a "few" would actually find the narrow road that leads to eternal life (see Matthew 7:13–14). To say that God's highest or ultimate purpose is to get the gospel to everyone contradicts Scripture and experience; it pronounces failure upon God in something He is not even attempting to do.

Maybe you're wondering, "Well, what *is* God's bottom line then?" Here's the hard truth that sets people free; God's bottom line doesn't have anything to do with you or me or any human being. This whole universe is not about us; it's about God. God does not exist to fulfill our purposes; we exist to fulfill God's purposes. The reason why He allows you and me to draw another breath is for His purposes, not ours. God changes us not to make us feel good or accomplish our plans. He changes us so we can accomplish His purposes. God is not here for us; we are here for Him.

IT'S ALL FOR GOD'S GLORY

You ask, "Well, what exactly does He want?" God's purpose is to bring glory to or display Himself. That's why God created the universe. **"The heavens declare the glory of God, and the sky above proclaims His handiwork"** (Psalm 19:1). God made all the planets and all the stars and the entire universe because He wanted to display Himself.

You ask, "Well, why did He make people?" God has already answered that question: "I have created [you] for My glory; I have formed [you], yes, I have made [you]" (see Isaiah 43:7). God made us so that we could bring glory to Him. That's why we're here.

Of course, everyone on the earth doesn't bring glory to God, just the people He has converted. **"He chose us in Him before the foundation of the world, that we should be . . . to the praise of His glory"** (Ephesians 1:4, 12).

The glory of God is what emanates from Him. As light is to bulb, as heat is to fire, as wet is to water, so glory is what emanates from the presence of God. No one has ever seen God (see John 1:18), but where He is, His glory is displayed.

Now here's the point: God wants to bring glory to Himself and display Himself through you. In fact, He wants to do it even in the most mundane things that you do. **"So, whether you eat or drink, or whatever you do, do all to the**

glory of God" (1 Corinthians 10:31). If you're a mom, understand that in every task—even the common and the repetitive—almighty God wants to display His presence through the way that you do it. If you're a factory worker or a medical doctor or a salesclerk or an astronaut, the truth remains the same: God wants to display His glory through you. Paul wrote, **"Or do you not know that your body is a temple of the Holy Spirit within you . . . ? For you were bought with a price. So glorify God in your body"** (1 Corinthians 6:19–20).

Now I am on the bull's-eye of why you are here. The reason why you are here is because *God wants to display His power and splendor through your life*, and if you realize that you are not doing it very well, then you truly understand why He wants to change you. He wants to get you to the place where no matter what happens to you or what you go through, you trust Him and follow Him and are committed wholly to His goodness. And so He's coming after you, and He's trying to change you. That process is called *sanctification*.

WHAT WILL I LOOK LIKE WHEN HE'S FINISHED?

Maybe you're thinking, "If I'm going to give this thing over to God . . . I'm kind of fussy about how I look. What exactly is God going to make me into?" Paul described us as those being made into "vessels" that honor God: **"For this is the will of God, your sanctification: that you abstain from sexual immorality; that each one of you should know how to control his own body in holiness and honor"** (1 Thessalonians 4:3–4). Notice the word *honor*. Whose honor? God's! As Paul compared us to a vessel (the word **body** is literally *vessel*, or *common jar*), he was teaching that the real you is not your body, but your soul. The body is temporary and the soul is eternal. The Bible calls us to live in our temporary bodies in a way that honors our Creator, **"not in the passion of lust like the Gentiles who do not know God. . . . For God has not called us for impurity, but in holiness"** (1 Thessalonians 4:5, 7).

If you're still struggling to picture what God wants to change you into, just think of Jesus Christ. He models who we are to become. That's why Jesus didn't simply drop down to spend three days on the earth, die for our sins, and rise again. Peter wrote, **"Christ . . . [left] you an example, so that you might follow in His steps"** (1 Peter 2:21). The essence of Christianity is to be like Jesus Christ, so that when people see you, they see the joy and the surpassing victory and the gentle graciousness of Christ. That's what God's trying to do. He's trying to make all His children like Jesus.

Let me show you a really cool verse. In fact, take a moment and read this: **"And we all, with unveiled face, beholding the glory of the Lord, are being transformed into the same image from one degree of glory to another. For this comes from the Lord who is the Spirit"** (2 Corinthians 3:18). God wants to change you to the point where you see Christ when you look at your life, the same way you see your physical self by looking in a mirror. People think that God is all about forgiving and trying to get as many people to heaven as He can. Wrong! God is about transforming people. He doesn't want the majority of Christians who are a tiny bit like Jesus. He wants the minority who are a lot like His Son. And He is transforming us, gradually, one step at a time. Notice how the text says *from one degree of glory to another.* Every little opportunity to display His glory, every little bump in the road of life equals an opportunity to change.

WHY HOLINESS IS ESSENTIAL

When you first realize that life after conversion is all about being changed, it can be a bit overwhelming. You may feel like, "Can't I just go to heaven? This is like way too much for me. I just wanted the fire insurance. I don't want all this heavy stuff—it hurts and it's hard, this change stuff. Can't I just be forgiven?" The Scripture's wise response is: **"For the moment all discipline seems painful rather than pleasant, but later it yields the peaceful fruit of righteousness to those who have been trained by it. . . . Strive for peace with everyone, and for the holiness without which no one will see the Lord"** (Hebrews 12:11, 14).

That phrase **"see the Lord"** is a reference to heaven. The verse is saying that without holiness, you're not going to heaven. Holiness is not the means to heaven or the road to heaven, but it is the evidence that you really are going there. Everyone whom God makes one of His own children—everyone who converts—is being made holy. If God is not changing you, you have to honestly ask, "Have I ever really converted?" To put it another way, "If your faith isn't changing you, it hasn't saved you." The people who really have the new birth—the people who really have that conversion experience—are changing.

"He who began a good work in you will bring it to completion at the day of Jesus Christ," Paul wrote (Philippians 1:6). It's not like God dropped down into your life and forgave you and then went on to somebody else. When He dropped down into your life, He came to stay. The moment you converted, God started something, and He's not stopping it until the very last day that you're on this earth. It's the process of transformation, and it produces holiness.

Are you ready to commit yourself to full cooperation with the work of transformation that God wants to do in you? It involves a crisis and a process. For life change to happen, you must commit.

Teacher Questions

1. What does the word "sanctification" mean? Is it a crisis or a process? What is that crisis?
2. What is the goal of sanctification? Can you prove it from Scripture?
3. How are you tracking your progress in sanctification?

Prophet Questions

1. Why is it that Christians are so often content simply to be forgiven and not actually transformed?
2. If we're not saved by being holy, how is holiness related to salvation?
3. What is the current state of holiness in your life?

Shepherd Questions

1. Why is it hard for you to accept the truth that God loves you?
2. How has your past been used by the Enemy to stall God's transformation in your life?
3. How often are you asking God to lead you into greater holiness?

LET'S GET TO WORK

Take a moment and make two lists. In list one, place all the reasons why people (1) don't trust God to change them, (2) don't want to change, and (3) are afraid to change. In list two, show all the reasons why we (1) can trust God, (2) should allow Him to change us, and (3) should desire that. Now evaluate the list. Which one is rooted in trust and faith? Which one is rooted in lies and doubt?

LOOK UP!

If you are a non-Christian, you cannot pray the "prayer of commitment" below until you have had a crisis of conversion, for change is not possible until you convert. Conversion puts you on the road to sanctification, the process of ongoing change.

Therefore, we begin "Look Up!" with a prayer of conversion. If you have not had that crisis of conversion, I invite you to pray this prayer.

Dear Father in heaven:

I know that I am a sinner and deserve Your rejection and punishment. Thank You for loving me enough to send Your Son Jesus into this world to die as payment for my sin. I repent of my sin and turn to You alone for my forgiveness. I believe that You are the only One who can cleanse my heart and change me.

Today I am making the choice to convert to following You and Your truth. I now receive Jesus as the Savior and Lord of my life. In the name of Jesus I pray. Amen.

The following is a prayer of commitment for Christians—a commitment to full cooperation with God's desire to transform you.

Dear heavenly Father:

Thank You that Your greatest passion is my transformation. Thank You that the painful circumstances in my life prove that I really am Your child. Please forgive me for resenting and resisting Your attempts to change me. I choose now to cooperate fully with Your desire to transform me. Anything You want to teach me I am willing to learn. Anything You want to change in me, I am available to receive. Thank You for loving me enough to make me like Jesus, in whose name I pray. Amen.

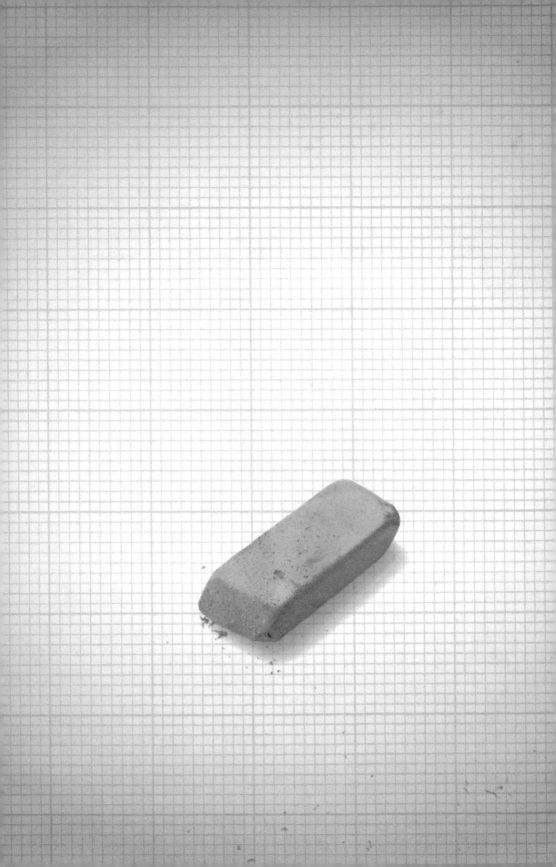

3

LET'S GET **SPECIFIC**

SAY IT IN A SENTENCE:

*For life change to begin, I must identify and isolate
one or two specific things God wants to change in me next.*

Did you ever play dodgeball as a kid? You know, where someone flings a large ball at a group of kids who scramble wildly as they try to dodge the ball; the last one remaining is the winner. I remember clear as a bell some wildly competitive games of elimination dodgeball in my elementary school gym. The teacher would roll the ball into the middle of the floor and shout, "Go get it!" All the kids would scatter away from the ball, and the biggest kid (not me) would saunter to the center of the floor, pick up the ball, and start firing rocket shots in all directions like guided missiles. We would huddle together and hide behind each other, terrified of being hit. We weren't trying to win, just survive.

Sometimes I observe followers of Jesus playing a spiritual version of the same game. Most Christians agree in principle that God is trying to change them, but they dodge the specifics. "Change? God change me? Absolutely!" we often say, but in reality we are dodging the process. Willing to buy into change in general terms, we squirm and twist and dodge when God uses a person or circumstance to begin working on the specifics.

Let me give you an example: One morning as I prepared to leave for work I was feeling a bit frustrated about some things I would face that day, and I knew my temperature was rising. Just then my oldest son, Luke, came into the kitchen venting frustration about the pants he was wearing. He had left an orange Magic Marker in his pocket, and of course it leaked during washing and had deposited several large ink stains. As he whined and complained, I reached the boiling point and proceeded to communicate with much intensity that it was not appropriate to vent his frustration on others simply because he was working through something that bothered him.

About three-quarters of the way through my speech on the subject, it occurred to me that I was doing the very thing that I was exhorting him not to do. Great teaching, huh? (More on how God is changing me later.) In this chapter, will you allow God to point out the specifics about what He is trying to change in you? In every situation and in every circumstance, through every person that you meet, God is working to make you more like His Son, Jesus Christ. That cannot happen unless you allow God to point out the specifics. As long as you "dodge" those specifics and relax in the land of generalities, you will not experience the transforming power of the gospel. Maybe you're wondering,

WHAT DO YOU MEAN BY SPECIFICS?

The Bible teaches that our God loves order (see 1 Corinthians 14:40), and you can be certain that He has an orderly plan for your transformation. He doesn't begin each day when you wake up trying to decide what to work on in you. He isn't swayed by your moods or circumstances, and He has a righteously stubborn way of ensuring that what He specifically begins to work on He will accomplish (see Philippians 1:6). By specifics, I mean we must identify (with God's help) the specific areas of failure or defeat so that God can give us victory.

In addition to specific sins that have to go, change is also about specific good things that God wants to add to your life. It's not just about what you need to stop doing; it's also important things He wants you to *start* doing. Specific things!

If you are truly serious about personal transformation, you must be willing to ask "What's the next step? What's the specific thing that God Almighty is working on in me today?" Until you can get specific like that, personal transformation for you will be just a concept: a nice idea, but only a pipe dream. I often hear people say: "Yeah! I want to be like Jesus, sure! Who wouldn't? So, where do I start?" Hey, listen, there is no true commitment to personal change without a willingness to get specific.

Can you name a *specific* area of your life that is not like that of Christ and is bringing you heartache and struggle because of it? What *specific* thing is God seeking to work on in you? Not "Someday . . . something . . . somehow." What does God need to work on in you now?

LET'S GET SPECIFIC

Let's get specific! Here are five steps to help you get specific about what God is working on in you.

1. Ask God in faith for wisdom to know exactly what He wants to change in you. (James 1:2–7)

God is the Architect. He is the Contractor and He is the Coworker in all personal change. We cannot begin without His blueprint in hand—His specific wisdom on where to go to work. But part of His wisdom is to use trials as His heavy construction machinery. Therefore, James wrote, **"Count it all joy, my brothers, when you meet trials of various kinds"** (James 1:2). The word **"meet"** in this verse actually means *a sudden, unexpected hardship*. That's the way that trials come, don't they? You're going along and all of a sudden you're like, "Whoa! I didn't see this steamroller coming." Also notice that other word, **"various"** trials. *Various* is actually the same as a word used in the Greek translation of the Old Testament to describe Joseph's coat of many colors. It means that trials come in all shapes and sizes. What you're going through is really a lot different than what I'm facing. Trials come in all different types, amounts, and intensities; i.e., financial, relational, physical, emotional, etc.

Notice James said, **"Count it all joy . . . when you meet trials."** The word **"count"** means to *press down upon your mind*. It means to think about it. The idea is that you take your specific trial in hand and you begin to focus your thoughts on what is going on and why. Is there a purpose for this? I mean, what really is joyful about hardship if you don't discover its specific purpose? But don't leave it there—deliberately label that trial *joy*. You can do this because of what you **"know"** (v. 3). Trials bring the steel treads of God's truth to the road of life. When contact is made, we can't forget what we know in the heat of friction. Trials help us to really know what we know.

According to verse 4, we know that the goal of all trials is to produce patience or **"steadfastness."** The New International Version of the Bible says **"perseverance."** The New American Standard version says **"endurance."** The Greek word for patience literally means *the ability to remain under*. God is trying to produce staying power in you—the ability to remain under the pressure. When hardship comes into your life, it puts pressure on you. And what's the thing that you want to do when you start to really feel the pressure? You want to get out from under it. "Ooohh. What is that on me! I don't like—this—get it off." Sometimes we pray, and we ask God, "Please take that out of my life! I don't *want* it anymore!" But God is trying to produce staying power in you!

Staying power is the ability to remain under that thing—as hard as it is. The determination to remain in that marriage—as hard as it is. The endurance to remain in that job—as hard as it is. The perseverance to stick with it in that difficult circumstance—no matter what. If God can produce in you that staying power, He can give you everything else.

Staying power is the funnel through which all Christian virtue flows. There is nothing good that God brings into your life by way of transformation that He doesn't bring through the funnel of perseverance. If God can get that characteristic into your life, He can truly make you what He wants you to be. Staying power is going to produce something. Look at the promise: **"Let steadfastness** (patience) **have its full effect, that you may be perfect and complete, lacking in nothing"** (verse 4). God can get every characteristic of Christ into your life if He can just teach you to persevere.

Listen, loved one. It's not how often you fall; it's how long you stay down. There is so much that God wants to do in your life and you have been resisting because you won't let Him produce perseverance in you. God wants *very much* for you to know what He's working on in your life. But it must begin here: Ask in faith for God's wisdom.

Now here is the good news: God offers wisdom regarding the specifics. **"If any of you lacks wisdom, let him ask God, who gives generously to all without reproach, and it will be given him"** (verse 5).

Change isn't coming like some big sweeping force over you, or like a large blanket. Here is how it *is* coming: It's arriving one adjustment at a time, bit by bit, measured progress on specifics. And this is the awesome thing about God. If you are already feeling the weight of the need for change you may be thinking, "It doesn't matter, man. I'm so lame. I always fail. UGH!" Here's a clue: that's the Enemy. That's the argument of the one who wants to keep you under his thumb and defeated.

Satan condemns in generalities: "Loser! Lost cause! You are hopeless!" That's the Enemy. He doesn't give anything to work on. He's not the corrector, instructor, or helper; he's the condemner and deceiver. He insists, "Oh, you are so messed up! You'll *never* get there! Not even God can help you." That's the Enemy of your soul whispering in your ear.

God doesn't come to us with condemning generalities. God comes to us with loving specifics:

☐ "You're going to need to be more patient."

☐ "You're going to need to grow in your faith and in your ability to trust Me. I have amazing things coming for you, but you don't have very much faith right now."

☐ "You need to become less selfish and more loving."

☐ "You need to become more generous."

☐ "You're harsh and angry. And that's not helping anything. We're going to work on *that* now."

God comes to us in specifics.

Now, how great is that promise? God loves you so much that He is willing to give you mega-wisdom about the specific things He is trying to change in you. He's not trying to hide it from you; just ask Him. I remember, back in school, partying with my friends till late at night and then going to take an exam the next morning and praying, "Lord, Your Word says that if we lack wisdom, that we should ask. . . ." That's not what this verse is talking about. This is a promise for wisdom regarding trials.

WHEN YOU GO THROUGH A TRIAL, ONE QUESTION IS ON YOUR MIND: WHY?

What's the number one question on the mind of every person going through a trial? One word: *why*. "Why is this happening? Why? Why? Why?" as in "What are You trying to teach me?"

God won't answer any old "why." Just the right one!

God does not answer the *existential why*, as in "Why do bad things happen to good people?" "Why is the world like it is?" Ask it if you want, but you'll feel like you're in an echo chamber—just a ringing silence.

God also doesn't answer the *ultimate why* as in "What will I ultimately look like?" or "Where is my life going?" and "Where will this all end?"

Here's another *why* He doesn't answer. God doesn't answer the *ultimatum why*, as in "You had better tell me what's going on or I'm not going to be part of this." When we pull that one, God's response may well be a hearty "Whoa! I am *so* scared now!" You see, we cannot threaten God. Okay? Threats are not a thing for Him at all.

You may be wondering, "Well, what kind of wisdom *will* He give?" The *why* that God loves to answer and does answer is, "Lord, why today? What are You trying to teach me this morning?" "God, what kind of a person do You want me

to be tonight?" And, "How do You want to use this thing to produce the righteousness of Christ in me today?" Notice that James said that God gives *that* kind
of wisdom, and He does so **"generously"** and **"without reproach."** The word
reproach literally means *He won't sink His teeth into the person who asks*. God never
shouts, "What are you asking Me that for?!" It's more like: "I am so glad you finally asked Me *why* I've allowed this." God wants to give you wisdom regarding
the specifics of what He's working on in you.

MAKE SURE YOUR REQUEST
FOR WISDOM IS "IN FAITH."

But here is the key, and this is why most people remain mystified about what
God is trying to do in their lives. **"But let him ask in faith, with no doubting"** (verse 6). Doubting what? Doubting if there is a God? No, or you wouldn't
be praying to Him. What would you be doubting when you're asking for wisdom
regarding your trial?

Verse 8 gives the answer: **"He is a double-minded man, unstable in all in
his ways."** The word *double-minded* there means literally two-souled. The doubter
of James 1:6–7 is saying in effect, "There is part of me, God, that really wants to
know why You've allowed this and really wants to work on it. And there's part
of me that's like, 'Okay, God, what are You trying to teach me, but it can't be this
or that. Okay, God, what is it You want to change about me, but I'm not willing to
work on these four things; but anything else—I'm wide open (sort of).'"

God will not reveal the specifics about what He is trying to change in us while
we are limiting the list from which He can choose.

There is a warning in verse 6—a warning not to become a "beach ball Christian." James wrote not to doubt, **"for the one who doubts is like a wave of the
sea that is driven and tossed by the wind."** Have you ever watched a beach
ball caught up on the waves? Between the wind and the waves, you never know
where it is going to go. It's all over the place. How much control does the beach
ball have over where it goes? None! And how much control does the believer have
over where his life goes if he is not sure if he really wants to be what God wants
him to be? None! Are you a "beach ball Christian," unsure from day to day if you
really want to be what God is making you into?

If yes, no wonder you have not received wisdom to understand why God has
allowed what He has in your life. As James explained, **"For that person must
not suppose that he will receive anything from the Lord"** (verse 7).

Let me summarize: God will not reveal what He is trying to produce in you unless you give Him a blank slate to work on and you can say from your heart, "No restrictions, Lord. Anything in my life, go for it, I'm Yours, period!" Bottom line: Until you are cooperating fully with God's desire to transform you (chapter 2), He will not give wisdom in regard to what He is working on in your life.

When you have made that full surrender, you are truly ready to "get specific."

2. Review biblical lists for attitudes and behaviors to change.

The New Testament is replete with lists of the specific things God is trying to accomplish in our lives. Attitudes and behaviors He wants us to "put off" and those things He wants us to "put on." Ephesians 4:22, 24, for example, has this exhortation: **"To put off your old self, which belongs to your former manner of life and is corrupt through deceitful desires . . . and to put on the new self."**

Begin by asking God for wisdom, then open your Bible to one of those lists, such as Colossians 3:5–10, and, believe me, God will get specific with you. Just pray, "Lord, convict my heart about something in Your Word that You want to change in me." And begin reading—slowly. Ask the "Lord, am I like that?" prayer after each specific item. In verses 5 and 8, for instance, you'll encounter these actions and attitudes that you are to put off: **"sexual immorality, impurity, passion, evil desire, and covetousness, which is idolatry. . . . You must put them all away: anger, wrath, malice, slander, and obscene talk from your mouth."**

As you read through such a list, you'll be like, "Uh, Okay . . . Okay . . . Okay." And then you'll say, "Ouch." Do you know what I am talking about? Has that ever happened to you when you were reading God's Word? You feel the jab of truth in your heart and know God is saying, "*That's* one of the things we can be working on anytime you're ready." Here's an example from verse 9: **"Do not lie to one another, seeing that you have put off the old self with its practices."**

Then we'll read how we must **"put on the new self"** (verse 10) and are told how we can respond, with **"compassionate hearts, kindness, humility, meekness, and patience, bearing with one another and, if anyone has a complaint against another, forgiving each other; as the Lord has forgiven you, so you also must forgive. And above all these put on love, which binds everything together in perfect harmony"** (verses 12–14).

I'll give you another example, Galatians 5:16. Now the picture is not "putting off and putting on." Now the picture is walking. The Christian life is a walk. Take a walk in Galatians 5:16–21 and see if there is anything that stands out to you. Grab a pen and underline something if God pricks your heart about it. In addition to items you read in Colossians 3, you find these additional **"desires of the flesh"** (and there may be some ouches you'll feel here, too. Mark them down as areas God wants you to work on): **"sexual immorality, impurity, sensuality, idolatry, sorcery, enmity, strife, jealousy** (that's an ouch; I'll underline it), **fits of anger, rivalries** (ouch), **dissensions, divisions, envy, drunkenness, orgies, and things like these"** (verses 19–21a).

So those things are going out; and here's what's coming in—the fruit of the Spirit —the evidence that the Spirit is present in my life: **"love, joy, peace, patience, kindness, goodness, faithfulness, gentleness, self-control"** (verses 22b–23a).

Why is all of this stuff in the Bible? Because God wants His people to be looking down the list and finding the specific things that He is trying to produce in their life. He hasn't left us clueless.

For many years I made it a habit when I was talking to Christians to ask, "What's God working on in your life?" Hundreds of times I have asked people, "So what's God working on in your life these days?" As a pastor I can get away with asking stuff like that, and when I do I get three main responses.

1. *The generic Christian response.* The generic response goes: "He's teaching me to love Him more," or "I need to trust Him more," or "I need to serve Him better." It's the generic, vague, Christianese kind of answer, and I wonder, Do you even have an answer?

2. *The evasive answer.* That's pretty common when I don't know the person as well. I say "Hey! What's God working on in your life?" And they are like, "Well, um . . . you know, I've never really had anybody ask me something, you know, quite that specific. It's really kind of um . . . personal, you know, to talk about what's going on in my own life here. I . . . I don't think I'm going to answer that." And I think to myself, You can't!

3. *The no-answer answer.* Some people just don't answer the question. I ask, "Hey! So what's God working on in your life? What's something specific He is challenging you about these days?" And they respond, "I . . . I . . . um . . . I . . . um . . . don't think the Bulls have a chance this year." They're practicing the not-so-subtle subject change.

As Christians we can be such liars. Sorry, but I have to say it—sometimes we are insincere; we lie. We sing songs and we say stuff when we're not even serious. Do you remember the old Joel Hemphill song, popularized by Bill Gaither, "He's still working on me"? Every time I hear that now I want to shout, "What!!" What's He working on?! Where has He made some progress?

WHAT SPECIFICALLY IS HE WORKING ON IN YOU?

Until you can answer with certainty about what God is *specifically* working on, you won't make a lot of progress.

Don't refuse to get specific about change by arguing that sanctification is *all* the Holy Spirit. Some Christians argue that; but if that were true, why is there all this biblical teaching on our part in change? When James instructs us to **"confess yours sins to one another and pray for one another"** (James 5:16), that sounds like specific language! Others counter that, "It's not the Holy Spirit; it's all us. We have to change ourselves." But Paul warned one group of believers, **"O foolish Galatians! Who has bewitched you? . . . Having begun by the Spirit, are you now being perfected by the flesh?"** (Galatians 3:1, 3). Recognize that it's a partnership between you and God, and He is willing to do His part if you are willing to do your part.

Do this: Isolate your own area of need. Not what your spouse needs to work on. Not what your dad needs to learn. Every follower of Jesus Christ should be able to articulate two or three things that God is trying to change in them; can you? You should have them on the tip of your tongue.

Also, don't refuse to get specific about change by hiding behind the strengths of your church. When God looks down at us, He doesn't say, "Oh, there are the people from Harvest Bible Chapel. Oh, there are the wonderful saints at First Baptist Church. Oh, there are those nice people down at St. Luke's Presbyterian Church." God doesn't look at us in groups. God looks at us as individuals. As Paul warned in Romans 14:10, 12, **"Why do you pass judgment on your brother? Or you, why do you despise your brother? For we will all stand before the judgment seat of God. . . . So then each of us will give account of himself to God."**

You *will* give an account of yourself to God. You're going to make a speech. And God may have to say, "Now, what was the problem exactly? Why couldn't we make better progress in the things that I wanted to do in you?" Everyone will give an account; and we don't want to be talking or blaming anybody else at that point.

3. Isolate your own areas of need.

Below and on the next page you will find what, I believe, are some of the most devastating character weaknesses common in the life of a believer. The list focuses on things that need to be "put off," according to the Scriptures. I am emphasizing what one needs to "put off," because nobody wants to put on a brand-new suit or dress before he or she takes the old one off. Let's focus first of all on the things that need to go, and I think very naturally you will see the things that need to go in their place.

I want you to know that the following list has been very significant in my life and in our church. Take some time right now and rank yourself on a scale of 0–10. Now in some of the categories, you'll say to yourself, "Absolutely not an issue in my life." If that's the truth, just put 0. If the attitude is extremely rare, score it a 1. If it is occasionally—but very occasionally—an issue for you, score it 2–3. If it is sometimes a problem, score it a 5. If it is often a struggle, then you're more in the 7 category. If you know it is one of your significant weaknesses, you are in the 8, 9, or 10 categories.

I'll give you a little head start. If you are thinking about closing the book because you just can't face the hassle of self-analysis, score yourself high in stubbornness. And if you want to write 9 or 10 beside every item, then self-deprecation is probably where you need to go to work. If you have 0s and 1s beside everything, then self-righteousness is your area for needed growth. If you want to change, but can't seem to find the energy to work on your life, possibly your need is to work on laziness.

GETTING SPECIFIC: MY NEEDS FOR CHANGE

Here is a list of attitudes and feelings that every follower of Christ needs to "put off" in his life. Place a number, from 0 to 10, before each item to indicate the extent of its presence in your life. Mark 0 if it's "not an issue at all" and 10 if it's present on a regular basis. (See the above for more information on rating each item.)

_ Addiction	_ Bitterness	_ Controlled by emotions
_ Anger	_ Boastful	_ Controlled by peer pressure
_ Anxiety	_ Bossiness	_ Covetousness
_ Argumentative	_ Causing dissension	_ Critical tongue
_ Bigotry	_ Conceit	_ Deceitfulness

_ Depression

_ Dominance

_ Drug dependence

_ Drunkenness

_ Envy (depressed by the
   good fortune of others)

_ False modesty

_ Fear

_ Feelings of rejection

_ Feelings of stupidity

_ Feelings of weakness or
   helplessness

_ Feelings of worthlessness

_ Gluttony

_ Greediness

_ Guilt (false)

_ Hatred

_ Homosexual lust

_ Hostility

_ Idolatry

_ Impatience

_ Impulsiveness

_ Impure thoughts

_ Indifference to others'
   problems

_ Inhibited

_ Insecurity

_ Intemperance

_ Jealousy

_ Laziness

_ Loner

_ Low self-esteem

_ Lust for pleasure

_ Materialistic

_ Must strive to repay any
   kindness shown you

_ Negativism

_ Occult involvement

_ Opinionated

_ Overly quiet

_ Overly sensitive to
   criticism

_ Passivity

_ Prejudice

_ Profanity

_ Projecting blame

_ Prone to gossip

_ Rebellion against
   authority

_ Resentment

_ Restlessness

_ Sadness

_ Self-centeredness

_ Self-confidence

_ Self-deprecation
   (or self-hatred)

_ Self-gratification

_ Self-indulgence

_ Self-justification

_ Self-pity

_ Self-reliance

_ Self-righteousness

_ Self-sufficiency

_ Sensuality

_ Sexual lust

_ Slow to forgive

_ Stubbornness

_ Temper

_ Unloving (of the
   unlovely)

_ Vanity

_ Withdrawal

_ Workaholic

_ Worry

Every single day we pitch our tent one day's march closer to eternity. It's coming; we're all going to be there, and if you have no desire to see almighty God do a work of transformation in your life, you need to check and see if you have lost your way.

4. Confess your sin to a friend.

Maybe it would help a bit at this point if I confessed to you the specific sins God isolated for me when I reviewed the list. You might be saying: "Wait, don't do that. I thought we were only to confess our sins to God." Yes, we confess our sins to God for forgiveness through the Mediator, Jesus Christ (see 1 Timothy 2:5). But we go to our brothers and sisters in Christ for support in the process of change. James 5:16 says, **"Confess your sins to one another"** (NASB).

That's where some churches have it wrong. It's not a whole bunch of people confessing their sins to one superior person; it's confessing our sins to each other. All Christians on equal footing acknowledging their struggles and their weaknesses with one another. The word "confess" means *to say the same thing*. When you go to confess your sins to your friends, you will be saying the same thing they have been saying for a long time. They will be like, "Whew! That is great that you finally see that." They will be thrilled to know that God has revealed to you personally something that the people around you may have been very aware of.

You say, "What would I do this for? Why would I confess my sins to a friend?" For two reasons:

1. *To get it in the open.* As the apostle John wrote, confessing our sins gives us fellowship with others and forgiveness through Christ: **"But if we walk in the light** (that is, get our sins out in the light where we can work on them) **as He is in the light, we have fellowship with one another, and the blood of Jesus His Son cleanses us from all sin"** (1 John 1:7).

2. *To get some prayer support.* When those around you become convinced that you are serious about change, they will become faithful prayer supporters of God's highest and best in your life. Everyone wants to pray about things they know God is willing to do.

So, as I said . . . let me go first. I went through the whole list again recently. I bowed my head and prayed for God's wisdom and then went over each one of those words. As I did, I asked, "Lord, is that me?" I am not proud to say that in twelve of the categories I had to write "8" or more. I highlighted those in green. With twelve things in the definitely-need-to-change category, I went back over the list, focusing on those twelve, and prayed, "God, I am serious about this. I really want to change and need to know what is next." As I prayed, the Lord seemed to emphasize something that was clearly next on His agenda of change in me.

I sensed God telling me, "James, it's time to work on your problem of outbursts of anger and frustration." Those who know me best and work closest with me would agree that I often fail during times of great stress or pressure. Whether with my family or my staff at church, and I say this to my own shame, I get frustrated and at times direct that toward others. I don't swear or throw things, and

I have never hurt anyone, at least not physically, but I know at times I have hurt those I love with my words.

So I began to pray, "Lord, I don't want to use pressures that I feel or a change in circumstances to excuse anger that is not pleasing to You and is hurtful to those I love." I will tell you more in the coming chapters of how God has used that prayer in my life, but let me say now that when we let God get that specific with us, change is on the way.

Each of us needs to know the power of confessing our sin to a trusted friend. If you haven't done it before, you might find it very hard to even say to one person, "I'm failing the Lord in this area." It's tough to say, "I'm not the woman that God wants me to be," or "I'm not the man God is asking me to be in this area." Here are some suggestions that will help you to confess your sins to a friend:

- Choose someone who also wants to change, so the confession can be mutual.
- If married, try not to choose your spouse, as your mate may struggle to be objective with someone so close.
- Choose someone of the same sex.
- Ask for and promise total confidentiality with the person you share with.
- After sharing, pray together, confessing your sin to God. If, later on, you doubt your sincerity, your friend can reassure you.

5. Express to the Lord your willingness to change.

The Scriptures include a phenomenal promise to every child of God who wants to change. **"And this is the confidence that we have toward Him, that if we ask anything according to His will, He hears us. And if we know that He hears us in whatever we ask, we know that we have the requests that we have asked of Him"** (1 John 5:14–15). Knowing that God will do whatever we ask if it is His will, and knowing that sanctification is God's will for us (see 1 Thessalonians 4:3), we can be fully confident that God will change us if we ask. If you go to Him in faith and confidence and say, "God, I am willing for You to change me, and I want You to work on this specifically; I know it's Your heart," you can be confident He will do that.

Teacher Questions

1. How do we know that God really wants to change us?

2. Why are we so reluctant to be specific about what needs changing in us?

3. When will you be completing that self-test on the previous page?

Prophet Questions

1. In what way(s) have you rebelled against God's work of transformation in you?

2. What areas of sin have you rationalized and shut God out of?

3. What have you decided to do about asking God to help you with those areas of needed change?

Shepherd Questions

1. Why is it essential that we believe God loves us before we "get specific"?

2. In what ways does it help you to know God will work on you one or two things at a time?

3. How do you recognize God's love in His willingness to help you change?

LET'S GET TO WORK

Complete and review the list "Getting Specific: My Needs for Change." Then arrange to meet with a friend for a time of mutual confession and prayer. (See guidelines for choosing a friend under the section "4. Confess your sin to a friend.")

LOOK UP!

Dear heavenly Father:

I thank You for Your persistent pursuit of my transformation. I believe You love me and have my best interest at heart so I come to You by faith, 100 percent willing to get specific. Please reveal to me the things You want to change in me next. Nothing is off-limits.

Lord, I want to be everything You would have me be and I'm ready to go to work now. Please be specific with me by Your Holy Spirit. I ask in Jesus' name. Amen.

PART 2

THE
PROCESS
OF
CHANGE

Good job! You have completed the first part, "The Preparation for Change." If you have followed through and done the homework you should have:

- rejected faulty methods for change,
- told God that you are ready and willing to cooperate with His desire to transform you, and
- gotten real specific about your sin, choosing one or two things you're willing to change and confessing those things to a trusted friend.

Now you can say: "I have done those things, so, help me change, God." You are also ready to move into part 2, which is very exciting. It's called "The Process of Change." If you haven't done those things, well, . . . maybe you could give the book to a friend or something . . .

Sound harsh? Remember, we're not trying to talk a better game; we're asking God to actually change us. For that to happen **we have to be willing to do our part!**

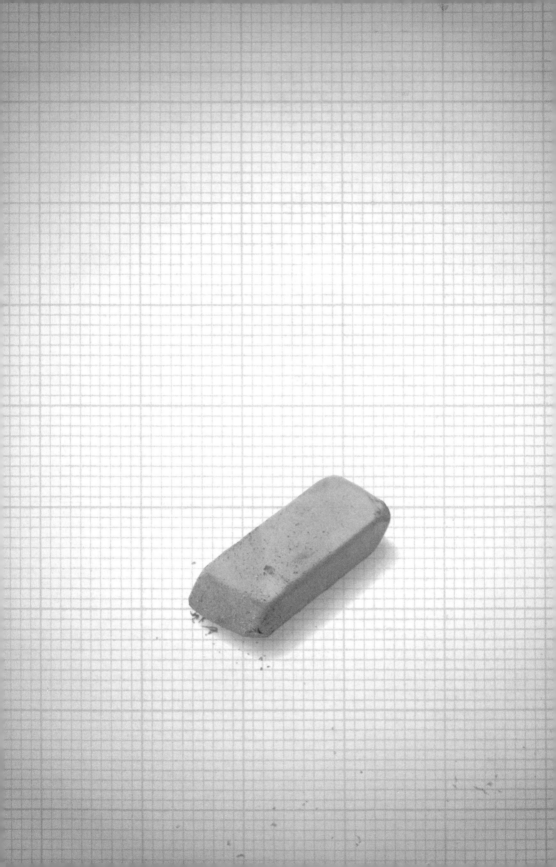

4

STEP ONE: REPENTANCE

SAY IT IN A SENTENCE:

True repentance is the first step in all change, but it is not easy.

This is a chapter on the first step in change. This is also a message that a faithful minister of the gospel has to deliver *repeatedly* in the life of his church—any church. This is a subject that I have preached from various passages many times. The application of this truth has come up frequently in my own life. It is such a central message to the life of every Christian.

We are going to look at God's instruction about how to deal with something called sin. And as we begin to wade into this, I want to make sure we are all on the same page when it comes to understanding the identity of sin.

SIN IS MORE THAN HARDNESS, BUT IT *IS* HARDNESS

Sin is not just temporary hardness. There's a stonelike character to my heart. Your most honest moments bring you up against that unyielding hardness in your own life. When I go to talk to someone about their sin, I have found that most people sense that there's a wall in there; a resistance to exposure. But it's not just hardness; it's darkness and blindness and stubbornness. That's how sin is rooted in us and what sin does to us. We are born fallen creatures.

How often in my preaching I have warned, "Choose to sin, choose to suffer." Well, if that was easy to understand *and* act on, everyone would be getting to a better place. We realize that sooner or later sin leads to suffering. We understand that when we reject the right and pick up the wrong, the choice produces pain. Most people get that! Yet we all regularly make the wrong choices. When I do the wrong thing; when I lash out at my wife; when I lie; when I lust; when I leave something good undone—all these confirm my status as a sinner. If you know to do good and don't do it, it's sin (see James 4:17).

When I sin, I have inflicted suffering upon myself. I am the one who suffers when I sin, yet I still do. Why is that?

SIN IS NOT JUST HARDNESS. IT'S ALSO DARKNESS.

Well, it's because sin is not just hardness; it's also darkness. Sin is darkness within and gravitation to darkness without: **"And this is the judgment: the light has come into the world, and people loved the darkness rather than the light because their works were evil"** (John 3:19). When you are in the process of choosing to sin, you can't always see clearly what you're doing. There is something darkened in our nature that, even if you are in Christ and you are dead to sin, there still is that old nature there, nipping at your heels. The darkness also creates the effect of blindness. Because a person in darkness could even have a sense of light as they move about, but we demonstrate an inability at times to even perceive the wrong. And sometimes I find myself lunging into a choice or action and only then discovering I have stepped into sin.

SIN IS NOT JUST HARDNESS AND DARKNESS.
IT'S ALSO STUBBORNNESS.

Sin is not just hardness; it is blinding darkness *and* stubbornness. What hardness is to stone stubbornness is to the heart. This is one of the things that I sense deeply. And frankly, in the last day or so, there's been a fairly significant spiritual buildup of personal awareness in this area. I have been doing this long enough to know that when you're going to move into enemy territory, you are also going to be met with some resistance. Confronting sin has been a long personal and ministry battle. Sometimes I get tired and think, "Well, wouldn't it be fun to preach something a little fluffier, something a little easier?" But I want to deliver the truth that sets people free. It's not easy to challenge people directly about their sin, but it really is the only way forward with God. Once we have recognized our impossible predicament with sin, we are ready for God's answer.

I want you to know that I really mean what I wrote in those first three chapters. God has been doing some fantastic transforming work in me and I have needed it. Right after I preached the first three chapters of this book in our church, I boarded a plane and flew to Canada for an intense week of ministry. I was working on anger, or more specifically outbursts of frustration, so I had specifically prayed that God would give me chances to work on that during the time that I was away ministering. All I can say is God heard and answered that prayer, as in "loud and clear; enough already."

I was coaching my oldest son's basketball game but left early. I wanted to avoid the kind of hurrying that leads to my sin of anger, so I got to the airport way early for me, like almost an hour before the flight left, but despite all my efforts, including missing the end of a close game (they won by one point in overtime), the plane didn't leave for four hours. In fact, they consolidated my flight with a later one, reporting snow problems. (There was no snow; they were just saving money by grounding a plane. I hate that!) Then I finally got on board—two-and-a-half hours late—and sat on the runway for an hour and fifteen minutes before we took off. As I sat there, I prayed, "Lord, here it is. Here's my chance to work on these things."

The coolest thing began to happen; as hard as that whole week was for me, it was good. I felt such a sense of partnership with the Lord as I yielded to His agenda for change. I began to experience victory at places where before there had been real defeat, and my heart filled with a kind of joy I have seldom known before. But I'm getting ahead of myself. At that point, I had already done the work I am going to talk about in this chapter. This is work each of us must do, in order to experience that surpassing joy. So let's get to work!

STEP ONE: REPENTANCE!

Repentance is the first step in all change. Imagine you could hold in your hand a specific area of personal defeat and/or sin. Take one of the ones you identified in the last chapter. It's before you, and you're asking God to change that area from the inside out. Repentance is the first step in that process. There is nowhere to go if you don't start here. This has always been God's way!

Jesus said, **"Those whom *I love*, I . . ."** (Revelation 3:19, italics added). There's His heart for you—unconditional love! His love is independent of your performance because it is rooted in His very nature and never changes. So what do you think He said next? "As many as I love, I . . . pamper? As many as I love, I . . . answer their prayers quickly and accurately? As many as I love, I . . . leave alone and let them enjoy life as they are"? No! Jesus said: **"Those whom *I love*, I reprove and discipline, so be zealous and repent."** God is always working to change us, and the first thing He asks of us is repentance.

I know some people have been taught only about the love and forgiveness of God. They wrongly believe that God's love overrides all His other attributes; that He will work to transform you in any moment that you have a fleeting fancy for freedom from sin. Sad but true, it's tough to find a preacher who even talks about repentance anymore, let alone proclaims it as God's nonnegotiable first step in change. So in case you're struggling to accept this truth, let me back this up with some Bible review.

A BIBLICAL OVERVIEW OF REPENTANCE

Repentance in the Old Testament

In the Old Testament, the prophets used to preach these one-word sermons. (My church would love it if I preached a one-word sermon. Ha!) Moses, Isaiah, Jeremiah, Ezekiel, Hosea, etc., all did it. Plagiarism to the max, each guy preaching the other guys' sermon. "Repent!" That was their whole message. And then they'd drive across town to their next engagement. "Good morning. Repent!" All through the Old Testament, one word echoes from the prophets' lips: *Repent*.

"What's your question?"

"Well, I want to get right with God. I want to learn how to do this. I want to grow in this or—"

"Repent!" The same message.

I love the verse in Ezekiel 18:30 which says, **" . . . Repent and turn from all your transgressions, lest iniquity be your ruin."** You have dreams for your family and for your future, but sin is crouching at the door. In Genesis 4:7 God warned Cain about the way sin lurks, **" . . . And . . . its desire is for you."** The only way you're going to keep that from happening, the only way you're going to see your dreams from being realized? Ask God for an awareness of sin and a willingness to repent. Otherwise . . .

☐ Sin will tear your marriage apart.
☐ Sin will tear your children apart.
☐ Sin will tear your finances and your future apart.
☐ Sin will tear your church apart.

The degree to which we are truly aware of the continual draw of sin in our lives will be measured by the way in which we live in continual repentance, tender toward God.

Repentance in the New Testament

Amazingly, as you go into the New Testament, the first message John the Baptist ever preached was not very original: **"Repent, for the kingdom of heaven is at hand"** (Matthew 3:2). Jesus Christ, while training the disciples to be excellent ministers, sent them out to preach. Guess what their message was to be? **"So they went out and proclaimed that people should repent"** (Mark 6:12). In Luke 15:7, Jesus said something incredible: **"There will be more joy in heaven over one sinner who repents than over ninety-nine righteous persons who need no repentance."** And by that He meant people who think they need no repentance. *Every person who will ever hold this book with a desire to change will need the exact same thing: repentance!*

Check out the first sermon in the early church. Three thousand people were converted. Peter stood up and guess what his message was? **"Repent"** (Acts 2:38). Second message? Time for some variety? Nope! **"Repent therefore, and turn back, that your sins may be blotted out, that *times of refreshing* may come from the presence of the Lord"** (Acts 3:19–20a, italics added).

Maybe you're reading this and you know in your heart that your spiritual life has become kind of dull or dry and you're wondering, "What happened to my love for Christ? What happened to my passion for spiritual things? How can I get those 'refreshing times' back?" I hope by now you know the answer: Repent!

In Acts 17:30, the apostle Paul revealed God's heart when he said, **"The times of ignorance God overlooked, but now He commands all people everywhere to repent."** Later Paul began to train the next generation of pastors. What did he teach the young Pastor Timothy to preach on? **"Correcting his opponents with gentleness, God may perhaps grant them repentance"** (2 Timothy 2:25). Peter taught the same, **"The Lord is . . . patient toward you, not wishing that any should perish, but that all should reach repentance"** (2 Peter 3:9). Step one, the first thing, is repentance.

GOD'S HEART FOR EVERY PERSON
IS THE SAME: REPENTANCE.

Maybe you're thinking, "That's fine for those brutal, harsh apostles, but that's not the heart of my Shepherd Jesus." Think again. Jesus Himself told the Ephesus church and, by application, all believers of all time: **"Remember therefore from where you have fallen; *repent,* and do the works you did at first. If not, I will come to you and remove your lampstand from its place—**

unless you *repent*" (Revelation 2:5, italics added). Here it is again: Jesus Christ was speaking, **"Therefore repent. If not, I will come to you soon and war against them with the sword of My mouth"** (verse 16). We're back where we started, Revelation 3:19: **"Those whom I love, I reprove and discipline, so be zealous and repent."**

Repentance is the first step in all change. If you really want to change—if you want lasting transformation—this is where you have to begin.

A DEFINITION OF REPENTANCE

I know you truly want to change or you would not have read this far. Yet sometimes you may feel trapped in your specific sin. Do you ever observe in yourself a vicious cycle: sin, then confess, try again; sin-confess, sin-confess, try again, always promising God to change but seldom really experiencing it? Could it be that you have not truly repented of that sin?

The New Testament Greek word for repentance is *metanoia*. It means literally to *rethink* or to *change your mind*. All change begins with a change of mind. Notice the word *mind*. Repentance is not a change of scenery. Repentance is not a new church or new job or a new marriage. Repentance is a change on the inside, a change in the way I think about something.

Down with Deception

In all sin there is deception. Just to illustrate that, let's play a little game of *Sinful Family Feud*. (Music begins:) "Welcome to *Sinful Family Feud*. Introducing on my left, the Pretender Family! . . . Introducing on my right, the Rationalizer Family!

"Okay, let's start the game. We've surveyed one hundred people, and the top five answers are on the board to this question: Name a self-deception people use when choosing to sin. Our survey said:

"Number 5: 'Just this once, I can handle this.'

"Number 4: 'I'll hide it, I'll cover it; no one will know.'

"Number 3: 'Everybody else is doing it.'

"Number 2: 'It can't be wrong if it feels so right.'

"And the number one answer (drum roll): 'I'll just do it, then ask God to forgive me.'"

Do you recognize any of those? The sad truth is that I didn't have to do a survey at all, just consult my memory bank. Every one of these and other self-deceptions are the mental gymnastics of choosing to sin. Repentance is when you detect and destroy the rationalizations that lead to your sin. It's changing your mind about those lies.

My favorite preacher in the history of Chicago—by quite a bit—is A. W. Tozer. And here's what Tozer said:

> Let us beware of vain and over-hasty repentance, and particularly, let us beware of no repentance at all. We are a sinful race, ladies and gentlemen, a sinful people, and until the knowledge has hit us hard, (what a great sentence), until it has wounded us, until it's got through and past our little department of theology, it has done us no good. A man can believe in total depravity (that great biblical doctrine) and never have any sense of it for himself at all. Lots of us believe in total depravity who have never been wounded with the knowledge that we have sinned. Repentance is a wound I pray we all may feel.

How to Know If You Have Repented

How can you know if you have truly repented? *First, genuine repentance leads to confession of sin.* The word *confession*, in the Greek *homologeo*, means *to say the same.* Confession is to say the same thing about your sin that God says. I believe we have greatly misunderstood the concept of confession. Many believers know 1 John 1:9 by heart: **"If we confess our sins, He is faithful and just to forgive us."** We become very glib with 1 John 1:9, carrying the verse around in our wallet and referring to it moment by moment.

"Sorry, God. It's sin."

"Whoa! Sorry, God. Did it again—sin. Thanks for Your forgiveness."

"Ohhhh! Sorry, God. Did it *again!*"

"Sorry, God. Did *it* yet again!"

"Sorry, God." That's *not* confession. You are not saying what God says about your sin when you put a little Post-it note on your behavior and label it "s-i-n." *You cannot confess your sin until you repent of it. You cannot say what God says about your sin until you see what God sees.* In fact,

REPENTANCE IS THE PROCESS OF
SEEING OUR SIN THE WAY GOD SEES IT.

Only when we see our sin the way God sees it will we be able to say what He says about it. Only then will we *break* the cycle of sin, confess, try again—

that spiritual game we play that doesn't bring glory to Christ and doesn't leave us changed. The first result of true repentance is a genuine *confession* of my sin to God.

Second, genuine repentance results in restitution. In Scripture, Zacchaeus is sort of the poster boy for restitution. Remember the short dude who climbed a tree to get Jesus' attention? Turns out Jesus got his attention. Zach had been a thieving tax collector, and when he repented of his sin to God, he immediately knew he had to make it right with others too; that's restitution. And so he told Jesus, **"If I have defrauded anyone of anything, I restore it fourfold"** (Luke 19:8b).

When we are truly right with God, we want to be right with others. It's the natural next step. After more than twenty-five years as a pastor, I have seen many Christians claim to be right with God when I knew they had not attempted to make things right with others. I've seen unbiblical divorces, where someone runs off with someone else, changes churches, and starts to worship with a new partner like nothing ever happened. How do you make restitution for a fractured relationship between a husband and wife that ends in divorce? When an unbiblical divorce occurs, the kinds of restitution are limited. You might write a letter, or meet to ask forgiveness. But does that suffice for the damage done to both people's lives? The difficulty in making proper restitution reinforces the truth that repentance is not easy.

If there is no restitution, there has been no true repentance. If there is no true repentance, worshiping God is a farce. I've seen people shatter churches through divisive, destructive gossip and then leave to worship elsewhere. Later I hear that they are serving as leaders in that church and yet they have never sought forgiveness for the vicious lies they spread. No wonder those churches struggle, with such hypocrisy at the top. God can't and won't bless that lack of integrity.

Genuine repentance results in restitution! We have to dispense with the notion that we can be right with God and not be right with others. You are not right with God until you've sought to be right with the people your sin affected. The two results of repentance in the heart are (1) confession of sin that goes vertically to God and (2) restitution for sin that extends horizontally to those my sin has injured.

When you are willing to go back to someone and say, "I'm sorry I wronged you. I have no excuse. I'm here to pay what I owe. I've asked for God's forgiveness and now I'm asking for yours"—when you are willing to do that, it proves your repentance is genuine. If you are always doing the business with God and never doing the business with others, you are not really repenting and that's why you are not changing. True repentance is the first step in all change!

THE CHALLENGE OF REPENTANCE

Repentance is not easy. I believe that genuine repentance is the greatest lack in our day. Not Bible knowledge. Not prayer. Not ministry. Not worship. Not the gifts of the Spirit. When genuine repentance happens, all those other things follow. Without it, they can never be. Repentance is the key that unlocks the door to all that God has for us.

Paul wanted the Corinthian converts to experience everything Christ had for them, and godly sorrow was the key to that. He wrote, **"As it is, I rejoice, not because you were grieved, but because you were grieved into repenting. For you felt a godly grief, so that you suffered no loss through us"** (2 Corinthians 7:9). The Greek term for grief (*lupeo*) is used twenty-six times in the New Testament—half of those occur in 2 Corinthians, and half of those come in this passage. Look; here we have, in this passage, twenty-five percent of the entire New Testament teaching on the feelings that accompany genuine repentance.

The term is grief—an *internal hurting*; literally a *soul anguish*. That's what the disciples felt when Jesus announced His crucifixion (see Matthew 17:23). It's what the rich, young ruler felt when " . . . **he went away sorrowful, for he had great possessions"** (Matthew 19:22b).

Repentance may not be easy, but its reward is great. **"Godly grief produces a repentance that leads to salvation without regret, whereas worldly grief produces death,"** Paul wrote in 2 Corinthians 7:10.

Feeling True, Godly Sorrow

Notice that repentance begins with grief—genuine sorrow over sin. We know what *sorrow* means; we're just not used to experiencing it in regard to our own sin. The word *sorrow* literally means *pain*; *internal hurting*; *soul anguish*. Notice that not all sorrow leads to repentance. Some sorrow is not godly sorrow. It's the sorrow of the world. As in, "Sorry I feel so bad." "Sorry I got caught." "Sorry I got hurt." "Sorry you don't like this, God." That's worldly sorrow, where the focus is on ourselves.

The results of worldly sorrow are twofold. First, worldly sorrow produces regret unlike godly sorrow, which is **"without regret."** We all feel the kind of worldly sorrow that produces regret; after all, we *are* citizens of this world, but worldly sorrow is worlds away from genuine repentance. "Why did I do this? Why don't I learn? Why am I like this? Why can't I change?" Regret is a useless emotion; it produces nothing. Regret focuses on what can never change. Repentance focuses on what *has* to change.

Notice how the text says that the result of worldly grief is also death. When the Bible uses *death* in that way, it doesn't mean to die physically. We're all going to die, so that would make it a meaningless statement. Death in this passage means *eternal* death, as in Romans 6:23a: **"The wages of sin is death."**

Please be warned. A lifetime of shallow worldly repentance leads to spiritual death—separation from God—to hell. The sad fact in our day is that the church of Christ contains many people who have never truly repented of their sin. That's why they don't change. Could that be true of you? Maybe you were standing in the mall or watching TV or sitting in a Sunday school class and somebody told you about Jesus. You didn't quite get it all, but you heard the gospel of the big offer: "Jesus loves you and Jesus wants to help you. He will make your life better. Don't you want your life better? Don't you want Jesus?" And you grabbed hold of it and pulled it to yourself and you think you have eternal life—but you don't. You are *not alive spiritually* because you have never truly repented of your sin, never grieved your sin before God. True salvation requires that we truly repent of our sin—agreeing we are going our own way—and then accept Jesus as our Savior and choose to let God lead our lives.

The cross of Jesus Christ is a *radical* thing. And God had to do a radical thing to get us back into fellowship with Him. He had to send His only Son to *suffer*, to *die*, and pay the penalty for your sin and mine. Now if you think you can get the benefits of the cross without ever facing up to the sin that required the cross, you are kidding yourself and trusting in a false gospel. All transformation starts on this point: repentance. Repentance is the first step in salvation, and repentance is the first step in transformation, but repentance is not easy. If it were easy, everyone would be doing it!

Repentance When Restitution Is Impossible

Some sins are more difficult to repent of than others. I know that no one ever comes to my office and says; "Oh, Pastor James, I am so heart stricken. I feel devastated. I just can't get right with God. I cheated on my income tax by $500 and I just don't know how to come to a place of true repentance about that. I'm not sensing God's forgiveness." That is like the easiest counseling session ever. "Get out your checkbook and write a check! If you are genuinely sorrowful over what you did, you'll pay it back!"

For those kinds of sins, we know that our repentance is genuine because we make it right, but there are two kinds of sin that are difficult to repent of, because you can't make them right. Satan goes after our failure in these areas because he knows if he can get us to stumble here, it will be much harder for us to repent.

Two categories of sin make repentance difficult; for in each case you can do little for restitution. *First, there are opportunities squandered.* How do you make restitution for an opportunity squandered? Let me give you some examples. The following are fictional stories. Any similarity to real persons—living or dead—is purely convicting.

- Kim had an abortion. She was young and impulsive. She was on the corporate ladder. She knew it was wrong, but she did it anyway. And now she has two things in her hand: the desire to make it right with God, and the freedom that resulted from the choice that she made to get an abortion. Now how do you repent of a choice that you made and at the same time continue to experience what you perceive as the benefits of that choice? It's not easy.
- Jeff was unbiblically divorced. He was willful, selfish, and rebellious. He knew it was wrong, but he got out. Now his former wife has remarried. He can't show his sincerity by making it right. He wants to be right with God, but in his heart he struggles to know if he is truly sorry for the decision he made. At times he wishes he could return to his wife, and at times he is relieved that she is remarried. Opportunity squandered. He can't go back now. He can't make it right. It's too late. How is he going to repent? It's not impossible, but it's not easy. This is a warning.
- Steve and Gail were a two-career family. With their three children, they were wealthy—and busy. Their kids had everything but them. There was no need for both of them to work; they know now it was just greed. Today their kids are grown and the seeds of neglect have come to fruition. Their kids want nothing to do with them and nothing to do with the Lord. How do you repent of that? You have the house by the lake. You have the extra cars you wanted. You've done the vacations. You've traveled to the places. You have the bank deposits. You went after something and got it and you have the results of those wrong choices, too. How do you repent of that? Opportunity squandered.

Second, there are the pleasures consumed. An alcoholic binge. A private pornography. A repeated gluttony. A strong compulsion. A homosexual tryst. A willful pursuit. A deliberate choice. Each of these represents a pleasure consumed. You have indulged in whatever momentary pleasure came from that temptation and now you are facing regrets and consequences. How do you make restitution for that? You had what you wanted. The problem is that you wanted the sinful pleasure *and* a relationship with God. That's where the rub comes, because you cannot have both.

You are struggling to convince yourself that you were sincere when you told God you were sorry because you have the "money in the bank," the outcome of the pleasure that you consumed—whatever it was. To come to the place where you are genuinely repentant about something you can't make restitution for is not easy.

"I THINK I'M SORRY."

Watch out that you don't play the game. You know: "I'm sorry or, uh, I think I am. Maybe I'm just sorry that I feel guilty. I'll do it again. I always do. I try to repent, but I can't. I plan to repent before I even sin. Even as I am feeling the temptation, I think to myself, 'Oh, I'll get right with God tomorrow.'" It's a game. And it is producing the spiritual poverty that so many of us experience so often.

Many Christians are trying to play a sin-confess-sin-again game with God that He will not play. God doesn't play games. If you are truly repentant, all the blessings of the grace of God are yours. If you are not truly repentant, you can pretend to be right with God, but your slavery to certain sins reveals that His transforming power is not being released into your life.

WHEN REPENTANCE IS IMPOSSIBLE

Here's a needed warning: Repentance is sometimes impossible. You say, "Is that true? Can we reach a point of no return? Can we resist and rebel and sin against the light of the truth to the point where it is too late for us to change?" Yes! Psalm 103:9a says that **"[God] will not always strive with us"** (NKJV). There comes a time when God ceases striving to change a person and stops striving to convict a person. Many people come to a place where God has been trying to get a piece of information to them and they are like, "Not yet. Not me. Not now. I'll hear You again on this on another day." And we always think we have another day. And the Scriptures warn: **"Today, if you hear His voice, do not harden**

your hearts" (Psalm 95:7b–8a). Do not assume that there will always be another opportunity.

Maybe you're thinking; "No way, man; I can *always* go back to God. God is loving. God is forgiving. He will always receive me. I can resist and rebel. I can be a lousy spouse or a lazy employee or a spiteful church member as long as I want to be. And when I want to wake up and get down to business, I can . . ." Wrong! That's called compounding or even *doubling down on* sin. The deeper sin becomes, not the behavior you are pursuing, but your blatant and offensive presumption on God's forgiveness.

If you need proof of this truth, consider two passages from the book of Hebrews. The first passage is Hebrews 6:4–8. Pastors seldom preach on Hebrews 6 because they fear it teaches that a person can lose his or her salvation. However, John 10:28–30, Philippians 1:6, and a host of other passages clearly teach that a genuine believer cannot lose their salvation. Hebrews 6:4–8 does not teach that you can lose your salvation; what it does teach is that you cannot resist God for as long as you want to and then tune in when you feel like it. **"For it is *impossible, in the case of* those who have once been enlightened, who have tasted the heavenly gift, and have shared in the Holy Spirit"** (Hebrews 6:4 italics added). The writer listed the characteristics of someone who is responding to God. Then he concluded that it's impossible **"if they fall away, to renew them again to repentance, since they crucify again for themselves the Son of God, and put Him to an open shame"** (verse 6 NKJV). Impossible to repent. Impossible!

Okay, so it is now beyond a doubt that there comes a time when it is impossible to repent, but the question remains, "When is that time?" Hebrews 12:14–17 provides an excellent illustration of when repentance is impossible. The context of Hebrews 12:14–17 is change. Verse 6 says, **"For the Lord disciplines the one He loves, and chastises every son whom He receives."** The purpose of God's chastening is to change us, to make us more holy (see verse 10), to give to us the **"peaceful fruit of righteousness"** (verse 11). A warning begins in verse 15, however: **"See to it that no one fails to obtain the grace of God; that no 'root of bitterness' springs up and causes trouble, and by it many become defiled; that no one is sexually immoral or unholy like Esau, who sold his birthright for a single meal"** (verses 15–16).

Do you know the story of Esau? Here's a quick overview (see Genesis 25–36). Abraham had a son, Isaac, who had two sons, Jacob and Esau. In Old Testament times the firstborn child was given special privilege; it was called his birthright. Part of that was a special bestowal of favor that came from the father called the *blessing*. With the birthright came a lot of financial favoritism such as livestock and land.

Jacob was unusually bitter about Esau's status as the firstborn, because he was a twin and missed the favored status by like eleven seconds or something. Somehow Jacob became his mom's favorite (you know how moms pull for the underdog), and together Jacob and Rebekah plotted to steal the birthright from Esau through deceit and trickery. Remember, Hebrews 12:16 indicates that Esau was a "profane person," which means he thought very poorly of the things of God. A profane person is like, "God? Whatever! What time is it? Who cares?" The mother and son tricked Esau, appealing to his appetite.

Have you ever felt hunger like tear-the-door-off-the-fridge, get-out-of-my-way-or-I'll-kill-you hunger? Well, Esau came home from hunting hungry like that. You say, "Well, I would never be so hungry that I would reject my birthright," but remember he was a profane person. The things of God and the blessings of God didn't matter to him. So he came and said, "Man! What's that I smell? What's that you're cooking? Give me some of that!" When Jacob refused, Esau went into a frenzy. The dialogue was something like this:

"What are you talking about?" Esau said. "I'll kill you. Give me that food!"

"Uh–uh–uh," Jacob answered. "Not so fast. Sell me your birthright."

"Birthright, smirthright," Esau said. "Get out of my way and give me that food!" (See Genesis 25:30–34 for the actual conversation.)

The crisis of life revealed something that had been happening for a long time. Esau had been turning from God and hardening his heart for a long time. Here he goes too far.

Notice what it says in Hebrews 12:17: **"For you know that afterward, when he desired to inherit the blessing, he was rejected, for he found no chance to repent, though he sought it with tears." "Rejected"** is from the Greek word *adokimos*. In Romans 1:28 it's translated "reprobate" (KJV). In 1 Corinthians 9:27 it is translated "disqualified." It is a very serious word, and in each instance that it is used, it describes a state in which God ceases to work for that person's transformation. **"He was rejected, for he found *no chance to repent*, though he sought it with tears"** (italics added).

The NIV and NRSV translations obscure the meaning slightly here by inserting the word "reward" in verse 17. It was not the blessing that Esau sought with tears;

it was a chance to repent. That is the whole point of the text. Esau resisted and rebelled against the Lord for so long that he could not repent. The King James, *New King James, New American Standard,* and the *English Standard* translations all support this reading. Esau tried really hard to repent. The word **"chance"** is literally "place"—Esau couldn't get to a place of repentance. In fact, he even shed some tears; not a tear or two, but the kind of tears that come from prolonged anguish. The kind of tears that come from a diligent pursuit of a solution to his grief. Try as he might, cry as he might, *Esau could not repent; he waited too long.*

You say, "You had better tell me how long is too long. If there is a point where it is too late, I need to know what that point is." You know what? The Bible doesn't tell us when it's "too late." If you are concerned about that, I would strongly exhort you not to wait until five minutes before midnight. Okay? If you are burdened about it and anxious that it might be too late for you, it probably is not. If you are wondering, "Why is he going on about this?" and don't really care, I'm concerned for you. Repentance is not easy and sometimes it is impossible.

HOW TO REPENT!

No matter how difficult repentance is, change cannot begin until we complete our repentance. The best biblical model of how to repent is found in the story of the prodigal son (Luke 15:11–32). Jesus had been teaching about how God loves it when lost stuff gets found, especially people. In Jesus' parable, the prodigal son represented each individual—you and me too—and the father represented God. The younger of two sons had run away from the father and got messed up with a lot of sin. The father knew that forcing him to stay would destroy their relationship, so he let him go and waited. The King James Version says that the son **"wasted his substance with riotous living"** (verse 13), which is a nice way of saying, "He lived like a pig and then ended up moving *in* with the pigs" (notice verses 15–16). Isn't it great to know that repentance is possible no matter how dark or desperate our sin has become, provided we don't wait too long?

Luke 15 indicates that there are three things involved in repentance: the mind, the emotions, and the will.

1. Repentance involves the mind.

Eventually the prodigal son **"came to his senses"** (verse 17 NASB, NIV). Repentance involves coming to the place where you look at the thing that used to be attractive to you and you say, "What is *that*? I used to *like* that? I used to find that attractive? Now I find it *repulsive*!" That's repentance! When at one time something used to look so good, now it makes you shake just to get near it.

With true repentance, you say to yourself, "That is *awful*. That is a world of hurt. Been there, done that. *Don't want it anymore!*" We come to our senses. That's the first part of repentance.

2. Repentance involves the emotions.

When you repent, you have deep feelings of grief over sin, a deep sense of shame for your sin and failure before a holy God. The testimonies of church history are replete with examples of people who have felt incredibly *undone* before God in regard to their sin.

The prodigal son was very emotional when he said, **"I am no longer worthy to be called your son"** (verse 19). Only when you see yourself as a guilty sinner and recognize what your sin did to Christ can you begin to feel what a repentant person should feel. If you are not willing to feel grieved about what you have done, how can you be confident that given the same opportunity you won't do it again? Yes, repentance involves our minds and also our emotions.

3. Repentance involves the will.

The prodigal son said, **"I *will* arise and [*will*] go to my father, and *I will* say to him . . ."** (verse 18, italics added). Notice that he was choosing, exercising his will to effect a solution to his sin. Even as repentance is completing itself, plans are forming in the mind of every truly repentant person on how he will avoid the same error next time—how he will change. *When the mind is changing and the emotions are feeling genuine grief over sin and the will is forming a plan of action for restitution and victory, repentance is taking place and life change is on the way.*

So repentance involves your mind, emotions, and will. Clearly, repentance is hard work. The reason many people do not experience cleansing and lasting change is that they don't do the hard work of repentance. Oh, they may say, "Sorry, God," and then they're back to it. But they do not experience the lasting change that they are longing for.

Yes, repentance is hard work, but here is an encouraging promise. Second Timothy 2:25 says God grants repentance. It is a gift. I believe that God wants to give each of us genuine repentance. In fact, I am convinced that God wants us to live in an attitude of continuous repentance and brokenness over our sin. He desires that we experience lives free from excuses and rationalizations. Lives that are being transformed by the power of God in every moment. The kind of lives that God delights to work in.

"HOW WILL I KNOW IF I HAVE TRULY REPENTED?"

"A broken spirit; a broken and contrite heart, O God, You will not despise" (Psalm 51:17). In Psalm 51, David was repenting of his adultery and subsequent falling dominoes of one sin after another (deception, betrayal, murder). David voiced the realization of his desperate condition in the words **"For I know my transgressions, and my sin is ever before me. *Against You, You only, have I sinned* and done what is evil in Your sight"** (verses 3–4a, italics added). A shattered David arrived at the "place of repentance" that Esau never reached. He was deeply broken, truly repentant, and completely forgiven by God. The Lord restored his joy and did many wonderful things in his life, but nothing good could have happened after David's failure until he repented. Repentance is the first step in all change.

You may be thinking: "If repentance is not easy and sometimes it is impossible, maybe I *think* I'm repenting but I'm *not* repenting. How will I know when I have repented?" John the Baptist said, **"Bear fruits in keeping with repentance"** (Luke 3:8). He was saying to produce behavior that is consistent with repentance. If the roots of the tree are healthy, the fruit will be there. If the human heart is right with God in repentance, the evidence of that will be apparent to all. Paul said, **"Repent and turn to God, performing deeds appropriate to repentance"** (Acts 26:20 NASB).

You say, "What are the appropriate deeds? What are the fruits of repentance?" The Bible teaches that at least four things will happen when we truly repent. Ask yourself how many of the following "fruits of repentance" are evident in your life.

1. *The absence of rationalization.* When you have repented, others won't hear you saying, "Well, it is hard for me." They won't hear, "You don't know my personality," or "My parents used to . . ." When you repent of your sin, excuses for sin become repugnant to you. The prodigal son said, "I've sinned against you and God. . . ." No "because." No "buts." No "Life is so hard for me." True repentance includes no rationalization of sin.

2. *Genuine sorrow.* With true repentance comes a genuine, heartfelt sorrow over sin. Does it involve tears? Sometimes. Sometimes they are there;

sometimes they are not. Some people reading this book haven't cried in years; others have cried through this whole chapter. Tears don't necessarily validate repentance either way, so don't labor for them if you are not that kind of person; don't overemphasize them if you are. Examine your heart and look for genuine sorrow, that is, genuine grief over displeasing God.

3. *Open confession of sin.* David hid his sin of adultery and murder for a whole year but when he repented, he repented before the whole nation. One of the proofs that your repentance is true will be a desire to openly confess your sin. People who are genuinely repentant may embarrass spiritual pretenders, who hear the confessed sin and say, "Dude! Cover that up! What are you talking about!?" But people who are genuinely repentant don't care who knows. The reason is that when one has done the business before the holiness of God, he has no energy to defend it before other sinful people. It's just not there. It's gone. Such openness about sin and confession in the church is very powerful. In our church in suburban Chicago, all sorts of people are saying, "These are my sins. Here's my struggle." In one sense it makes church an ugly place, but on the other hand, God is changing us, and that, of course, is a beautiful thing.

4. *Restitution.* I've mentioned this already, but here are some final thoughts. When I'm right with God, I cannot wait to get right with others. I rush to my spouse and I rush to my employer. And I rush to my coworker. Yes, I may even rush to my parents. And I make it right. I pay what I owe. I tell them what God has been doing in my heart and ask for their forgiveness. Now, if you say, "I'm okay with asking God to forgive me but I am not doing that," you are not repenting. Genuine repentance—like that of Zacchaeus—leads to restitution. "I am going to make this right with those I have injured."

LET'S GO TO APOLOGY SCHOOL

One test of the genuineness of repentance has to do with if and how we approach those we have hurt. Repentance begins with God and flows into our relationships with others. An apology combines all four of the traits we just reviewed. A genuine apology includes no rationalizations, expresses sorrow, confesses, and is ready to make restitution. Apologies are not optional for a person who is repentant. Let's start there. Ready?

Only one apology gets a passing grade. All other "apologies" fail the test of authenticity. You know, I used to hate it when I got an *F* on a test. Back in school I saw too many of those. I *hate* that feeling, man! I *hate* that. When it comes to repentance and apologies, I want to get it right. So here it comes. This is the only passing grade apology:

"I am sorry. I was wrong when I hurt you by _____. I have no excuse. Please forgive me."

That's it. An apology is an open confession, without excuses or "explanations," and it leaves us vulnerable to a counterattack by the person we have offended. By asking for forgiveness we are giving them permission to hurt us back, but hoping they will be merciful. This is why genuine apologies are hard. We lay down our shield and weapons before someone we've wounded, knowing they may choose to take advantage of the moment. This is why a genuine apology ends with a humble request: *Will you forgive me?* If we haven't handed over the initiative to them, we haven't apologized.

Here are some failing apologies:

☐ *"I'm sorry."* The most frequent and most ineffective attempt at an apology. It misses by a mile. "I'm sorry" by itself basically says, "I care about how *I* feel; not necessarily how *you* feel."

☐ *"If I hurt you, I'm sorry."* ENKK!! Not an apology. This is a rationalization followed by information. It means, "I'm not taking responsibility for pain you were just caused, and even if it could be proven that it was my fault, the best you're getting from me is a vague bad feeling." It is likely to provoke a thought or statement like, "Were you in the room three minutes ago when I said how much you hurt me?"
"Well, *if* I hurt you . . ."
"IF?!? IF?!? There's no 'if' on the table!
Just a '*when*!' I just *told* you that you hurt me."
So all of those, "If . . . " "If . . ." "If . . ." apologies are pathetic.

☐ *"I'm sorry I hurt you, but that was not my intent."* Apology? No! This is information followed by a lame rationalization. "I'm sorry that I hurt you, but here, let me climb up on my intent. My intent was so noble that it invalidates any pain I may have caused you. And I preserve an element of nobility in my apology."
That's another useless excuse for an apology. It compounds the pain by

minimizing our responsibility for the hurt we have caused. You should be ashamed of an apology like that. It's a world away from repentance.

☐ Here's the worst one: *"Hey, I'm sorry that you got hurt,"* which translated means, "I'm sorry that you're so sensitive and weak that my minor offense was so hurtful to you, you lame person. It's really your fault you got hurt!" An apology like that is absolutely pathetic.

There is only one apology that reflects a repentant heart that God will use to carry forward the relationship that needs healing.

"I'm sorry. It's my fault. I was wrong when I hurt you. I have no excuse. Will you please forgive me?"

That genuine apology will bring grace into that relationship. If you can't say those words, you haven't yet repented.

Over one hundred years ago, Charles Spurgeon was preaching a series of messages on repentance. Week after week after week in his church, the same message: repentance . . . repentance . . . repentance. After several weeks, a lady came up to him after the service and asked, "When are you going to stop preaching on repentance?" And he said, "When you repent." The questions, exercise, and prayer that follow will help lead you to that place of true repentance.

Teacher Questions

1. What is repentance?
2. What part does repentance play in Scripture?
3. How do you know if you've repented?

Prophet Questions

1. Can you think of a time in your life when you genuinely repented? How do you know?
2. What is meant by the statement that repentance is sometimes impossible? Does that concern you? Why?
3. In what specific areas are you now pursuing an attitude of repentance before God?

Shepherd Questions

1. Why does biblical teaching on the method and importance of repentance build hope regarding change?
2. What does the father's response to the prodigal's repentance teach us about our heavenly Father? (See Luke 15:22–24.)
3. In what ways can you identify with the prodigal son?

LET'S GET TO WORK

Notice that the "Look Up!" prayer below is incomplete. Take an extended time with God to complete the unfinished prayer from your heart. Then contact each person your sin has directly affected, asking their forgiveness and making restitution where possible.

LOOK UP!

Dear heavenly Father:

I come to You today seeking repentance regarding the specific things You are asking me to change. I ask You to grant me genuine repentance. I ask Your forgiveness for rationalizing and blaming others. I acknowledge that I have no excuses for my areas of failure . . .

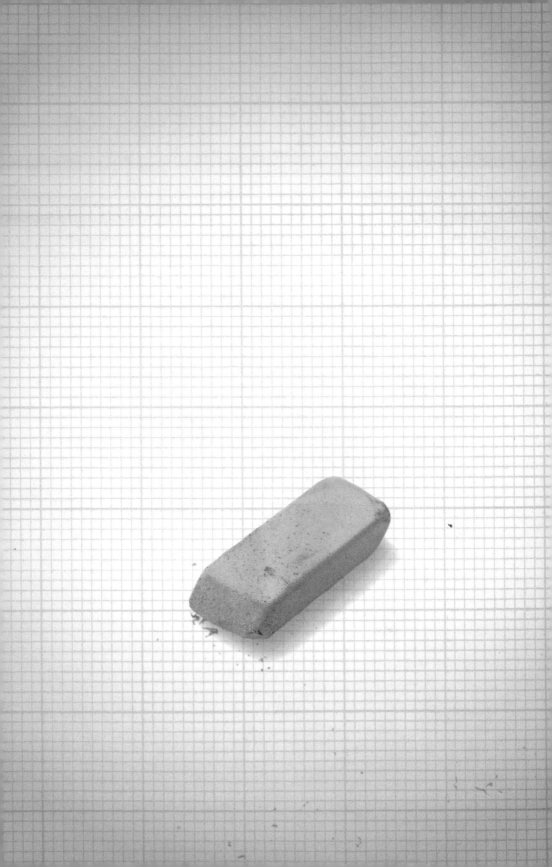

5

STEP TWO: NOW I CAN **CHOOSE**

SAY IT IN A SENTENCE:

*I can never be different unless I believe with all my heart that
the power of sin has been broken in my life—that I am dead to the
power of sin because of my relationship with Christ.*

At one point a number of years ago now, both my sons were in separate but significant basketball games. Let me tell you, it was very intense. Two tournament championship games—and I was the head coach of both teams. Historically those settings have been points of great temptation for me. Far too often in the past my desire to be a godly man has been overcome by my desire to win and help my boys' teams win, ending in some display of frustration that would leave me feeling very defeated whether we won or lost.

To make matters worse, the referees on this particular day acted semi-insane. A blind, amputee Civil War veteran could have done a better job of calling the game than these guys. The refs were beyond awful, and I felt I had every reason to give them an earful. But before the game, I had knelt down in a private place and done what I am going to teach you to do in this chapter. I'll tell you what happened a little later on. . . .

BELIEVING THAT CHANGE IS POSSIBLE

Do you believe in the "power of positive thinking"? I don't! In fact, I thank God for those who have exposed and repudiated the so-called preachers who promote positives and possibilities. While I seriously doubt that positive thinking has any inherent power, I do believe in the power of negative thinking. I believe that negative thinking is often nothing more than a lack of faith and therefore sin (according to Romans 14:23). If you didn't want to change, you would not still be reading this book on change; but I have to stop you now and say as plainly as I know how, "You will never experience life change unless you *believe within your heart that change is truly possible.*"

Believing that failure is inevitable is a self-fulfilling prophecy. We must believe that we have a choice in what we do, that by God's grace we can choose to do what is right. If we don't believe that we can make the choice to change at a specific moment in time, we will always only wonder why others are changing while we are stuck in the rut of sameness year after year.

Take a moment and mentally gather in your hands the thing in your life that most needs to change, the thing that you may have anguished over countless times. Possibly it comes with a deep sense of shame and regret. Maybe you find it painful even to focus your mind on it and have chosen many times to label it hopeless and bury it somewhere out of sight. Go ahead, you know what that is; dig it up if you need to and pick it up. Good; now bring it to a wonderful passage of Scripture that teaches that change is truly possible and shows us how to choose what is right.

BEFORE ROMANS 6

The passage I have in mind is Romans 6. Now you cannot jump right into Romans 6 any more than you can start reading a letter you receive at page five. Paul had already said some important things earlier in this letter. Let's quickly review what he'd already written.

In Romans 1, Paul described how all Gentiles are sinners. Paul, of course, was a Jew, and in Romans 2, he indicted all Jewish people as sinners too. In Romans 3:23, he summarized the issue of sin, declaring, **"For *all* have sinned and fall short of the glory of God"** (italics added). We're all the same; we all need God. We may be different on the outside, but the problem on the inside is the same—we are sinful. And unless we find God's solution, we will never change.

Romans 4 began to talk about the solution. Paul was saying, "Hey! Some of you think that faith is a *new* plan and that change *used* to be by works, but you're wrong!" He presented Abraham's life as proof that transformation by faith has always been God's program. **"Abraham believed God, and it was counted to him as righteousness"** (4:3). In Romans 5 we learn that God accepted the faith of Old Testament believers, knowing what Christ would ultimately do on their behalf. Then in Romans 5:20, Paul wrote something pretty amazing: **"Now** the law [God's system of rules and regulations] **came in to increase the tres-pass."** Paul's point was that rules and regulations about how to live don't help us change, they only make us want to sin more. Then he added: **"But where sin increased, grace abounded all the more."** Paul was teaching that the grace of God is greater than all of our sin.

BEING DEAD TO SIN: ROMANS 6:1-7

Next the Holy Spirit prompted Paul to caution us against using the grace of God as an excuse to keep on sinning. This is Romans 6, our focus. Paul wanted to make sure that we not abuse the grace of God by repeatedly requesting forgiveness for the same offense while stubbornly refusing to change. So he wrote:

> **What shall we say then? Are we to continue in sin that grace may abound? By no means! How can we who died to sin still live in it? Do you not know that all of us who have been baptized into Christ Jesus were baptized into His death? We were buried therefore with Him by baptism into death, in order that, just as Christ was raised from the dead by the glory of the Father, we too might walk in newness of life. For if we have been united with Him in a death like His, we shall certainly be united with Him in a resurrection like his. We know that our old self was crucified with Him in order that the body of sin might be brought to nothing, so that we would no longer be enslaved to sin. For one who has died has been set free from sin.** (verses 1-7)

Take a moment and notice how Paul used repetition throughout Romans 6 to teach a powerful truth: **"Do you not know," "we know," "we know that Christ,"** and **"do you not know"** (verses 3, 6, 9, 16, respectively). Clearly there is something here he wants us to know. And it is this: In Christ I am *dead* to sin. Again notice the repetition: **"We who died to sin"** (verse 2); **"baptized into His death . . . buried therefore with Him . . . into death"** (verses 3-4); **"united with Him in a death like His"** (verse 5); **"We know that our old self was crucified"** (verse 6); **"for one who has died"** (verse 7).

You'd have to be clueless to miss the theme in those verses. Paul wanted us to know that in Christ we are dead to sin. He was not saying that we are weakened to sin. He was not saying that we are distanced from sin. He was not saying that we have suddenly grown a bit cold toward sin. He was saying that we are *dead* to sin!

I know what you're thinking—"If I am dead to sin, why do I feel so alive to it?" *Dead* is the *last* word most of us would use to describe our experience with sin. *Forgiven* maybe. *Cleansed*. Even *changing*. But *dead*?

There is a lot of confusion over what **"dead to sin"** really means. No doubt Satan causes this confusion, because he knows that if we really got hold of the truth that in Christ we are dead to sin, the "demonic jobless rate" would skyrocket. Pretty tough to tempt a dead person.

What "Dead to Sin" Doesn't Mean

Before we get to what it does mean, I think we should take a moment and eliminate three false understandings of what "dead to sin" means.

First, dead to sin doesn't mean sinless perfection. Some people have said that this idea of being dead to sin is teaching sinless perfection—the idea that real committed mature believers reach a place where they stop sinning completely. Actually, I'm not sure who teaches this, because whenever I teach this passage publicly I ask those who have reached sinless perfection to stand and no one ever has. If someone ever does, I will lay on them 1 John 1:8, **"If we say we have no sin, we deceive ourselves, and the truth is not in us."** "Dead to sin" does not mean sinless perfection is possible.

Second, being dead to sin doesn't mean our old nature is gone. The old nature is our inclination to sin, the part of us that wants to sin and fights the part of us that wants to do right. Those who believe this teach that in Christ our inclination to sin has been fully eradicated. Again, the problem with that is that it contradicts Scripture. James 1:14 teaches that each one of us is tempted when he is first **"lured and enticed by his own desires."** The tragic fact is that even in Christ there is still something in me that wants to do what is wrong. That is the whole point of Romans 7: "The things I don't want to do I still do." (See especially verse 15.) Also, Galatians 5:17 says, **"For the desires of the flesh are against the Spirit, and the desires of the Spirit are against the flesh, for these are opposed to each other, to keep you from doing the things you want to do."**

I wish it was true, but sorry; "dead to sin" definitely does not mean that the old nature is wiped out.

Third, it doesn't mean "blah, blah, blah." It doesn't mean gibberish. Some people water down the phrase "dead to sin" completely. "Well, 'dead to sin' just means that we are identified with Christ and when He died, we died." Wow, that's so unhelpful. Every time I read a statement like that in a Christian book or commentary I scream, "Dead to what? Something clearly died when I came to Christ and I have to know what it is." I hate it when people try to smoke-screen the fact they don't understand something with a lot of Christian "blah, blah, blah."

What "Dead to Sin" Does Mean

Well, if it doesn't mean sinless perfection, the end of our old nature, or some vague identification with Christ, what does it mean? Simply yet profoundly this:

WE ARE DEAD TO THE **POWER** OF SIN.

The apostle Paul is talking about the *power* of sin. The *penalty* of sin is what sends us to hell if we have not repented of our sin and by faith embraced Christ as Savior. Most Christians understand that they are not under the *penalty* of sin. What we miss so often is that the *power* of sin has also been eliminated. Before we are in Christ, sin is the master and we are the slave. We have no choice but to sin because we are under its power. But in Christ all that changes; in Christ we are dead to the power of sin.

Picture yourself at a fork in the road. You're facing an alluring temptation that may have beaten you many times before, or you're facing a brutal interaction with a painful person before whom you often fall. Do you believe that person or temptation has power over you? Do you believe that you will fail again because you always have before? Or will you begin to accept by faith that because of your union with Christ, more specifically with Christ's death, that the power of sin is broken in your life and you can choose victory instead of failure and defeat?

In my past when I would come to a fork in the road and have to make a decision about change, there is a part of me (based upon my own résumé for the last fifty-two years) that would always say, "I'm gonna fail again; here it comes." Deep inside me there was something that believed very strongly, "I cannot do differently. I won't change. I'm always going to be like this. Oh, I may change for a time. I'll go through a little phase. But I will always revert back to those sinful inclinations in me."

If you have been hearing those same kind of things, believing that you will never change and that certain persistent sins will always have power over you, I tell you Scripture says *that is a lie*! The power of sin is now nothing but a bluff by the Evil One.

When I first wrote this book, Kathy and I were living in a two-bedroom apartment with our whole family because we were building a house having sold our other house. We were caught in home construction limbo. And that's not great. And it's especially not great to rent if you have a bad landlord. You know; that loud guy who arrives unannounced. He hardly knocks before entering. He doesn't even *have* to knock; he has his own key. It stinks to live in a place where somebody has a key to your place.

The landlord barges in and says, "Oh yeah? What's for supper? You don't own this. This is *my* place! I own this!" He can say what he wants; he can walk in when he wants.

That's what it's like to be a non-Christian. Satan is that landlord that can bust in anytime; who can control everything. He is in charge. He tells you what to do. But the locks get changed when Christ owns us. Satan's ownership is terminated.

Here's the thing though—the sad thing. Some Christians still listen to their former landlord even though he's not in charge anymore. And if we listen, he's happy to keep up the illusion that he's still in control. The point of this chapter is that you don't have to sin anymore. There was a time where that was all you could do. You were capable of nothing else but sin. But in Christ, the power of sin is broken. It's defeated. It's not in charge. You have a new Master. You have a new Landlord. This Landlord wants to help you choose. You can choose.

The incredible, transforming promise of Romans 6 is that the power of sin is broken in your life. Now you have a choice. Before you were in Christ, you had no choice; you were a slave to sin. *In Christ, we may choose to be a slave, but we don't have to be.* We can choose to do what is pleasing to the Lord. Say it out loud by faith: "Sin does not have power over me! In Christ I am dead to the power of sin."

BEING DEAD TO SIN:
PART OF GOD'S TRANSFORMING WORK

Being dead to sin is foundational to God's transforming work within us. In Romans 6, Paul explained why being dead to sin is foundational.

1. God's grace demands it.

When we properly understand the grace of God, we begin to hear it calling, even demanding, that we change.

To fully comprehend the grace of God is difficult, because no parallel exists, and no comparison comes close. We who follow Christ max the category of un-deserving, and God maxes the category of loving benevolence. In every believer's life are times when he glimpses, just for a moment, how desperately lost he really is. During those seconds, the abundant mercy and amazing grace of our loving God dawns briefly upon our forgetful minds. Right at that moment we understand deep within that God's grace cannot be abused or ignored. Such grace should fuel our passion to be like Him.

In verse 1, Paul asked, **"Are we to continue in sin that grace may abound?"** You can see how a person might start to tell himself, "Well, hey! If God is into grace and I'm into sin, and if the more I sin, the more God shows grace . . . and if God's grace is limitless and my desire to sin is limitless . . . Hey, hey, hey! This could be a great partnership! I'll just keep on sinning and God will just keep on showing grace and forgiving. Wow! We both get to do what we do best. What a great partnership!"

Now you say, "Nobody really thinks that." Grigori Rasputin did. He was the religious advisor to the ruling Russian czar, Nicholas II, in the early 1900s. Rasputin taught that the more you sin, the more God shows grace, so let's go crazy—and Rasputin did. He was a very immoral advisor. He seems to have also had a lot of influence over Nicholas II's wife, Alexandra. Interestingly, the Russian people began to deeply resent Rasputin. History records that conditions deteriorated to the point that citizens laid hold of him, murdered him, and threw his body into a river. Once people were roiled, chaos ensued. Within thirty days, there was a revolt in Russia that led to the overthrow of the czar and set the stage for the scourge of communism. The idea of sinning so that God can showcase His grace is satanic to the core.

Modern-day Rasputins are everywhere. This philosophy has actually grown right here in the good old USA—the idea that God is so loving and incredibly merciful and wonderfully forgiving that we can pretty much do what we want and God will look the other way. The all-loving, all-forgiving, never-angry, never-demanding God of modern evangelicalism is gaining popularity all the time. We've tried to turn God's grace into hyper-grace. Bestselling Christian books are about the psychological God who just wants to forgive and affirm His rebellious children; a God who would never dare to spank His children. Some of the most popular Christian songs, and several of the largest Christian churches preach "the heavenly Father who never chastens and His Son who never rebukes," a far cry from the biblical Jesus who said, **"Those whom I love, I reprove and discipline, so be zealous and repent"** (Revelation 3:19).

My guess is that most of the people reading this book have heard that kind of false teaching so often they hardly recognize it for what it is. We cannot eliminate false teaching from our world, but we can eliminate it from our minds. Let me ask you a few questions right now to help you determine if you have been using God's grace as an excuse to sin.

1. Do you have certain areas of disobedience that you are apathetic about? Do you have certain areas of disobedience that you are just, "Oh, whatever. Someday. I doubt if that will ever change in me. I always handle things that way. This is just the way I am." Hyper-grace treats God's holiness with carelessness.

2. Do you emphasize the love of God over the justice of God to lessen your own sense of responsibility? Have you been cultivating a desire to hear truth about the love of God more than other biblical truths because it lessens your sense of responsibility to be holy? Hyper-grace deliberately ignores God's righteousness.

3. Do you abuse God's promised forgiveness by choosing to sin and saying while you choose, "Oh, well. God will forgive me anyway"? Hyper-grace abuses God's grace with callous disobedience.

If we think that Jesus suffered and died to provide an excuse to sin, we are out to lunch! If we think that Jesus endured the abuse and the ridicule and the scorn of that cross and suffered and died to make payment for sin so that we could just keep on sinning, we desperately, desperately need a change of perspective. Have you ever had your perspective changed?

I heard once about a sweet lady who was seated near the departure gate in a large airport. Having some time before her plane took off, she had bought a newspaper and a little bag of cookies. After she began to read in her seat, though, she heard a tearing of paper. Looking down, she saw her cookie bag being torn open and the man beside her reaching in and taking out a cookie. Not one for confrontation, she flipped the paper up and thought to herself, "The nerve of this man to have one of my treats." So she flipped the paper down and took a cookie herself.

As she ate her cookie and read the paper, she struggled to concentrate because of her outrage at the cookie thief. Just as her anger began to fade she heard him in the bag again and peeked from behind the corner of her paper to see him in the very act and thought, "What is this world coming to? People have no respect for property!" Then she reached in frustration for a second cookie of her own. Back and forth they went until there was only one cookie left. Unable to muster the courage for confrontation, she sat and stewed, wondering what he would do next.

Well, she didn't have to wonder long, because the next sound she heard was the final cookie breaking in half! Fighting mad, she opened her paper only to see the kleptomaniac man walking away with the final half cookie lying on top of the bag. In complete frustration she grabbed the final morsel off the bag, stuffed it in her mouth, and right then heard the loudspeaker, "Final call for flight 507." Of course, she jumped up, gathered her things, and ran toward the gate.

After showing her ticket, she took her seat on board, exhausted but relieved to have the ugly incident behind her. Opening her purse to file her ticket stub she froze and felt the blood rush from her face . . . there before her eyes was *her* bag of cookies, unopened and untouched. As the plane took off she thought back to her angry treatment of the "generous" stranger and marveled at how quickly her perspective had changed.

Like the misguided woman at the airport, many of us need a change of perspective. Be honest with yourself. Have you allowed God's marvelous grace in your life to become an excuse to keep on sinning? Is there a way in which His long-suffering, His mercifulness, His graciousness has become to some degree a "freedom" not to change? Let's be honest together. Have we not many times allowed God's gracious, forgiving nature to be an excuse to struggle with the same old sins instead of seeking with all our hearts to be changed?

Paul chose the strongest words he could choose to say about using God's grace as an excuse to keep on sinning, **"By no means"** or "Certainly not!" The NASB translates verse 2, **"May it never be!"** The Greek phrase is *me genoito*—the strongest idiom of repudiation in the entire New Testament. I think the best contemporary translation is, **"ABSOLUTELY NOT!"**

Let us embrace this great truth: Christ in you is not a reason for sin but the power to not sin. In Christ *you* are dead to sin. God's grace demands it, loved one. God's grace demands that you seek to live out the truth that the power of sin is broken. Not generically in Christians everywhere, but in *you*! You have a choice now; you don't have to keep on sinning.

Here's a second reason to embrace this truth:

2. Christ's victory assures it.

Notice in Romans 6:3-4, **"Do you not know that all of us who have been baptized into Christ Jesus were baptized into His death? We were buried**

therefore with Him by baptism into death." Paul is teaching that, in some way that we can't understand, when God saw our repentance and faith in Christ, something happened. Somehow when you came to that crisis and turned from your sin and received Christ by faith, in God's eyes you were identified with Christ's death. Paul's point is that if we have been **"united with Him in a death like His, we shall certainly be united with Him in a resurrection like His"** (verse 5).

In other words, don't just claim the forgiveness of Christ based on His death for your sin; also claim the resurrection of Christ as your promise for life and victory and personal transformation. God doesn't just want to forgive us; He wants to transform us. God doesn't want us to be identified only with Christ's death for our cleansing but also with His resurrection for our *victory*! What a fantastic truth!

I recognize there's a lot of confusion about what is meant by the word "baptism" in this passage, and we must clear it up to experience the powerful truth that lies behind it. Recognize first that the word "baptism" doesn't always mean "immersion into water." In common English, for example, we use the phrase a "baptism by fire" to describe someone who is getting into something tough in a hurry. The word *baptism* just means to be immersed into something. Submerged. Plunged under the surface, right into the middle of something. There are four common positions on what Paul meant when he said we have been baptized into Christ's death, so here they are, from weakest to strongest.

1. *Infant baptism.* I don't want to offend anybody's tradition, but these verses are not describing infant baptism. In fact, the Bible doesn't talk about infant baptism anywhere. Except for Moses, there is not a single place in the whole Bible where you can even find infants and water in the same chapter. Infant baptism is the product of church history, and those who defend it must admit that it did not emerge from a study of Scripture but in trying to answer the difficult question of what happens to infants when they die. (The Bible is almost entirely silent on that subject; cf. 2 Samuel 12:23.)

2. *Spirit baptism.* First Corinthians 12:13 teaches that all believers are baptized into the body of Christ at the point of conversion. That is a wonderful truth, but Romans 6 is not talking about Spirit baptism. In fact, the passage does not even mention the Holy Spirit. We must always remember that the Bible is meant to be understood. It's not like God is up in heaven kind of snicker-

ing like, "Tee hee hee; they'll never figure out what I mean in that verse." The Bible is provided by a loving God who wants us to understand what He has written.

3. *Baptism in a figurative sense.* Some people argue that Paul was describing not a literal water immersion but an immersion into something else. An example of this would be found in 1 Corinthians 10:2, which describes how we were baptized into Moses. The idea there is that the children of Israel were immersed in Moses's leadership. I think that is possible, but I don't think that is what Romans 6:3 is talking about.

4. *Literal water baptism.* After you make the private decision to trust Christ inwardly, you get baptized to kind of "go public" and let others see outwardly that something inward has changed with you.

I agree with this final interpretation. The reason people miss this obvious meaning is that we have so de-emphasized believers' baptism in the church. If you look at the text objectively, Paul appears to be almost equating salvation and baptism. Salvation and baptism *are* separate decisions, but in the modern church we have made them far too separate.

In Paul's mind, conversion and baptism were so closely related that in Romans 6, while thinking about the death, burial, and resurrection of Christ that baptism pictures, Paul used conversion and baptism synonymously.

Here's an important aspect of Christ's victory on the cross that we must not forget: His resurrection gives us a new life, which water baptism pictures. **"Do you not know that all of us who have been baptized into Christ Jesus were baptized into His death?"** (Romans 6:3). That is why Paul said at the end of verse 4b, **"As Christ was raised from the dead by the glory of the Father, we too might *walk in newness of life"*** (italics added).

Get it? *We're to be different!* In Romans 6, Paul is teaching that water baptism identifies us with Christ's death for our cleansing; next he teaches how identification with Christ's resurrection assures our victory.

ONE OF GOD'S FAVORITE WORDS IS "NEW."

Do you like new things? I love stuff when it's new. I like new cars and new seasons and new restaurants and new kids (not in that order). To me, new is a really good feeling. I like new jobs (even though I'm in somewhat of a rut at this point—and twenty-five years happily so). I like getting new clothes. I like having new friends, but here's a wonderful truth: God loves new things. Do you know that about your heavenly Father? He loves stuff that's new too!

Did you know that God loves new things? All the way through the Bible, He is talking about new things. And these new things He has given to us. Here is a list we should not ignore:

- God gives us a new heart (see Ezekiel 36:26).
- God gives us a new spirit (see Ezekiel 18:31).
- God puts a new song in the hearts of His children (see Psalm 40:3).
- He has given us a new name (see Revelation 2:17).
- He has given us a new self (see Ephesians 4:24).
- He makes us wholly new. Second Corinthians 5:17 pulls it all together and says, **"Therefore, if anyone is in Christ, he is a new creation."**

God loves new stuff. In fact, among the final words that God will speak in human history, recorded in Revelation 21:5, are: **"Behold, I am making all things new."**

The Christian life is about being new, different, and changed. If your faith in Christ has made no difference in you, then ask yourself if it has made any difference to God. If you are not changing, being transformed little by little, day by day feeling His victory, then what is up with your faith? The people who are in Christ are being changed. The Christian life is all about change. The words **"newness of life"** from Romans 6:4 translate a Greek word that does not mean new in time, but new in character, new in quality. A different person.

Now don't miss this: God wants to make you new. That is His thing. He is trying to change you. And that is why it says in the text that if then we have been identified, through baptism, with the death of Christ, we should also be identified with the resurrection of Christ and **"walk in newness of life"** (verse 4).

When you get right down to it, church history is nothing more than a list of the lives God has made new. Let me tell you about one, John Newton. (*New*ton is an appropriate name . . . right?) Early in his life he ran away from his home in England because he was rebellious and hated his parents. He joined a slave ship crew, but when he fell out of favor with the captain, he was given as a slave to the African wife of a white slave trader. For many years he lived the life of a slave in Africa and eked out an existence on table scraps and wild yams that he dug up at night. Finally he was able to escape from his master and worked his way back into the shipping/slave-trading business. Over several more years he actually became a captain, transporting captured people back and forth from Africa to America. Wicked, evil, filthy, rotten, and profligate things were done on Newton's ship, and those were the darkest days of his life.

One night in 1748, John Newton was transporting slaves across the northern Atlantic Ocean when a violent storm arose to nearly sink his ship. In that hour of desperation, although he was a very wicked man, John Newton cried out to God for forgiveness and was converted to Christ. He returned to London and became a tireless, powerful minister of the gospel. He had a profound influence on William Wilberforce, one of the young political leaders in Britain who led the long struggle for the abolition of the slave trade. Though Newton was not perfect, he was dead to sin—dead to the old way. He was changed. The film *Amazing Grace* several years ago captured the profound shift in perspective for John by having him summarize his view as knowing two things: his own identity as a great sinner and the marvelous identity of his great Savior!

After spending the final days of his life preaching the gospel, he wrote his own epitaph, which stands to this day as a testimony to the marvelous transforming power of God. He wrote:

> Here lies John Newton.
> Once an infidel libertine,
> A servant of slaves in Africa
> Was, by the rich mercy of our
> Lord and Savior Jesus Christ,
> Preserved, restored, pardoned, and appointed
> To preach the faith
> He labored so long to destroy.

John Newton is best known for writing the hymn "Amazing Grace." In its familiar first verse, he testified that grace "saved a wretch like me." Another verse of the hymn details Newton's awareness that conversion was just the beginning of transformation, not the end:

> Through many dangers, toils, and snares,
> I have already come;
> 'Tis grace that brought me safe thus far,
> And grace 'twill lead me home.

John Newton was a man in process. Are you a man or woman in process? The truth that we are learning here from Romans 6:3-5 is that the power of sin is broken in us. We are free to choose what we do; in Christ we are dead to sin! Why? Because God's grace demands it, and Christ's victory assures it.

3. My experience confirms it.

Think back to the time before you committed your life to Christ. Do you remember certain sins that you were a slave to? No matter how you tried, prior to coming to Christ, you fell back into those same patterns again. The good news is that when we confess Christ as Savior, God connects us with the very resurrection power of Jesus Christ and the power of sin in our life is broken. Sin may call us or tempt us or try to get our attention but it cannot boss us around anymore.

To make sure you understand this critical truth, take a moment and return to that apartment building we described a few pages ago. In that tragic arrangement, remember how your "landlord" was a brutal taskmaster who extorted extra rent money and stole food from your fridge and made your life miserable with tempting promises that always turned out bad? You didn't want to do what he said, but you knew that you had little choice in the matter if you wanted to live in his building. In fact, when you questioned him at all, he quickly threatened to bounce you and your family into the street.

Next, remember how you discovered in Christ that you could report him to the housing authorities, and when you did they agreed that he's a criminal and quickly had him fired. Not long after this, as you sat in your apartment on a warm summer night, rejoicing in your new freedom from tyranny, you heard a loud pounding at the door and in came the old landlord with the same attitude and the same demands. Of course, now things are different. Before, you *had* to do what he said. Now, though it may be tough, you can say no to him. He has no power over you and though he can still threaten, he cannot follow through. So, why do you keep taking his word for it that he's still in charge?

THAT BRUTAL LANDLORD HAS TO GO!

That is the picture Paul is trying to communicate in Romans 6:1-7. He wanted you and me to know that we do not have to be under the demands of sin anymore. That need not be our experience, and by the power of God, it is *not* the experience of those who live in His resurrection power. Tragically, most Christians are still living like they are under the power of sin. Are you? I challenge you in this moment to embrace the truth that can set you free. You don't have to sin! You can choose! Before Christ you had no choice. Now you have a choice.

We can believe we are dead to sin's power because of our own experience. Most Christians can recall the dramatic change within when they initially trusted Christ.

When I look at my own life, I recognize that something happened when I came to Christ. That inner transformation, of becoming "a new creation," took place. That is why Paul said in Romans 6:6, **"We know . . ."** Paul was appealing to accepted understanding. Paul said in effect, "If nothing else, certainly you have learned this; that our old man was crucified with Him." That phrase *old man* doesn't mean old chronologically, it just means *worn out, useless, fit for the scrap heap*. That old way of living and thinking. That selfish, getting-my-needs-met mentality. The power of sin was broken when it was crucified with Him. Why? **"That the body of sin might be done away with."** By **"body of sin"** (verse 6), Paul meant the sum total (as in "body of truth") of our being, of our specific sinful patterns. The words **"brought to nothing"** or **"done away with"** (NKJV), from the Greek *katargeo*, mean "rendered inoperative" or "nullified."

Keep that in mind, because you know by experience that there is still a part of you that wants to sin; the old inclination to sin is still present in you and me. It is not gone. It is there, but sort of unplugged. It's like toast; you can't make toast if the toaster is unplugged and you can't sin if the old man is unplugged, but you can go plug him in again.

When Paul added that you have **"been set free from sin"** (verse 7), he was letting you and me know that the power of sin is broken in us. All who receive Christ personally have had their inclination to sin cut off or rendered inoperative. It's not in charge anymore; you don't have to do what it says.

If you're still struggling with a certain sin, it is because you choose to remain in that sin. If you are trapped in a pattern of sin-confess, sin-confess, it's because you have not known or not acted on the truths in these pages.

A TRAGIC STORY

It's a tragic story, having the means to escape but not acting upon it. In his historical book *The Three Edwards*, Thomas Costaine described such a tragedy. During the fourteenth century a duke named Ranald lived in the region that is now Belgium. Ranald was grossly overweight. In fact, he was commonly called by his Latin nickname "Crassis," which means *fat*. Eventually Ranald became the king, but his brother, Edward, was very jealous. After a violent quarrel, Edward rallied a group of people together and led a revolt, taking over the castle and the kingdom.

Now you would think the younger Edward would kill his older brother, as was often done, but somehow he had an odd form of compassion on the hefty guy. He built a dungeon for his brother—a very specific kind of cell. Edward removed Ranald from the throne and built a large, circular room, which had a doorway but no door. Inside the room was a bed and table and all the essentials Ranald would need. The doorway to the room was a regular-sized doorway but Ranald was too big to get through it. Edward placed Ranald in the room and said, "When you can fit through the doorway, you can leave."

Every day Edward would have his servants bring to the room a smorgasbord of pies and pastries, along with massive platters of meat and other delicacies and lay it all out in front of old "Crassis." People used to accuse Edward of being a cruel king, but Edward had a ready answer. "My brother is not a prisoner. He can leave when he chooses to."

Ranald remained in that same room, a prisoner of his own appetite, for more than ten years. He wasn't released until after Edward died in battle. By then his own health was so far gone that he died within a year, not because he had no choice, but because he would not use his power to choose what was best for his life.

Now if you are in Christ, you are no longer a slave to any sin. In Christ you absolutely have the *power* to be the person that God wants you to be. There is no pattern of thinking that holds you unless you believe Satan's lies. There is no pattern of behavior that necessarily enslaves you unless you choose to let it. You are not a slave to any sin. That power has been broken through your identification with the death and resurrection of Jesus Christ that took place when you turned from your sin and accepted Christ by faith. The chains of sin are broken in you; you are free to do what is right.

In the next chapter, I am going to tell you how to begin to experience this truth, but you can't live it until you believe it. You can't appropriate it until you accept it. So take a moment just now and pray about it. This chapter ends a little differently, with the "Look Up!" prayer first. That prayer is a great opportunity to express your faith. I urge you to pray it now.

LOOK UP!

Perhaps the power of sin has continued to enslave you in one or more areas. Even though you are a child of God's, you are not living in His resurrection power. Take a moment just now and pray about how your life is expressing your trust in Christ. Maybe you would like to kneel down and say these words to God out loud and from your heart.

Dear heavenly Father:

Thank You that You sent Your Son to die in my place so that my sins could be forgiven. Lord, I thank You for that cleansing, but I don't want to use Your amazing grace as an excuse to keep on sinning. And I have. I'm sorry for that; please forgive me, Lord. You say that somehow You see me as connected with the death and resurrection of Your Son and I thank You for that truth. I accept it as true whether I feel it or not, and I believe that the power of sin is broken in my life.

Thank You, Lord, that I can change. Thank You that with Your help I can be different. Lord, help me to live out this truth. As I come to that critical fork in the road where I would choose to live a certain way—the way I have always chosen—help me to believe that I can choose differently with Your help. I can choose, and with Your help, I am going to do what pleases You. With Your help, I am going to choose to do what is right.

By faith, I thank You for the promise that the power of sin is broken in my life. I rejoice in Your victory, and I claim it for myself and for my life so that You would be glorified in me. In Jesus' precious name I pray. Amen.

Teacher Questions

1. Does Paul assume that all Christians have been baptized? What are the implications of your answer? Where does that leave you?
2. How does Christ's victory also mean victory for the follower of Christ? Can you show that in the Bible text of Romans 6?
3. What are some of the sins that typically bluff their way into ongoing control of believers after they have been saved by Christ?

Prophet Questions

1. If life in Christ is about change, am I unsaved if I'm not changing?
2. Have you seen a tendency in your own life to abuse the grace of God, as shown in the three areas discussed on page 108? If so, in which one(s)?
3. Which sins do you now know you need to exercise the authority of Jesus Christ over in your life?

Shepherd Questions

1. What does it mean to you that the power of sin is broken in your life? How should that affect your attitude toward your greatest struggle or area of defeat?
2. How would your attitude change if you really believed that victory over sin was possible for you this week?
3. Who have you enlisted to pray with and for you as you choose the freedom you have in Christ over sin?

LET'S GET TO WORK

Write a list of things that you know are true, even though you can't prove them. Then answer this question: How is the truth of your being dead to sin like that?

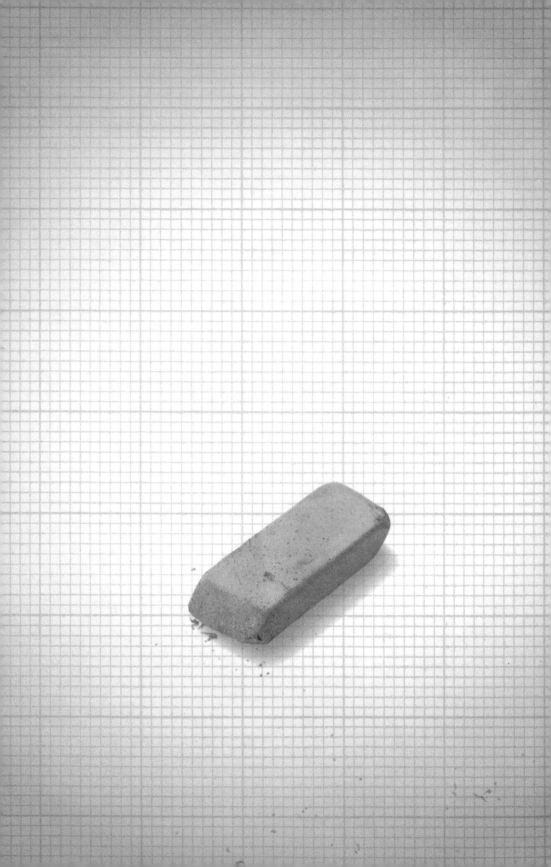

6

I'M DEAD TO THAT

SAY IT IN A SENTENCE:

*For life change to happen, we must apply the power of
our identification to Christ at the specific point of temptation.*

If we refuse to change personally, we'll be the only ones not changing—because everything around us is sure changing! I was born in 1960, so a recent article entitled "Information Overload" caught my attention. If you were to gather all human knowledge from the beginning of time through 1960 into one massive pile—calculating all that mankind has ever learned or discovered from the beginning of time until 1960, that amount of information would have doubled from 1960 until 1990. In only thirty years! Then that thirty-year pile of info would have doubled again by 1995. In only five years!

When I wrote the above paragraph a decade ago, I was stunned at the rate of change. But that amazement didn't prepare me for the accelerating rate of knowledge accumulation since then. The CEO of Google was speaking recently in Lake Tahoe at an event called Techonomy. And he said (try to imagine what this means): "Knowledge, by the end of the year, will be doubling every two days." I thought my head was going to explode!

It is unbelievable how fast things are changing. Consider just four areas:

1. *Public media.* Only fifty years ago, there were basically three television stations and six national magazines. Today most people can choose from several cable and satellite delivered television networks and their TV remotes can scroll through hundreds of stations. They can choose from an apparently endless supply of magazines with all kinds of special interests and

specializations, many still issued on paper, but increasingly available digitally through an ever-widening assortment of devices.

2. *Personal communication.* Less than a century ago, the ways to communicate with people included mail, telegraph, and a primitive form of the telephone. It's hard to comprehend how telephone developments changed our access to one another. And now it's out of control, with e-mail, cell phones, and texting. As a kid I watched *The Jetsons* cartoon and figured that video phones would be so cool, but of course would never happen. It's here! It's happening. People immediately get creative with new technology. Families use Skype to keep in touch with loved ones.

3. *Travel.* Only a generation ago the average person traveled only locally or to a nearby state, and most people considered a trip to another country the trip of a lifetime. As I write this I am stuck on a runway at O'Hare International Airport in the middle of the night. (Yet another chance to work on change!) I was in Orlando this week. I was in Toronto two weeks ago. In the last twelve months I have been in numerous countries around the world. And that's not a big deal; there are people in my church who fly internationally every week. The whole matter of travel has changed so fast. When I noted those changes in the late nineties, we were two years ahead of the tragic events of 9-11. I couldn't imagine all the ways our travels would be altered by security inconvenience as a result of global terrorism!

4. *Moral change.* During the 1960s, men and women sharing the same house and bed before marriage were said to be "shacking up" and condemned; in the 1970s—and today—they are "living together" and applauded. As proponents say, "Who would buy a car without driving it?" (Logical, yes, but historically and biblically inaccurate.) Once Americans trusted their presidents; with Watergate, a Congressional vote to impeach a president, and an almost daily effort by the media to reveal the hidden lives of politicians, we wonder if our leaders ever tell the truth. And we must explain to our children that lying is still wrong. The moral decline in our country has been so thorough and so rapid that it has made us numb to how drastic the devastation really is. Sexual perversity is now commonplace and behaviors that used to be relegated to the "red light" district and the dark corners of society are now paraded on the nightly news and defended from our nation's capitol. No one blushes anymore.

Now here's the sad news I have to give you, though I wish this were not true. In spite of the dramatic alarming rate at which our world is changing,

MOST CHRISTIANS ARE NOT CHANGING.

Most born-again, Bible-carrying followers of Jesus Christ are not changing. The "leavening" (Matthew 13:33), "salting" (Matthew 5:13), and "lighting" (Matthew 5:14–16) effects that Jesus said His true followers would have in society are spotty at best. Every study and every survey indicates the same thing. The Barna Report (by pollster George Barna), a sort of Gallup Poll of evangelicals, has been tracking trends among contemporary Christians for many years (see www.barna.org for the most recent statistics). In his ongoing research, Barna has surveyed and then compared the attitudes of self-described born-again Christians with their secular, or pagan, counterparts. Surprisingly, there is very little difference. The most recent of Barna's many books is *Maximum Faith: Live Like Jesus.*[1] In it, Barna explores from a research base why it is that Christians are not changing. His conclusions are similar to the ones we are tracking here from God's Word: we're not changing because we're stuck. And we're stuck because we haven't moved very far into the new life we claim Jesus gave when we believed in Him. In reflecting on current conditions in the church, Barna said, "Most Christians mirror cultural goals, desiring happiness, comfort, security, belonging, and popularity. Surprisingly few are focused on completely cooperating with God to experience the kind of whole-life transformation described in the Bible and made possible only through a partnership with God."[2]

Only a relative handful of believers in Barna's surveys actually demonstrate they understand the meaning of salvation and the lifelong process of sanctification that God has called us into. When asked to describe the top reasons for which they live, less than 20 percent of the population describe themselves as "totally committed" to growing spiritually. And only one in seven self-reported Christians confess that their relationship with God is the central pursuit and priority in their lives.[3] Reviewing Barna's latest statistics while updating this book was a discouraging exercise. Christians are not changing. They are not demonstrating with their lives a connection with the God who brings about change. So we conducted a survey about what Christians are doing *instead* of changing. Confronted with the need to change, here are the four alternatives most Christians are pursuing:

☐ **Rituals.** Now I know the word "ritual" usually makes us think of main-line and Catholic churchgoers and the ritualized forms that shape most of their experience, but that's not who I have in mind. We orthodox evangelicals have our own tried-and-true rituals, too. Our practice of faith can boil down to a routine. "This is what I do every week. I come to church and I usually sit in the same place. We sing our songs and we raise our hands. We have our little holy habits that we do. It's the spiritual part of our week, but it doesn't come down into our lives. It affects me while I'm here at church. But when I leave here? I'm a lot like my sister who doesn't come. And I'm a lot like my neighbor who thinks I'm crazy for coming to church." Not that much different really.

☐ **Debates.** I'm currently out on a limb trying to get some Christians to-gether who don't normally talk in our conference, the Elephant Room. I'm having a whole fresh experience with people who not only don't appreci-ate what I'm going for there, but also are intent on letting me know how deeply offended they are that I would even engage others in conversation unless they have been preapproved by the guardians of orthodoxy. I end up limiting contact with critics, not because I don't want to hear their con-cerns but because it becomes clear after a while that they simply want to debate rather than pursue the truth. And they're not even debating people who are unbelievers or declared opponents. They are attacking other people who do believe but don't believe it exactly like they do. Internet cru-sades against other believers are a colossal waste of time. They are also a massive substitute for sanctification and detour from humble obedience to God. This is the will of God—not our rituals; not our debating skills; **"This is the will of God, your sanctification"** (1 Thessalonians 4:3).

☐ **Sentimentality.** Some of us are living on yesterday and long-time-ago faith. The fact is you don't have a great thing with God anymore. You had a growing thing with God in college or when you were first married or when you used to live in that other city. And now what you're looking for is a place where they'll sing those same songs. (I love, by the way, singing "How Great Thou Art." I appreciate that song and many others from my upbringing.) But I'm concerned about this: Is it stirring up in me a remem-brance of a time when I had a lively relationship with God, but maybe I don't have one anymore? Watch out for sentimentality. Watch out for spiri-tuality that is not current and not actually changing the way I talk to my wife. It's just stirring up warm feelings of a day gone by when I was actually close to the Lord.

☐ **Carnality.** Just flat-out living in the flesh. Some believers seem bent on reclaiming their way of life from before they met Christ. "I just want what I want. I just do what I do. And I go to church to help me feel a little better about how awful I really am!"

All these alternatives to change are symptoms of settling for an incomplete or distorted gospel. Sometimes they are even evidence that the gospel may have been heard but it was never understood or believed.

ONLY THE BEGINNING . . .

Many professing Christians presume that once a person has made peace with God in Christ that his or her spiritual journey has, for all intents and purposes, come to an end.

God's forgiveness was never intended to be the end of anything. If you think that almighty God sent His Son to die on a cross just so He could get your and my sorry selves into heaven, you are wrong! He wants to display the power and the glory of who He is. He wants to complete in your lifetime the process of transformation that He began at the cross. So why are Christians having such a hard time believing that? There are approximately 350,000 churches in North America and 85 percent of them have either plateaued or are in decline.[4]

Even the emergence of "megachurches" in the last two decades hasn't made that great a difference in the overall state of Christianity in our nation. Large groups of immature Christians meeting together in one place are not further along spiritually than many smaller groups of immature Christians attending struggling churches. Why are so many churches dying? Because the people inside them are dying! They are refusing God's agenda for their lives and rejecting His transforming power. For two thousand years of church history, Christians have believed in a gospel that not only transforms our destiny, but also transforms our character. They believed wholeheartedly that the gospel isn't just about going to heaven; it's about becoming like Jesus along the way. But during desperate times along the way, large parts of the church have gotten off-track. People have not been taught nor have they lived out the truth about the Christian life that scripture teaches. We are in one of those times (at least in the Western world) when the unchanged gospel is being ignored and people are therefore living unchanged lives. Have we arrived at a description of your experience?

Let's get very serious. Up to this point you could read and do everything that I have written without actually changing the behavior or attitude that you are working on. This chapter—if you apply it—brings actual change. Let me say it a different way: "You can't do what we're going to talk about in this chapter and not actually be changed."

May I say to you directly, as a follower of Jesus Christ you have been forgiven and placed into a family? Your place in God's family is as secure as the Word of your heavenly Father who cannot lie, but now you have a responsibility to express your gratitude. You must demonstrate your gratefulness for the gift of eternal life by living like the One who died to redeem you. Anything less than that is blatant ungratefulness.

Pressing on in the process of change

Let's quickly review how we have reached this point. We had three chapters on *preparing to change:*

1. Eliminating faulty change methods from my thinking
2. Committing to cooperate fully with God's desire to change me
3. Choosing specifically what needs to change in me next

Next, we began the *process of change:*

1. Repentance is changing my mind about a particular sin or weakness. It is turning from all rationalization and sincerely purposing within my heart to be different.
2. Sin's power to rule our lives is broken when we come to Christ. We can now embrace the liberating truth that because of our identification with the death of Christ we have a choice. We don't have to sin anymore; we can choose to do what is right; we can choose to change.

THIS CHAPTER IS ABOUT HOW TO ACTUALLY
MAKE THAT CHOICE—THE CHOICE TO CHANGE.

The third step in the process of change is: "I must reckon myself dead to sin moment by moment." When that happens, change happens. Here's the passage that teaches that, Romans 6:7–11:

For one who has died has been set free from sin. Now if we have died with Christ, we believe that we will also live with Him. We know that Christ, being raised from the dead, will never die again; death no longer has dominion over Him. For the death He died He died to sin, once for all, but the life He lives He lives to God. So you also must consider yourselves dead to sin and alive to God in Christ Jesus.

Living for Him *Now*

Notice how strongly Paul stated that forgiveness is just the beginning of life in Christ. Know it. Forgiveness is not the end of something; it's the beginning. Instead of saying after we come to Christ: "Man! I'm all set! It's done! It's settled! I'm on my way to heaven," we ought to be saying, "This is just the *beginning*." That's why Paul said here, **"If we have died with Christ** [that's His death for my forgiveness], **we believe that we *will also live* with Him"** (verse 8, italics added). In Greek, as we do in English, the future tense is used to describe certainty. My point is that Paul was not talking about someday living with Christ in heaven. He was saying we must be living with Him now!

Not only must we live *for* Him now, but we must live *by means of Him*. All of our life is plugged into His life. We cannot live *for* Him *without* Him living out His strength in us. Forgiveness is just the beginning of life in Christ. The grace of God demands that we be pursuing with our whole hearts the life change Christ died to bring us.

SIN'S POWER BROKEN ONCE FOR ALL

Now here's a second thing: *The power of sin is broken once for all. Believe it.* **"We know that Christ, being raised from the dead, will never die again; death no longer has dominion over Him. For the death He died He died to sin, once for all, but the life He lives He lives to God"** (verses 9–10). Paul was using *sin* and *death* synonymously. When he spoke here of sin, he had death in mind; when he spoke of death, he had sin in mind also. All through the Bible, these two are connected. **"The wages of sin is death . . . Therefore, just as sin came into the world through one man, and death through sin, and so death spread to all men because all sinned"** (Romans 6:23; 5:12). There it is: sin and death. Cause and effect. In Genesis 2:17 God said to Adam and Eve that if they would eat from the tree, **"In the day that you eat of it you shall surely die."** In Revelation 20:14, we learn that at the end of the age death and hades will be cast into the lake of fire. Sin and death are synonymous in Scripture. Ezekiel wrote, **"The soul who sins shall die"** (18:20).

Don't Trust Feelings

So hear this: When Christ stepped out of the tomb on that first Easter morning, the power of sin was broken. Sin can no longer take control of you if you are in Christ. It can't tell you what to do. It can't boss you around. Its power is broken.

"I don't feel like it's broken," you say. Don't trust your feelings! It's the same as when you came to Christ; at first maybe you didn't *feel* as though anything great had happened, but you believed the Word of God and acted upon it. As you look back, you know you haven't been the same since that moment. In the same way, if you, by faith, accept the truth that the power of sin is broken in you, you might not feel different, but over time you will *be different.*

"Well, why do I still feel so aware of the power of sin?" you ask. Picture a very tall oak tree in the center of a park. The whole park is full of oak trees. And the tallest one—the strongest one—in the center has a big, tall trunk extending up into the sky. It's a beautiful oak tree. But planted at the base of the oak tree is a strong, thick vine. It's been there for many years; in fact, the vine has grown up and wrapped its way around the trunk of that oak tree and out along the branches. Now, after many years, the entire tree is covered by that vine.

Now imagine for a moment that your life represents the oak tree, and the vine represents sin. When you came to Christ, it's as though God Almighty took an ax to the base of that vine and cut that thing off! And let me tell you something: The vine is dead! You say, "It doesn't *feel* dead. It is still all over me!" Right. And if you will begin to cooperate with God and do what I am about to teach you, that old vine can be cast off in your life and you will begin to experience the victory that is rightfully yours.

Remember Lazarus in John 11? Jesus and Lazarus were close friends, but Lazarus was dying. Jesus, ministering elsewhere, didn't get to Lazarus's home before he died. By the time Jesus did arrive, Lazarus's two sisters, Mary and Martha, were just crying all over the place. They were messed up—really bad. Acknowledging their grief and confusion, Jesus started ministering to them. He was like, "Guys, just calm down (I'm paraphrasing now); I'm going to raise Lazarus from the dead." Everyone was shocked and said, "He's been dead for three days; he's going to stink."

Then Jesus said this powerful truth, **"I am the resurrection and the life.**

Whoever believes in Me, though he die, yet shall he live, and everyone who lives and believes in Me shall never die. Do you believe this?" (verses 25–26).

Then Jesus walked toward the tomb. He stopped, and I wouldn't be surprised if the ground began to shake after the stone was removed (verse 41). Then Jesus shouted, **"Lazarus, come out!"** Lazarus came walking out of the tomb all wrapped up in graveclothes. Jesus said, **"Unbind him, and let him go."** He wanted the people to untie him because he wasn't dead anymore.

Now what if Lazarus had said, "You know . . . just hold off for a minute. I'm not feeling very alive right now. I think I may go back in the tomb and just lie down for a few minutes. I'm not sure what happened exactly, and I can't tell how long it's going to last. I don't want to get too far from my tomb in case I need it again."

Sound ridiculous? But we do the very same thing. We linger by our old sinful tombs. We claim God's forgiveness but refuse His transforming power. It is such a tragedy, and that kind of thinking makes a travesty of the gospel and God's intent for us. Will you begin by faith to act upon the truth that the power of sin is broken in you? Personal change is available to you right here, right now, but you cannot go any further unless you begin now to exercise your faith toward this truth: The power of sin is broken. `

Living for God Day by Day

Here's the third thing: Living for God is day by day. Choose it! Choose to live for God. You can choose it. Look at Romans 6:10, **"For the death He died He died to sin, once for all, but the life He [Jesus] lives He lives to God."**

That biblical phrase belongs in a frame over every Christian life: **"The life He lives He lives to God."** God the Son lives toward the Father. He lives for the Father's pleasure. He lives for the Father's joy. He lives for the Father's glory. He lives to God. Say it out loud as you read: "Jesus lives to God." Yes, "Jesus lives to God." Now as His followers, can we do any less? This is where living like Jesus begins, with our living to the Father.

GOD'S ROLE—AND OUR ROLE

Some Bible teachers argue that it is all about God and not about us at all. All we really need to do in order to experience the transforming power of the gospel, they say, is lean back in our recliners, put our feet up, and let God do it all.

Now hear this: That is not what the Bible teaches! Of course we need God's help, but we cannot be changed without making the choice to change ourselves. Notice Paul's command in Romans 6:12: **"Let not sin therefore reign in your mortal body."** What's that if it's not a choice?! *Do not let sin reign in you!* Make a choice.

"Well, sin has been ruling my life," you say. Listen; it doesn't have to. Don't let it; make a choice. The power of sin is unplugged—don't plug it in. Don't let it rule you.

The next time temptation steps up to you and says, "Do it! Go ahead, do it! Go ahead," just answer: "Get off me! You are not in charge! Shut up! Stop bossing me around. Don't tell me what to do! I'm not that person anymore! I'm a new creation in Christ!" That's what Paul meant when he said, "Don't let sin reign."

Get involved! Choose to change! With your commitment and God's help, you can.

HERE'S HOW TO CHOOSE!

Maybe you're saying, "Well, how do I choose? Teach me how to choose. I want to choose." Here's a neat little story my mom gave to me, called "Choosing to Change in Five Days." I don't know the source, but it's helped me out of a few "holes" in my life.

Day one: I went for a walk down a street. I fell into a hole. I didn't see it. It took me a long time to get out. It's not my fault.

Day two: I went for a walk down the same street. I fell in the same hole. It took me a long time to get out. Why did I do that?

Day three: I went for a walk down the same street. I fell in the same hole. I got out quickly. It is my fault.

Day four: I went for a walk down the same street. I saw the hole. I walked around it.

Day five: I went for a walk down a different street. I can't handle it when I go down that street. Every time I go down that street, I feel something sucking me down that hole! I'm not going down that street anymore! I don't like what happens on that street. And when I get there, I can't handle it. I don't want sin to reign in my body so I'm not going down that street anymore.

Living for God is day by day. Choose it.

THE BEST PART OF THE BOOK SO FAR!

Now we are ready for victory, and I am so excited to be with you at Romans 6:11, which says, **"So you also must consider yourselves dead to sin and alive to God in Christ Jesus."** Notice the word **"So"** or **"likewise"** (NKJV). What Jesus has done, likewise we also must do. If we know and believe that in Christ we are dead to sin, we also can live like it.

The phrase **"consider yourselves dead to sin"** also has been translated **"reckon yourselves to be dead indeed to sin"** (NKJV) and **"count yourselves dead to sin"** (NIV). No matter the translation, *Romans 6:11 is the absolute center-piece of Christian victory* in the entire New Testament. I have seen more and faster transformation in my own heart and life because of my willingness to take seriously Romans 6:11 than any other verse in the entire Bible. The word **"consider"** or **"reckon,"** *logizomai*, means *assessing the facts, pressing your mind upon, calculating the importance of.* It means considering myself dead to sin. Please believe me when I tell you that there is incredible power here.

Here's how it works. Imagine yourself at the point of temptation. Deep within you a struggle is going on. You are tired of your old pattern of behavior and the pain and guilt that comes with it, but you feel strangely compelled to make that sinful choice again. Right then you must exercise your faith and consider yourself dead to sin. It doesn't matter whether you *feel* dead to the temptation. It doesn't matter whether you feel dead to the sin. *If you will exercise your faith, you will experience victory.*

HOW TO EXERCISE YOUR FAITH

If you are in Christ, you know how to exercise your faith. **"Therefore, as you received Christ Jesus the Lord, so walk in Him"** (Colossians 2:6). You exercise your faith in Christ the same way you came to Christ. Romans 10:9a says, **"If you confess with your mouth that Jesus is Lord and believe in your heart . . ."** That's how you exercise faith.

Speaking Four Little Words

Please note: It is no different in sanctification than it was in conversion. If you want to be different at that point of temptation, exercise your faith. Believe in your heart that you are dead to sin and confess with your mouth—speak it out! There is great power in verbal confession. I can't fully explain it, but somehow almighty God honors faith expressed at the point of temptation. Believe in your heart and confess with your mouth those four words: "I'm dead to that." If you say those words—if you will speak them out—your behavior, your speech, your attitudes, whatever you are working on *will be changed*!

"Well, how can that be?" you ask. "It's just four words. What difference will that make? To speak out by faith that I'm dead to a certain sin when I feel so very alive to it? How can that possibly make a difference?" Let me answer that question with a story of success that started very small.

Small Beginnings

Back in the late 1800s, residents of Niagara Falls wanted to build a suspension bridge across the Niagara Gorge at Niagara Falls. Remember, of course, that engineering then was not what it is today. The problem they faced was how to initially span the wide gorge with the rushing Niagara rapids beneath them. The engineers were stumped, so they held a contest inviting the locals to submit their best ideas. The person who won the contest suggested they take a kite, when the winds were favorable, and fly it across the gorge, landing it on the other side.

Incredibly, the majestic suspension bridge that stands to this day began with a little kite and string. To the string they attached a rope and pulled it across. The rope was used to pull across a chain. The chain was used to pull across a set of cables. Upon those iron cables they began to build the concrete structure which became the mighty Niagara Bridge. All that strength and power began with a frail, little string.

Maybe you feel that the words "I'm dead to that" are like that little string, and maybe this truth seems flimsy when facing a pattern of sinfulness that has held you so long, but I challenge you in this moment to begin by faith. Begin, by faith, to express those words at the point of temptation and say, "I'm dead to that." Look the temptation in the face with the eyes of faith and say the words out loud, "I'm dead to that! I don't feel dead to that. But in Christ I believe and choose to confess with my mouth the truth that I am dead to that." And pull that string across and pull that rope across and pull that chain across and pull that cord across and say, "I'm dead to that. I'm dead to that. *I'm dead to that!*"

You can build an entire life of victory and transformation upon that rock-solid truth, regardless of how you feel. In Christ, the power of sin is broken. "I'm dead to that. I can choose. I don't have to live like that or do that anymore."

President Abraham Lincoln wrote and signed the Emancipation Proclamation on January 1, 1863. Lincoln proclaimed once and for all that all men and women in the rebelling Confederate states were to be free. He wrote into law the righteous precept that slavery in every form was immoral and must be eliminated. At the moment that proclamation was signed into law, hundreds of thousands of slaves in the rebelling Confederacy were freed. In an incredible moment, each slave was 100 percent free. Yet history records that many of them continued to live like slaves. Because slavery was the only life they had ever known, they struggled to believe that things could really be different. Some slaves said, "This is all I've experienced; I don't see how life could be better." Others said, "It's too late for me. It will be easier just to stay with my old master."

What a tragedy! The day after slavery was abolished it should have been eliminated, but it wasn't because so many slaves could not believe they were free. Refusing to embrace what they had been given, they never experienced the freedom that was rightfully theirs.

NOW HEAR THIS!

Sin's power over you is broken. If you will begin to believe that and exercise your faith at the point of temptation, if you will begin to confess with your mouth and believe in your heart the powerful words, "I'm dead to that," you will begin to change.

Remember what I promised? . . . that *you can't apply the truths in this chapter without actually changing.* Let me say it one last time: God is not content simply to forgive you. He wants to change you! The day you came to Christ the power of sin was broken in your life. Isn't it about time you started living like it?

You can begin by confessing your faith in the face of temptation. The sample prayer in "Look Up!" will help you do that. Then experience the powerful truth of your victorious relationship to Christ.

Teacher Questions

1. If the power of sin is broken, why do we sometimes feel like it is not broken?

2. Why is it important that we believe the truth even when we don't feel like it?

3. What does it mean to "reckon yourselves to be dead indeed to sin"? How do we build our faith in that truth?

Prophet Questions

1. What is the specific thing that God is trying to change in you? How is it going so far?

2. What do we mean when we say that living for God is a day-by-day choice? Is it harder for you some days than others? If so, why?

3. What points of temptation have you faced today?

Shepherd Questions

1. Can you share a story of your own or a close friend's victory in applying this truth?

2. What should you do immediately after you experience defeat in the area you are seeking to change with God's help?

3. What should you do immediately when you realize you have had a victory in an area that has been a place of defeat for you?

LET'S GET TO WORK

Experiment with the phrase "I'm dead to that." You know the things you've chosen to work on when you "got specific" in chapter 3. In chapter 4 you repented of those areas of sin and defeat. Now when they rear their ugly head, by faith say out loud, "I'm dead to that." Say it several times if you have to, and see how the Lord begins to work.

LOOK UP!

Dear Father in heaven:

Thank You for the powerful truth that I am dead to sin because of my personal faith in the shed blood of Jesus Christ as sufficient payment for You to forgive me. I believe that sin's power is broken in me. Please bring that truth to mind each time temptation rears its ugly head. Give me faith to believe I can choose against sin and speak the words "I am dead to that."

I claim my victory in Jesus' name. Amen.

NOTES

1. George Barna, *Maximum Faith: Live Like Jesus* (Ventura: Metaformation/SGG/WHCP, 2011).

2. See http://www.barna.org/transformation-articles/480-research-on-how-god-trans-forms-lives-reveals-a-10-stop-journey. Accessed 1/2012.

3. See http://www.barna.org/transformation-articles/480-research-on-how-god-trans-forms-lives-reveals-a-10-stop-journey. Accessed 1/2012.

4. Class notes, "The Nature of the Church," Paul Borden, director of the D.Min. program, Denver Seminary, July 1990.

7

LORD, I'M **YOURS**

SAY IT IN A SENTENCE:

*Victory is accomplished when we offer
ourselves alive to God moment by moment.*

A long time ago I found a dead guy. I was twelve years old and headed back to school after a doctor's appointment. I jumped off the city bus and chose a shortcut between two houses and through the woods because it was pouring rain. As I ran up the muddy trail toward the woods, with houses on either side, I froze in my tracks. There sprawled on the ground in front of me was a man with his legs tangled under him and his right arm flung across my path. I knew in an instant that he was dead because his eyes and mouth were wide open and his face was knotted and blue. I wanted to run for help but my legs refused to move.

How did he get there? Had he been killed? Was I in danger? It seemed like an hour but it was only a moment before I silenced a thousand questions in my mind and ran to get some help. As it turned out, the poor soul had died of a massive heart attack while trying to dig a trench in his backyard to reroute the rainwater that was flowing into his basement.

My ministry as a pastor often calls me to places where I see those who have died, but I have never fully gotten over that first, sudden encounter with the reality of death. Death is very cold. Though the promises of heaven are real and comforting to me, I hate death. It is an ugly and cruel enemy.

BETTER ALIVE THAN DEAD

I am so thankful that there is more to the process of change than simply confessing the words, "I'm dead to that." You may have been wondering at the close of chapter 6, is that all there is? Is that the Christian life, just being dead to stuff?

I have great news for you. Like the famous outlaws of old, we are worth far more to God alive than dead. God doesn't want us to spend the rest of our days focused upon our sin and simply claiming the reality of what we are dead to. *Far more important than what we are dead to because of Christ's death is what we are alive to because of Christ's resurrection.*

That truth is contained in the Bible passage we will consider next. Take a moment and read this truth for yourself:

> **What then? Are we to sin because we are not under law but under grace? By no means! Do you not know that if you present yourselves to anyone as obedient slaves, you are slaves of the one whom you obey, either of sin, which leads to death, or of obedience, which leads to righteousness? But thanks be to God, that you who were once slaves of sin have become obedient from the heart to the standard of teaching to which you were committed, and, having been set free from sin, have become slaves of righteousness. I am speaking in human terms, because of your natural limitations. For just as you once presented your members as slaves to impurity and to lawlessness leading to more lawlessness, so now present your members as slaves to righteousness leading to sanctification** (Romans 6:15–19).

NOT UNDER LAW BUT GRACE

Not Losers . . .

There is so much in those verses to fuel the personal transformation that you are seeking. Notice the phenomenal promise from God that you **"are not under law but under grace."** When you are under the law, you feel like a failure and are constantly attacked by messages of condemnation: "Loser! Blew it again!" or "You're such a failure; you never measure up and you never will." Those messages come from the Enemy of our souls, Satan, who is called the **"accuser of our brothers"** (Revelation 12:10). If we listen to those lies, we can become greatly discouraged and even despondent about our need to change.

The purpose of the law was to *reveal* sin, and that is all it can ever do. The law just makes us feel bad by rubbing our noses in our failure. But now hear this: None of God's children is under the law. All who know God in Christ are under grace. God has immersed us in a system of grace so that when He sees us, He sees what He is changing us to be and not what we are.

We must dispense with the notion that God is looking out of heaven with a furrowed brow and clenched teeth, saying, "What is *wrong* with you?! Why can't you *get* it?" God has placed us under His system of grace so that when we fail in the process of change we can hear the liberating message, "I love you; I forgive you. Get up and keep trying. I am going to help you!"

... But Embraced As His Children

Do you understand that since you came to Christ your "stock" has never risen in God's estimation, because it reached the top the day He embraced you as His child? It doesn't rise—and it doesn't fall—because it has nothing to *do* with you. It has to do with grace and the fact that God has chosen to set His love on you.

Isn't that great news? We want so much to be changed from the people we are into Christ's image, but sometimes we get discouraged when we fail and even want to quit. Into the middle of that struggle steps the Word of God with an authoritative pronouncement: **"[You] are not under law but under grace."** You are under a loving God who is committed to supporting your transformation, giving you divine resources for as long as you live on this earth. When you fall and fail, get up! And go on in the strength of His grace and love for you.

WHOSE SLAVE ARE YOU?

One of the amazing truths from this passage is that we are all slaves to something. **"Do you not know,"** Paul wrote in verse 16, **"that if you present yourselves to anyone as obedient slaves, you are slaves of the one whom you obey . . .?"** Even as Christians who are freed from the power of sin, we still serve a master. The question is, which one? Sin still has its appeal, even to the born-again Christian.

ALWAYS A SLAVE TO SOMEONE

If you do whatever your boss says, without hesitation and without question, you are for all intents and purposes the slave of your boss. If you do whatever your spouse says without evaluating or considering if that is really best, then you are a slave to your spouse. And if you do whatever your sinful nature says, without resisting or discerning the wisdom in that choice, then, for all intents and purposes, you are a slave to your sinful nature.

The only other possibility is becoming what Paul calls a "slave of righteousness." A slave of righteousness is a person who has as his or her consuming desire, doing what the Master wants.

A Slave to Sin . . .

Whose slave are you? There are countless sins that people can be enslaved to. Just to give you an example, let me flip open my "Sin Rolodex" and let's see . . . down to letter "S". Yes, here we go . . .

- *Stuff.* Some people are slaves to stuff: more money, new car, nice clothes, a bigger house. They are consumed with acquisition. Indeed, they are slaves to that sin.
- *Sexuality.* I have known and counseled with men whose mind is focused almost exclusively on women and sex. They can't think about anything else. No matter what the subject, they find a way to draw the conversation over to sexuality. They're slaves to the sin of immoral sexual thoughts and actions. Sexuality, a gift from God, has been perverted in their minds.
- *Substance.* A substance can call some people's names, and they are like, "Duh . . . okay, I will do whatever you say!" Cocaine, alcohol, tobacco, caffeine, sugar—they're slaves to substance, when the Bible commands us not to be brought under the power of anything.
- *Someone.* For these people, someone in their life controls them. That person "has their number." That person can push their buttons and pull their chain at will. An individual can get the "slave" to say or do things that he will regret yet still do because of the control that that person has over him. It's bondage!

As a pastor, I often observe that people wrongly view Christianity as too restrictive. I hear things like, "Man! Christianity has way too many rules," or "Doing all this Christian stuff is like a prison; I've just gotta be me." Certainly, Jesus has given us a description of how He wants us to live, but it doesn't even come close to comparing to the imprisonment—the bondage—that is involved in being a slave to sin.

I remember reading the newspaper account of the Texas court verdict on John William King, sentenced to death for the cruel death of a black man. King was convicted of chaining James Byrd Jr. by the ankles to the back of his pickup truck, then dragging Byrd at high speed for more than three miles. You would think the impact of a sentence like that would rattle his decadent thinking, but as he was walking out of the courtroom, a reporter asked him for a comment and all he could do was curse the sorrowing family members.

I said to myself, *Sin is a ruthless, heartless, vicious master.* Genesis 4:7 says, **"Sin is crouching at [your] door. Its desire is for you."** Remember, sin equals slavery, and the only way to be truly free is found in the gospel of Jesus Christ (see Romans 6:17), the One who said, **"You will know the truth, and the truth will set you free"** (John 8:32).

... Or a Slave to Righteousness

This will really encourage you. Paul continued in Romans 6:18 with the words, **"Having been set free from sin, [you] have become slaves of righteousness."** That's not "Hey, maybe someday"; it's "Right now you have it." There's a new slavery that has taken the place of slavery to sin. It's called *slavery to righteousness.*

Again the point is emphasized through repetition: **"You are the slaves of the one whom you obey, . . . of obedience, which leads to righteousness"** (verse 16); **"slaves of righteousness"** (verse 18); **"slaves to righteousness"** (verse 19); **"slaves of God"** (verse 22).

Even though I don't know you personally, I know something about you if you are truly in Christ, especially if you came to Christ after childhood. There used to be a time in your life when you hardly thought about sin at all. Oh, there may have been some vague feelings of guilt or regret, but not a true, consistent conviction over sin. When you came to Christ, however, all that changed. Where once you used to be able to say and do all kinds of things without giving it a second thought, now you feel convicted that it is wrong. Before, you seldom thought about sin, but since you gave your life to Christ, sin is everywhere. You see it in others and you're especially conscious of it in your own life. Before we come to Christ, we are slaves to sin and hardly ever think about righteousness. After we come to Christ, we are slaves to righteousness and frequently think about sin.

Has that been your "testimony," or experience? Are you a slave to righteousness? Maybe you're not sure. Why not take this simple three-point test? If you are not a slave to righteousness, you are still a slave to sin, and you are not in Christ. So this is a test you want to pass.

"I know I'm a slave to righteousness if . . .

1. "I'm acutely aware of unrighteousness in me." You're aware of it. When you sin, there is this megaconviction thing that happens. Your heart is grieved. You feel badly about it when you break His standard. Now when you set your eyes on something unrighteous . . . if you say words that are unrighteous . . . if you choose an action that's unrighteous, you're convicted about it.

2. "I can't ignore personal sin, and I have to make it right." When the Holy Spirit convicts you of a certain sin, you have to make it right. You feel the need to ask for God's forgiveness and to go to a brother or sister who has been injured by the sin and say, "I've sinned against you and I'm truly sorry. Please forgive me."

3. "I constantly wonder if I'm pleasing Jesus." Can you honestly say, "I think of Christ a lot. Not every moment, but every day." Real slaves of righteousness have the Holy Spirit inside them constantly asking, "Would this be pleasing to Jesus?" It's more than message bracelets, bumper stickers, or catchy T-shirts. It's our hearts asking, "Is this what He wants me to do?" And it's following through on the question with an authentic answer.

THE FRUIT OF RIGHTEOUSNESS

Somebody says, "Well, hang on for a second; I'm not acutely aware of sin. I can choose to ignore it, and not have to make it right with God or with others. I'm not constantly seeking to please my new Master, but I still consider myself a Christian; I've just backslidden." Many supposed Christians live this way and then wonder why they're not becoming more like Christ.

But if you are truly a slave to righteousness, the fruit of your life will show it. A man I'll call Jack came up to me after a church meeting recently and said, "I'm worried. I have all this stuff in my head, but I'm not really sure if it's in my heart. I'm not really sure if I'm a Christian." I knew what was troubling him. He was reviewing the biblical evidences of genuine faith in Christ and not seeing them in his life, and he wanted me to give him assurance that he was truly born again. Why would I try to give him peace when the Spirit of God was convicting him and bringing unrest? What I did do was ask Jack if he saw any of the fruit of righteousness in his life. I explained to him that Jesus said, **"Thus you will recognize them by their fruits"** (Matthew 7:20).

I told him that the New Testament instructs us to **"work out your own salvation with fear and trembling"** (Philippians 2:12) and to **"examine yourselves, to see whether you are in the faith"** (2 Corinthians 13:5). If your life does not bear any of the fruits of righteousness, then it's time to stop pretending that you know Jesus, who said, **"Whoever abides in Me, and I in him, he it is that bears much fruit"** (John 15:5). It's time we stopped giving people more assurance of salvation than God's Word gives. If you're not bearing the fruit of righteousness with consistency, then you must question whether you have ever been **"free[d] from sin [to] become slaves of righteousness"** (Romans 6:18).

If you do recognize the fruits of righteousness in your life, then you know the joy they bring and you are hungering for more. In fact, that's why you're reading this book, because you really want to change. Fantastic!

Here's the final point in the process of change:

VICTORY IS ACCOMPLISHED WHEN
WE OFFER OURSELVES WHOLLY TO GOD.

After repenting of my sin and believing that the power of sin is broken in my life, "It's all done but the choosing." Choosing to confess the powerful words, "I am dead to that," and reckoning myself dead to sin is the first part of the choice to change. But those actions alone will not guarantee change. There is a second part.

Maybe you have experienced the pain that follows standing before a certain temptation and saying, "Well, I am dead to that, I am so dead to that. I'm dead to that, but it seems to be growing in me this very moment; in fact, I'm not as dead to it as I was a few seconds ago." Then you hear yourself saying, "Why do I feel so alive to this?" And then failure comes!

You can't just be dead to sin if you want to change. You have to act on what you are alive to because of Christ's work in you. The second choice you must make is to present yourself to God, offering yourself as a servant of His.

This point is made repeatedly in Romans 6:

"Consider yourselves . . . alive to God in Christ Jesus" (verse 11).

"Present yourselves to God as those alive from the dead" (verse 13 NASB).

"Present yourselves . . . as slaves for obedience . . . resulting in righteousness" (verse 16 NASB).

"Present your members as slaves to righteousness, resulting in sanctification" (verse 19 NASB).

IT FEELS LIKE VICTORY, NOT SLAVERY.

Don't be discouraged by all this "slavery talk." In verse 19, Paul explained, "I speak in human terms." What he meant was "Hey, guys, I'm using an analogy to help our finite human minds comprehend supernatural truth. Don't press the analogy too far here." In the truest sense, God's children are not slaves to anything. We are victors. We are sons and daughters of the Most High God. Before we were in Christ, no one had to teach us how to sin; we just did whatever sin told us to do. The purpose of the "slaves of righteousness" analogy is to make sure we don't make following Christ too complicated. If we are as obedient to our new Master as we were to our old one, we will be very successful at following Christ. Beyond that, Paul wanted to make sure we didn't transfer the negative imagery of slavery to living for God.

SHUNNING SATAN FOR A LOVING MASTER

Serving Satan and serving Christ are as different as two things could possibly be. It's amazing that we are often tempted to waver in choosing who will be our master. Take a moment and reflect on the difference between them.

First, Satan hates those who serve him! Did you know that? He hates you and wants to destroy you! I've never been able to understand this modern "church of Satan." What do they do at their services? Curse and swear at each other. Tear each other down and abuse each other. Spend themselves trying to advance the goals of their master. How stupid is that? Satan hates people! In contrast, Christ loves us and has given Himself for our joy and ultimate fulfillment in knowing and following Him. Don't ever think of that as slavery!

Second, Satan consumes us for his own purposes. He's just using and abusing people. In contrast, Christ changes us for our own good. He never allows one thing into our life that He will not use for our benefit, to produce something good. Now, which one should I choose as my master?

Third, Satan condemns us with generalities that produce despair. I have already pointed out to you that Satan never says anything specific when he accuses us about sin in our life. The Bible says Satan is the **"accuser of the brothers,"** but he never says anything specific. He would never say, "Hey, Lyn, you need to be a little more . . ." Do you know why he never says that? Because he never wants you to be any better than you are. He doesn't want you to improve. He doesn't say, "Hey, Rick. I wish you'd work on this . . ." Or, "Hey, Shawna, why are you so . . . ?"

He doesn't get specific because he doesn't want to help you. Instead he condemns us with generalities like, "You stink! You're a failure. Give it up. You're just playing a game. Who are you trying to kid?" He tries to trash us with general accusations.

In contrast, through the Holy Spirit, Christ works with surgical precision. "Hey, you. Stop neglecting your wife." Now I can go somewhere with that—specific points of conviction. The Holy Spirit will reveal specifics you can work on. "Hey, Brad. You're addicted to . . . Let it go and lean on Me for that strength," or "Hey, Cheryl. That's a sinful thought that needs to be replaced by anything on the list in Philippians 4:8." "Hey, Martha. That's not a loving thing to say."

Offering ourselves to God feels like victory, not like slavery. When I do what Satan says, I feel like garbage, but when I do what God says, I feel like a million bucks because I have victory and hope for the future.

MAKING THE CHOICE

You can't study Romans 6 without seeing that we're being called to make a choice. We know how to make a choice; we do it all the time. It involves our will. It's a decision. "I'm going to go here. I'm going to sell this. I'm going to choose you." This passage is filled with willful choices for righteousness:

"Let not sin therefore reign . . ." (verse 12).
"Do not present . . ." (verse 13).
"Are we to sin . . ." (verse 15).
"You present yourselves . . ." (verse 16).
"You obeyed from the heart..." (verse 17 NKJV).
"For just as you once presented . . . so now present your members . . ." (verse 19).

Since I went public—telling my church family—about the specifics of what God is changing in me right now, He has been giving me a significantly increased number of "opportunities to grow." I have been finding that the busier I am, the harder it is for me to choose patience over frustration at the point of temptation. In every instance, I have had to remind myself of this truth:

OFFERING MYSELF TO GOD
IS ALL ABOUT CHOOSING.

It is early summer as I write this, always a tough time because it is right before a family vacation; and so I am trying to wrap things up and get some time away. Adding to that pressure, I have promised to have this book completed in about a month, and on top of that, Pioneers, whose board of directors I serve on, called an emergency board meeting. Pioneers is an international missions agency to the unreached, based in Orlando, with more than seven hundred missionaries worldwide. Most of the men on the board are businessmen, but do they call the meeting at the toughest part of their week? No! They put the meeting on Friday right when I am scrambling on top of everything else to get my most important message of the year ready for Sunday. It's the message where I take the people back through all that we have learned since last September and challenge them to evaluate themselves in light of what they have been learning.

So there I am at O'Hare Airport, the busiest airport in the world, at the busiest time of my year, in the busiest year of my life, and we are sitting on the plane waiting to take off for Orlando. I'm trying to have a good attitude, but in the back of my mind I can't help wondering, "Why did I say I would do this? I don't have time for this."

Buzzzzzz. "This is the captain speaking. I regret to inform you that weather patterns over Florida are so severe that we have not been cleared for takeoff, and won't be for at least three hours." "Oh, well," I thought, "back to the terminal, and I'll plug in my laptop for three hours of concentrated work." Not a chance! The captain proceeded to inform us that we would not be able to return to the gate. With so many planes lined up to take off, we were stuck in line and would have to sit on the runway for three hours. I could spend three more pages describing the way this entire trip became a trial. Suffice it to say that was just the beginning:

- A terrifically draining meeting in Orlando which I had to leave early to fly home;
- Five more hours sitting in the Orlando terminal as our return trip was delayed in twenty fifteen-minute increments, without explanation;
- Another hour on the runway in Chicago after we landed, so that my two-and-one-half-hour return trip turned into a twelve-hour nightmare.

Maybe it would not have been a significant thing for you to get through all this and not lose your cool, but for me it required a miracle. More specifically, a choice!

By God's grace, I sat and endured the entire ordeal with not a moment of anger and not a word of frustration. I didn't even complain, though there were lots of people willing to commiserate. As I walked off the plane at almost 1:30 A.M.

and headed for the baggage claim, I remembered that I had forgotten my hat on the plane. I laughed out loud as I turned to go back for it, my heart was filled with so much joy. God had given me a whole day to imprint in my heart the lesson that victory is a choice.

Earlier in the week I had arrived at the church feeling defeated because I had lost my patience with one of our children before leaving for work. I knew that I had no one to blame but myself; I knew I had made a choice to do wrong. How essential it is if we are really serious about personal transformation that we recognize the power of a choice in any given moment—the choice to do right or wrong. That leads us to the next part of this truth.

OFFERING MYSELF TO GOD
IS MOMENT BY MOMENT.

Even when I began this book I did not fully understand that concept. I've come to see and understand in a brand-new way that change is not so much about the crisis as the process. Change is about thousands upon thousands of little decisions we make every day. "Here I am at this point. I always do this, but now by God's grace I choose in this moment to do this instead. Lord, I'm dead to that and I offer myself to You."

It's a million decisions. Change is moment by moment by moment by moment by moment.

My spiritual upbringing was marvelous in so many ways, but the above truth was something that was not understood or taught. I was always taught that change was about the crisis. So many Sunday mornings, the service would end and the church would sing, "All to Jesus I Surrender . . ." or "Lord, I'm Coming Home," or "Just As I Am." All wonderful hymns, but each focused on the crisis part of change. And people would walk up the aisle at the end of the service and have a crisis where they promised God that they were going to change.

In the summertime we would go to camp and have another crisis. The whole week would build to that last night where they'd have a big bonfire and everyone would "sell out for God" and put a stick in the fire. And things would go phenomenally until the end of Labor Day weekend. And then you'd ask yourself, "Where did that go?"

I'm not opposed to the crisis, but I am persuaded more than ever that real transformation is about the process. It's about a thousand choices in the moment. Chris Rice is a popular Christian music artist who wrote a fantastic song called

"The Power of a Moment." In it he noted, "Right now's the only moment that matters."[1]

Instead of sitting in church and waiting for the crisis and waiting for the preacher to move us in some deep way so we can have a crisis that's more of a crisis than any crisis we've ever had before, why not make a choice to change? Not a big emotional crisis kind of choice but a little one, then another and then another, one at a time. It's thousands upon thousands of those little choices that lead to real transformation.

LET'S GO FOR A WALK

The Holy Spirit uses many pictures to describe the Christian life in the Bible. We are told that living for Christ is like working in a vineyard (Matthew 20), building a house (Matthew 7), and running a race (1 Corinthians 9). Many other examples could be given, but by far the most common picture of the Christian life in the New Testament is the walk. Living the Christian life successfully is like going for a walk. Let's take a quick walk through six New Testament passages.

> **"There is . . . no condemnation for those who . . . walk not according to the flesh but according to the Spirit"** (Romans 8:1, 4).
> **"Walk by the Spirit, and you will not gratify the desires of the flesh"** (Galatians 5:16).
> **"If we live by the Spirit, let us also keep in step with the Spirit"** (Galatians 5:25).
> **"I therefore, a prisoner for the Lord [Jesus Christ], urge you to walk in a manner worthy"** (Ephesians 4:1).
> Also in Ephesians you'll find, **"No longer walk as the Gentiles do"** (4:17), **"Walk in love"** (5:2), **"Walk as children of light** (5:8), and **"Look carefully then how you walk"** (5:15).
> **"As you received Christ Jesus the Lord, so walk in Him"** (Colossians 2:6).

Many more could be given, but maybe you're thinking, "Well, that's Paul. He was a missionary. He probably walked a lot, so what's the big deal about him expressing himself that way?" No, it's far more than that. Remember that the Holy Spirit inspired the writers of Scripture to express the very words of God: **"Men spoke from God as they were carried along by the Holy Spirit"** (2 Peter 1:21). Luke, Peter, Jude, and John also described life on this earth as a *walk*. Even in the Old Testament the prophet Isaiah promised teachers from God who would say, **"This is the way, *walk* in it"** (30:21, italics added).

When we understand that the process of change is like walking, we begin to see that all we need to focus on is the next step. Often we become discouraged in the process of change because a lifetime of battling sin and seeking victory seems so overwhelming. If you and I are ever going to walk with Christ and be the person that God wants us to be, our focus has to be the next step. Just that and nothing else. Satan gets us all intimidated about the long-term victory and we miss the opportunity to live for Christ in this moment. We've got to honor God as we step-by-step make our way through the day. Just have a great day today! "Tomorrow will take care of itself," Jesus said (see Matthew 6:34). Victory comes one step, one moment at a time.

Norman Grubbs wrote in his insightful booklet, *Continuous Revival*, "At this moment—right now if your walk is being clouded with the rising of some motion of sin in you, listen as God points to that and says, 'There, right there, just that, get *that* under the blood and walk with Me again.'"[2] This truth has brought me so much freedom, and it can do the same for you. A lifetime of transformation is so intimidating, so why not lay that down, and pick up instead this next moment for Him.

READY FOR A PRACTICE SESSION?

It's time for a practice session—time to consider a specific area and how we can call upon God for help. Suppose that your struggle is lying. Have you ever told a lie before? (If you answer yes, continue; if no, you just did.) Let's imagine that the Lord has revealed to you that lying is the next thing that He wants to change in you. You have come to a crisis of understanding that. You see that sin for what it is in your life and God in His grace has brought you to a place of true repentance about that. As always happens before you get too far past the crisis, you see it coming, the situation where time and again you fall and lie. But this time, in this moment you face that temptation and refuse to give in, believing that you don't have to fall and fail because Christ has broken the power of sin in your life.

Of course, the sense of temptation does not vanish immediately. So you decide to pursue victory by confessing out loud the powerful words, "I am dead to that!" In that moment, the temptation withers slightly, but you know it's coming back with a vengeance. Standing still won't be enough for long, so you make the choice to offer yourself alive to God, by praying: "You know, Lord, I used to use my mouth to speak lies, but I am offering myself alive to You in this moment." Then open your mouth and speak truth. Any appropriate truth. Truth about God, truth about the situation itself, *truth*! In that moment you are changed.

Now if you can substitute that story for a thousand different sins, you understand the process of sanctification. Paul wrote, **"Let the thief no longer steal [be dead to that] . . . but rather let him labor, doing honest work with his own hands [offer yourself to God in the moment], so that he may have something to share with anyone in need"** (Ephesians 4:28). It's not just a matter of standing in front of the refrigerator and saying, "I am so dead to that chocolate cake. I am so dead to that. I am going to kill the person who put that in there. I am so dead to that." There has to be a turning from that and investing my energies in something else. Moment by moment by moment.

Maybe your problem is materialism. You go over to the local mall with a family member and before you know it, you find yourself in that expensive store. You're standing in front of a suit or piece of furniture or whatever with your Visa card in hand, knowing you can't afford this purchase and saying to yourself, "I don't want this. I am dead to that thing. I am dead to it!" Don't stand there too long, though, or you know you're gonna fail. Instead, why not get out of the store? And as you leave, try praying, "Lord, I typically use this time to buy something to gratify myself, but now I offer my time to You. I'm going out into the mall while I wait for my family and I pray that You would give me someone to minister to. Lord, show me somebody that I can encourage. Give me a way to use myself and my life for You. I offer myself to You in this moment."

The second part is as critical as the first: After saying you're dead to that sin, remember that you are alive to God. And pray, "I'm dead to that. Lord, I offer myself alive to You." Several Bible versions translate Romans 6:13 differently. One says **"present yourselves"** (NKJV); another says **"offer"** (NIV). The King James says, **"yield yourselves."** The point is to give God that struggle. Make *that* choice. Give the right to self-serving choices over to God moment by moment.

Teacher Questions

1. Why must we move past simply being dead to things in order to have lasting victory?
2. How often do you think you will have to offer yourself afresh to God this week? Why?
3. What is the difference between the crisis of offering to God and the ongoing process of offering yourself to God?

Prophet Questions

1. What parts of your life have you refused to give to God?
2. What consequences have you experienced because you have withheld yourself?
3. How are you planning to settle these points of resistance? How has this chapter helped?

Shepherd Questions

1. Why do we often fear giving our lives completely to God?
2. In giving our lives to God, what can we be sure of because we know He loves us?
3. What was your last moment of victory in surrender to God? How have you expressed your gratitude for the help He gave you?

LET'S GET TO WORK

It's time to go public with your process of change. Invite a close friend out for coffee or breakfast. Share with him or her what God has been teaching you. Then ask your friend to pray for you as you complete this book.

LOOK UP!

Dear Lord:

I praise You today for the victory that You won over my sin through Your death and resurrection. I confess that I have not been experiencing the victory that You have provided for me, and I ask forgiveness for that. In this moment, as never before, I am turning my life over to You. As best I know how, I will seek to live the truth that I am Yours. When I forget or regress, I ask You to bring this pledge to mind, and I will offer myself afresh to You.

Thank You for making this choice possible through Your marvelous grace. In Jesus' name. Amen.

NOTES

1. Chris Rice, "The Power of a Moment," © 1988 Clumsy Fly Music; from the CD, "Past the Edge," Rocketown Records.
2. Norman Grubbs, *Continuous Revival* (Ft. Washington, Penn.: Christian Literature Crusade, 1977), 11.

PART 3

THE
POWER
TO
CHANGE

Remember that kids' game "Hot and Cold," where you hid something and then challenged the other kids to find it simply by responding to your clues of "warmer, warmer" or "colder, colder; you're getting very cold"? Did you ever play that? I remember best the enthusiastic shouts of the prompter as I would be very close to winning the game: "Hot! You're getting red-hot!"

Of course, personal transformation is a difficult and sometimes painful process. It's certainly not a game, but I want you to know, if you have done everything we have covered in this book so far, "You're getting hot, red-hot!"

Lasting change and victory are almost within your grasp. Part 3 offers you the final element to lasting change: the power to change.

In part 2 we examined from God's Word the **crisis** and then the three-step **process** in personal life change. If you have followed through and done the homework, you should have:

- Repented of a specific behavior or attitude that God wants to change in you: the crisis.
- Begun by faith to live out the truth that sin's power over you is broken by virtue of your relationship with Christ.
- Experimented with the life-changing words "I am dead to that" at the moment of temptation.

- Experienced the joy of turning from that behavior or attitude and offering yourself in that moment to God.

If you can say, "I have done those things; Lord, change me," you are ready to move into part 3.

And now a warning. So far, after seven chapters, we have the process. Now, it's an excellent process; it's a biblical process for change. But so far it's like a grill with no gas, like a house with no electricity, a car with no motor. Without part 3, your momentary victories will be very short-lived. You will quickly return to an excruciating cycle of sin-confess, sin-confess. You may go back to the same sin or you may replace it with another one, but without the content in the final three chapters of this book you will not experience lasting transformation. So don't quit while you're ahead!

The very best part of this book is still ahead of you. It's about the power to change. It's about a kind of Christian life that you may have never experienced before. Put into effect the principles of part 3, and you will experience a consistency of victory that most people never knew was possible.

8

THE POWER **SOURCE**

SAY IT IN A SENTENCE:

For life change to happen, we must access the power of God for change,
admitting that we do not have the strength within us.

Most of the Christians I meet are tired; many of them very tired. They don't have the passion for God they once had and feel a kind of vague guilt about it. The sequence is always the same: countless seasons of (1) renewed expectation, (2) energetic pursuit, (3) encroaching disappointment, and finally, (4) exhaustion.

"What's wrong with me—why don't I learn? Why don't I change? Will things ever be different?" They have tried serving, spending themselves to the limit in the work of Christ as they look for a fuller Christian experience through ministry involvement. Exhausted, they "pull back" for a season and then try "Bible knowledge." "That's the key—staying focused on God's Word," they're told, so they make plans to immerse themselves in Scripture. They undertake Bible studies, quiet-time schedules, and books about spiritual disciplines. Again, the new direction lasts for a season and some good certainly comes from it, yet they feel like the joy they were promised at conversion is still eluding them somehow. As faithfulness and regularity give way to dull routine, they can't help but feel they have just traveled another set of seasons toward exhaustion.

Other seasons of worthy pursuits come and go. Worship, helping the poor, missions and evangelism and prayer and, and, and, . . . In all of this there is a sincere intent to live as God desires, followed by failure, frustration, and exhaustion. Sound familiar?

THE EXHAUSTING CHRISTIAN LIFE
Paul's Dilemma

Paul described something very similar in his life: a desire to do good but an inability to get it done. He wrote:

For I do not understand my own actions. For I do not do what I want, but I do the very thing I hate. Now if I do what I do not want, I agree with the law, that it is good (Romans 7:15–16).

In other words, Paul wanted to do something. The fact that he wanted to do it proved that the law is good. "I'm just not getting it done," Paul exclaimed. Then he indicated why: the "sin that dwells within me. For I know that nothing good dwells in me, that is, in my flesh. For I have the desire to do what is right, but not the ability to carry it out (verses 17–18).

What Paul was describing in Romans 7:15–18 is *the exhausting Christian life.* The victorious Christian life was eluding Paul, and amazingly, under the inspiration of the Holy Spirit, Paul admitted it. Paul acknowledged that at a certain point in time, his Christian life was not working for him. For him it was a temporary problem, but sadly, for many of Jesus' followers, it's all they ever experience. I know, because for many years this is the Christian life that I lived. Precept without power. Rules without resources. Laws without life. Initially exhausting and ultimately excruciating, it is the powerless Christian life. It causes many people to slip into what Paul calls "the carnal-minded life," or the "fleshly Christian life" (see Romans 8:1–10). Forgiven—yes. But failing and falling into a lukewarm mediocrity, believers begin to view the dynamic, spirit-filled, victorious Christian life that God promised like a carrot on the end of a stick.

Charles Price's Dilemma

Charles Price, a British author, has written a book called *Christ for Real.*[1] In the book he explains, "When I came to Christ, I got three things: a ticket, a certificate, and a catalog. The 'ticket' stated: 'One way journey to heaven.' . . . The 'certificate' stated: 'this is to certify that Charles Price has had all his sins forgiven . . . signed, God.' . . . The catalog . . . was called the Bible." And so with his ticket and his certificate, he started to read the catalog. He pictured heaven as this heavenly supermarket with rows and rows of shelves stocked with things that God promised in the catalog to give him. If he came across something in the catalog he wanted, he just needed to pray. Prayer was like ordering online, direct from God.

Price would read God's Word, and it would say that God promised to give him love and to make him more loving. And so he would say, "That's what I want, God. Send some of that." Price then pictured the Holy Spirit as a heavenly errand boy, who would go up and down the rows and fill the order. The Holy Spirit then would come and sort of pour love all over him, so that he was more loving for a short time.

But then he would be reading in the catalog and see that he was supposed to be more patient—so he would put in another order. The Spirit would come and give him some patience for a while. Being in ministry, he sensed very strongly the need for power. Since God promised to give him power, he would pray for it. According to Price, the Spirit would come and light the fuse and boom! there would be power for a while. But always, always, always—no matter what he ordered from the catalog—it was short-lived.

When I first read that concept from Charles Price, it deeply impacted me because it was exactly how I felt. He was describing my own personal experience in trying to be a godly man. Now *that* is the Christian life that I lived for many years. And the message that I'm sharing with you here is probably the single, greatest breakthrough in my own walk and relationship with the Lord. If you're not on this, you *have* to get on this. When I've gotten off of it—even in the last decade— I've had to get right back on it again!

My Dilemma

The problem with approaching sanctification that way is that the results are always temporary: Be loving; be patient; be self-controlled; pray; study the Bible; and witness. And we get all these things going in the air like some kind of professional juggler wanting like anything to keep the "act" going, but growing in our awareness that very soon it is all going to come crashing down on top of us. That kind of living, though well-intentioned, is really nothing more than self-powered sanctification, and it always leads to exhaustion. Always!

Take it from me. I say to my own shame that I spent too many years—too many pastoral years—trying to be a godly man in my own strength. Growing up I was never taught the concept that follows in the pages ahead. Growing up I remember singing a song that kind of summarizes the problem:

> Obedience is the very best way to show that you believe
> Doing exactly what the Lord commands, doing it happily

Action is the key, do immediately, joy you will receive,
Obedience is the very best way to show that you believe!
O – B – E – D – I –E – N – C – E
Obedience is the very best way to show that you believe!

The problem with the song is that the "what" is very clear but there is not a shred of "how." Like most Christians, I assumed that the "how" was me. "Get to work, buddy. If you really love God, you will make it happen." I never heard anyone say that, but that's what I saw everyone doing.

Over the course of many years, I turned from a kid who didn't know how to "power" the Christian life, into a preacher who proclaimed the "what God wants," without the "how." Oh, maybe I gave four or five little explanatory steps on how to "go to work" on change but never a full explanation of how to access the power of God to change. *Without the power of God flowing through us, personal transformation will always remain a mirage.*

THE TYPICAL SUNDAY MORNING DILEMMA

This dilemma over obedience plays out in most churches every Sunday morning. You come to church already exhausted, having failed at living the Christian life in your own strength the past week. The pastor stands up and says, "Be more dedicated. Be more committed, you people. Sell out to God! Obey the Lord on this or that important matter. If He's not Lord *of* all, He's not Lord *at* all. Obedience, obedience, *obedience*!" The whole service builds to an emotional song or prayer at the end where we "surrender all" for the ten thousandth time.

Eventually most Christians tune out the challenge to change, concluding that they "just don't have what it takes," and settle into a sort of numb, passionless, pseudo-Christian experience.

We sit and listen to preaching like that week after week (I can criticize because I have done so much of it myself), and we feel guilty about our disobedience. We promise God we will try harder, and some weeks if we are really serious, our promises will last all the way to Tuesday or Wednesday before we fall flat on our faces, exhausted and frustrated.

WHY IS JESUS ALIVE?

This kind of living is a knife in the heart of Jesus Christ who not only died for our forgiveness but rose again that He might live His life through us. Let me ask you something: Why is Jesus Christ alive today? Yes, I know, "because He rose from the dead." But why? Yes, I agree, "because He is God and death could not hold Him." But why? What purpose does His present life serve? He's got eternity on His hands; what is He doing with it?

Over and over the New Testament tells us that Jesus is alive to make intercession for us, to come before the throne of heaven as our mediator, to make requests before the Father for our moment-by-moment needs. **"He always lives to make intercession for [us],"** the Scripture says (Hebrews 7:25). Payment for sin is complete; that is a past accomplishment. Someday Christ will rule the earth; that is a future promise (see Revelation 19:15).

But what about today? *Today Christ lives to bring His victorious power to bear upon your and my character.* Yes, He offers victory over sin and death, and He gives forgiveness to all who believe; but He also wants to live His life through us. That is what Christian living is all about.

I'm afraid sometimes the Lord Jesus has looked down at my Christian experience and possibly at yours and said, "This is *it*? *This* is what I rose for? *This* is the degree to which you are going to draw down upon *My* resurrection power? *This* is the degree to which you're going to let Me live My life through you? This is the sum total? This is as good as it gets?"

I challenge you right in this moment as you hold this book to come to the turning point that I had to come to. A once-and-for-all decision to be done with the exhausting Christian life! A choice to be done with all the silly posing and posturing and "look at me, how hard I'm trying to be a good Christian."

MAKE A PERSONAL DECISION
TO PICK UP THE TRUE CHRISTIAN LIFE.

"Christ in you." As we will see, it's a way of living that is far superior to the Christ-in-my-own-strength program. It's a way that will have you wondering why you wandered around this reality so long without seizing it for yourself.

THE EXCHANGED CHRISTIAN LIFE

You cannot experience the kind of power I'm talking about until you come to the end of yourself. Just as a person cannot come to Christ until he comes to the end of himself, so you cannot experience the power to change until you are done with your own efforts. That's what Paul did when he confessed, **"Wretched man that I am! Who will deliver me from this body of death?"** (Romans 7:24).

Those are not easy words to say from your heart. Until you and I fully recognize that *we* are the problem—*we* are the reason that Christ is not seen in us—until we stop trying to live the Christian life and let Christ live His life through us, we will always be exhausted.

Such a desperate cry from Paul in Romans 7:24, **"Wretched man that I am! Who will deliver me from this body of death?"** deserves an answer and it comes immediately in verse 25: **"Thanks be to God through Jesus Christ our Lord!"** There's the answer right there. It's Christ! He is the only one who ever lived the Christian life successfully! Our only hope is to get out of the way and let Him live His life through us.

No Power in Ourselves

Christ has made no provision for you—on your own—to live the Christian life. Sure, we can get knowledge and understanding. We've been working on that for seven chapters, and of course we can serve and worship and walk with Him, but we have no power, no personal strength to resource that kind of obedience. Do you know how much actual power or strength Christ has given us personally to live for Him? Zero! Nothing! There is absolutely nothing in you—not an ounce of strength . . . not a smidgen of anything . . . not a thimbleful. And until we recognize and embrace that truth, we will always inevitably fail in the process of change.

Bible Time

Maybe you're wondering: "Are you taking all of that from Romans 7:25?" Absolutely not; this truth—the power's in Christ alone—is all through the New Testament. We could spend a lifetime studying the verses, but let's check out a few of the major ones together.

In Romans 5:10, Paul wrote: **"For if while we were enemies we were reconciled to God by the death of his Son, much more, now that we are reconciled, shall we be *saved by his life*"** (italics added). In this context, "saved" does not mean forgiven. Paul used the word "reconciled" to describe that part; here he uses the word "saved" to mean saved not from the penalty of sin but from sin's power—the power it holds on us even after we come to Christ. An accurate paraphrase would be, "Having been forgiven through His death you are now being changed by His life." There's the source of power—the exchanged life, Christ living through me.

Many years ago I preached a message on 2 Corinthians 4:8–9, which says, **"We are afflicted in every way, but not crushed; perplexed, but not driven to despair; persecuted, but not forsaken; struck down, but not destroyed."** I stood behind a pulpit and tried to give our congregation hope from those promises. But verses 8 and 9 themselves offer little hope—the situations are almost devastating. It's only great news if you read verse 10. **Always carrying in the body the death of Jesus, *so that the life of Jesus may also be manifested in our bodies*** (italics added). When people see some spiritual energy in me, whose is it? It's Christ's! Not mine. It's not me at all.

Verse 11 repeats this important message: **"For we who live are always being given over to death for Jesus' sake, *so that the life of Jesus also may be manifested in our mortal flesh*"** (italics added). Paul was saying that if people see anything worthwhile in your body—your shell—if there is anything eternal and lasting that they see, it is the actual life of Christ flowing through you. The only true resource—the only power for lasting transformation—is Christ in me. Only that is eternal and lasting and transforming.

CLASSIC BIBLE PASSAGES ON THE EXCHANGED LIFE

Galatians 2:20 is a classic New Testament passage on this truth. Paul wrote, **"I have been crucified with Christ."** There's the dead part. Then he explained, **"It is no longer I who live, but Christ who lives in me."** When you received Jesus Christ as your Savior, He came to live within you, and that is the *life* of the Christian life. Jesus will not wrestle or fight with us; as long as our flesh wants to be on top and in control, it will be.

Personal Transformation in Four Words

For many years I taught our people that the gospel can be summarized in four words: *Jesus in my place.* Always carrying about in the body the dying of the Lord Jesus, that the life of Jesus also may be manifested in our body. That certainly captures what Christ did on our behalf. More recently, I have come to see that God's plan for sanctification can also be summarized in four words: *Not I, but Christ.* This captures what Christ continues to do on our behalf. That's the message of Galatians 2:20. There's the power for change.

You come to Christ when you figure out that you can do absolutely nothing to save yourself. God's not interested in our efforts. God only wants us to repent of our sin and receive Christ by faith. "I cannot do it myself." That's how you come to Christ.

Now how do you *grow* in Christ? The same way! **"Therefore, as you received Christ Jesus the Lord, so walk in Him"** (Colossians 2:6). It's the same complete laying down of all my own strength. And yet how many of us have lived the exhausted life, where we say, "Okay. You saved me; I can't do that. You forgave me. I can't do that. But now get out of my way. I am going to live this Christian life . . ."? It's exhausting!

Kids, Don't Try This at Home

Have you seen those crazy TV stunt shows where people jump off buildings, swallow fire, wrestle wild animals, etc.? Inevitably, on that kind of show, you will hear the disclaimer: "Now kids, these stuntmen and women are professionals; don't try this at home." I always laugh when I hear this, wondering to myself, "What kind of maniac would ever try to pull a stunt like one of those in his backyard?"

In the middle of 1 Thessalonians 5 there is a pretty exhaustive list of dos and don'ts for Christians: **"Rejoice always, pray without ceasing, give thanks in all circumstances. . . . Do not quench the Spirit. Do not despise prophecies, but test everything; hold fast what is good. Abstain from every form of evil"** (verses 16–22). You start reading a catalog list like that and you feel like, "There is no way I can get all of this stuff done!"

Fortunately, Paul concluded the list of appropriate Christian behaviors with a sort of "now kids, don't try this at home": **"Now may the God of peace *Himself sanctify you*. . . . He who calls you is faithful; *He will surely do it*"** (1 Thessalonians 5:23–24, italics added). How do we miss this? Paul isn't changing the subject; he's finishing the thought! God doesn't just call me to do it; He will do it if I will just get out of the way.

As you study the New Testament with this truth in mind, it will amaze you how many descriptions of what Christians are supposed to be doing are followed up or preceded by that warning, a sort of "now kids, don't try this at home." That's the exchanged life—where we allow Christ to live His life through us. Other Bible verses you can study describing the exchanged life include John 15:1–5; Romans 5:10; 6:5; 8:10; 2 Corinthians 2:14; 4:10; Philippians 4:19; Colossians 1:27; 2:6; 3:3.

LIFE-CHANGING EXPERIENCES

My wife, Kathy, and I have served at Harvest Bible Chapel since we planted the church after seminary in the fall of 1988. It has been exciting, fruitful, and fulfilling, but also, at times, difficult and draining. As we approached our tenth anniversary at the church, the elders agreed that an extended time away to be refreshed and renewed would be profitable for us and for the church. With that goal in mind, we left in the spring of 1998 for a three-month sabbatical. Through the generosity of our church family, we were able to divide our time evenly among England, Scotland, and France. I did not know at first how I would use so much time, but one thing I was sure of, I was going to come home a different man. I had to find a way to serve Christ with the same passion but with a new energy source.

Turning Point #1

A little background might help you understand. At the time this book was originally written, Harvest Bible Chapel had a weekly attendance of more than three thousand, with over forty people on staff in various capacities. From 1988 to 1992 the church grew from our original group of eighteen people to approximately three hundred. During those initial years God had to teach me some very difficult lessons about my own version of the flesh and how it affected people. My commitment to truth was unwavering, but my ability to express it in love left something to be desired. (People were quite willing to point that out.) Frankly, I was driven to build a great church, to do something exciting for God, to make a difference in people's lives. Praise God; I didn't neglect my family, but at times I was hard on some of the people who worked with me and through my aggressiveness caused some to walk away from our ministry shaking their heads.

What I came to see, through several painful experiences, was that God was more interested in working in me than He was in working through me. January of 1992 was a turning point for me in my understanding that character formation in James had to be the number one goal in my life. The changes did not come all at once, but, looking back, there has been a steady and growing balance between truth and love in my ministry since that day.

Since that key lesson in 1992, God poured out abundant fruitfulness upon my ministry and upon our entire church. During the following eight years our church grew tenfold, our radio ministry began and continues to expand greatly (now more than 1100 stations), and many are coming to Christ. In the eight weeks prior to writing this chapter originally, we saw more than one hundred seventy adults baptized in our church, most of those being very recent converts to Christ. This year (2011), we have baptized nearly one thousand new believers. Harvest meets on seven campuses each weekend with an average attendance of over thirteen thousand. All of this is what God has done!

Turning Point #2

At the time of my sabbatical in 1998 the ministry was clearly bearing the kind of fruit that any pastor would rejoice in, yet I was not filled with joy and it troubled me. I had always known *Who I was serving*, Jesus Christ the Lord. So I thought that once I settled *how to serve*—finding the balance between truth and love—I was off to the races. I set out on my time away never imagining for a moment that God had an equally dramatic turning point for me on the subject of *who actually does the serving.*

I can think of specific places in Europe—on my face on a beach on the south coast of France, in a chapel over five hundred years old in a small village west of London, in the north of England in an isolated castle known as Capernwray—where the Lord spoke as clearly to me as He has at any time in my life. "You cannot live the Christian life; only I can. Stop trying and failing, and let Me succeed." During this time I came across a book that impacted me as deeply as any I have ever read. It is called the *Saving Life of Christ*. It was written in 1960 by Major Ian Thomas, an evangelist and founder of the Torchbearers conference centers and Bible schools, but it is far from out-of-date. Many of the truths you are reading here are the result of what I read in that book and the other books it led me to, most importantly a fresh look at God's Book.

On July 12, 1998, while in England and reflecting on Thomas's insights, I wrote this prayer on the bottom of a page: "Lord, I *am so weak*! Every day of failed effort to live a righteous life is painful and a penetrating truth of that fact. But today I turn as never before to You alone. Christ in me. I die to myself by faith and today, Lord, I trust You to live Your life through me."

Simple words, but a powerful, powerful turning point in my life. I commend it to you this moment—the exchanged life. That simple truth has absolutely changed my life, and it can yours too.

THE EMPOWERED LIFE
Powered by the Spirit

Here's another biblical picture of where the power to change comes from. Let's call it the *empowered* life. If you continue to read on, you come to Romans 8, where Paul expanded what he only hinted at in Romans 7. Beginning in Romans 8:2, the apostle repeated a key word that indicates the source of a powerful life in Christ.

> **For the law of the *Spirit* of life has set you free in Christ Jesus from the law of sin and death . . . in order that the righteous requirement of the law might be fulfilled in us, who walk not according to the flesh but according to the *Spirit*. For . . . those who live according to the *Spirit* set their minds on the things of the *Spirit*. Those who are in the flesh cannot please God. You, however, are not in the flesh but in the *Spirit*, if in fact the *Spirit* of God dwells in you . . . the body is dead because of sin, the *Spirit* is life because of righteousness. If the *Spirit* of him who raised Jesus from the dead dwells in you, he who raised Christ Jesus from the dead will also give *life [power] to your mortal bodies through his Spirit who dwells in you* . . . But if by the *Spirit* you put to death the deeds of the body, you will live.** (Romans 8:2, 4–5, 8–11, 13; italics added)

See that? Spirit . . . Spirit . . . Spirit . . . Spirit. If you want to get precise about exactly what it is—Christ in me—it's the Holy Spirit. We cannot change ourselves. On our own, we cannot be like Jesus. We can try to emulate the current Christian marketing versions of Jesus until we are blue in the face. But until we let Jesus live His life in us by His Spirit, we are going to be exhausted.

Allow me to paraphrase the simple command of Jesus to His disciples just before He left this earth. Jesus was saying, "Guys, I am out of here. But wait here! Don't go *anywhere*. Don't preach any sermons. Don't make any cold calls; don't do a thing! Just get in a room and wait for the Holy Spirit. 'Cause if you guys try to do this stuff without My Holy Spirit controlling you, you're going to mess everything up. I have poured three years into you and if you just wait for the Holy Spirit it's going to be phenomenal, but if you try to make it in your own strength it's going to be ugly, fast!" I believe that is an accurate expression of the context and meaning of what Jesus said in Acts 1:8, **"You will receive power when the Holy Spirit has come upon you, and you will be My witnesses."**

What Being Filled with the Spirit Means

Ephesians 5:18 says, **"And do not get drunk with wine, for that is debauchery, but be filled with the Spirit."** The Greek word for "filled" means *controlled; intoxicated; permeated; thoroughly influenced.* If you want to understand what a biblical word means, look at how it is used in other places in the Bible. The same word is used in Luke 4:28, where people who were angry about Jesus' teaching are described as **"filled with wrath."** In Acts 13:45 some of the Jews, resentful of Paul and Barnabas's ministry, are described as **"filled with jealousy."** The word means *to be overcome by a power greater than your own.* To be controlled. That's filled.

One of the memorable illustrations from Major Thomas's book that I mentioned earlier was the idea of a glove representing our relationship with the Holy Spirit. In this picture, we're the glove. We are gloves washed clean and pure by the blood of Christ. What can a glove do? Not much. In fact, a glove can do nothing. That's you. That's you living the Christian life. Until the Holy Spirit comes into you and fills you and totally permeates you, that's what "filled" means.

Several years ago I was playing basketball with some guys I know, and I was holding the ball on offense, trying to make a play while the defender swiped at the ball and tried to swat it away. In a split second, just as I swung the ball to the right, he swiped at its previous location and stuck his middle finger in my eye socket right up to the second knuckle. Talk about pain . . . I felt like I was one huge eyeball. I fell on the ground. I ceased to exist. I was filled with pain.

I also know what it means to be filled with joy. The day I married Kathy, I remember seeing my beautiful bride sitting up on the back of a convertible as it drove up toward the back of the wedding area, sun shining and faces glowing at the outdoor wedding. I can still see Kathy now, coming up the aisle to meet me. There will never be another day like that.

It maxed my joy meter—or so I thought until our kids were born. Even though my oldest son is twenty-six years old, going back now I can remember the moment each of my three children came into the world, and I stood there and held them for the first time. If you have ever experienced that, you know what it means to be filled with joy.

The filling of the Holy Spirit is very similar to being filled with pain or joy. It means to be overcome by a power greater than yourself, to be controlled by it.

FOUR TRUTHS ABOUT THE SPIRIT'S FILLING

Ephesians 5:18 says, **"Do not get drunk with wine, . . . but be filled with the Spirit."** Four essential truths come from that little verse in God's Word:

1. *The filling is commanded.* God does not give suggestions like, "Hey, if you get some time you might want to consider being filled with the Spirit." It's a command—"Be filled"—and because God commands it, it is possible. Nowhere in Scripture are we commanded to be indwelt or baptized or sealed with the Spirit because those things happen to us at conversion, but we are commanded to "be filled." It's a command.

2. *The filling is passive.* Remember your English grammar class? We do not perform the filling. We are the object being acted upon. God is implied as the source of the filling. God does the filling when we ask Him. We cannot do it for ourselves.

3. *The filling is for everyone.* You can't see this in the English, but in the Greek it is plural: *"All of you* followers of Jesus, be filled with the Spirit." This filling is for every believer. This is not for the spiritually elite, or for certain people who have had certain experiences. This is for all of God's children— it's for you.

4. *The filling is not permanent.* Some translations have it "be being filled." We are to be continuously filled. Day by day filled and filled again. Never in the New Testament do you see a believer baptized by the Holy Spirit more than once. However, you do see multiple fillings. Believers at Pentecost were filled once (Acts 2:4), and Peter was filled again (Acts 4:8). Paul was filled once, in Acts 9:17, but then again in Acts 13:9. So there's one baptism at conversion but many fillings.

PROOF OF THE HOLY SPIRIT'S FILLING

The eighth chapter of Romans includes five indications of the Holy Spirit's filling and controlling presence:

☐ **Leading** (v. 14)

In Romans 8:12, Paul writes, **"So then, brothers, we are debtors, not to the flesh, to live according to the flesh. For if you live according to the flesh you will die, but if by the Spirit you put to death the deeds of the body, you will live. For all who are led by the Spirit of God are sons of God."**

The Spirit of God is leading God's children. I could give reams of examples of how the Lord has led me personally; how the Lord has led Kathy; and how the Lord has led our church. For example, I am sure that the Holy Spirit led us not to do a planned church campaign a year ago. The specific reasons may be known only to God, but I am so thankful for the leadership of the Holy Spirit that at one point said, "No" and confirmed that leading in moving the leadership team to urge holding off. And I am so thankful for the leading of the Holy Spirit—confirmed by a group of people leading our church together—when the Holy Spirit said, "Yes," He led us to say, "Yes."

I have no idea where our church would be without the leading of the Holy Spirit, but I know I wouldn't want to be there!

☐ **Confidence** (v. 15a)

"For you did not receive the spirit of slavery to fall back into fear" (Romans 8:15). One of the truest indications of life in the flesh and not in the Spirit is fear.

"What's going to happen to my son? When is he going to come back?"

"What's going to happen to my marriage?"

"Where are we going to be five years from now? I am so *filled* with fear."

That's flesh talking, expressing lack of trust in God. That's **" . . . the spirit of slavery to fall back into fear."** That was life *before* Christ—a life of fear.

Now in Christ, as you look ahead, you're like, "I don't know what's going to happen. I don't know where this is going to end up, but God is for me—right in this moment, and He's got no problem with the future. **"If God is for [me], who can be against [me]?"** (Romans 8:31). Further, **"[I am] more than a conqueror through Him who loved [me]"** (Romans 8:37).

When the Spirit takes up residence in the life of a believer? Paul said to Timothy, **"God has not given us a spirit of fear, but of power and of love and of a sound mind"** (2 Timothy 1:7 NKJV). The Spirit's presence increases confidence and eliminates fear.

☐ **Intimacy** (v. 15b)

Filled with the Spirit also means intimacy with God. Notice the second part of Romans 8:15, **" . . . You have received the Spirit of adoption as sons, by whom we cry out 'Abba! Father!'"**

Frankly, this is harder for men than it is for women. God is our Abba, Father. Men who are accustomed in every other place to have to be strong find it difficult to seem weak with God. Men think they have to "hold it together." People are counting on them. I understand that. But there is to be a private place—a secret place—where you can lean on Someone who needs nothing from you. God, your Abba Father is waiting in that place.

Men often mumble, "I don't know, man. Depending on God is a little freaky. That makes me uncomfortable."

I *get* it. And that's why the Spirit was sent into your heart so that He could cry out "Abba! Father!" through you and get you to that place of total intimacy with God.

☐ **Security** (v. 16)

Those filled with the Spirit experience security. Romans 8:16 says, **"The Spirit Himself bears witness with our spirit that we are the children of God."** You get security in God's family. Are you a person who doubts your salvation? It's the job of the Holy Spirit to confirm that you are among God's children. But if you sin against the Holy Spirit—as we're going to talk about a little further—and you grieve and quench the Holy Spirit, what happens?

On a good day when you're walking with the Lord, He's like, "You're *Mine*!!"

But sin a little bit and don't deal with it? The volume drops, "You're Mine."

And don't deal with that, and He whispers, "You're Mine."

And don't deal with that, and you can hardly hear, "You're Mine."

And don't deal with that, and you strain for, "You're Mine."

And then you're like, "I wonder if I'm a Christian."

Well, it's the Spirit's job to confirm your security as He fills you again and again throughout your Christian life.

☐ **Identity** (v. 17)

Romans 8:17 completes the thought, **" . . . And if children, then heirs— heirs of God and fellow heirs with Christ . . ."** Of course, that's the Holy Spirit indicating to us who we were really are—heirs with Christ! I mean, do you have any idea what's in store for you? I don't know what's coming in the next two weeks or the next two months or the next two years or the next twenty years. But do you have any idea what an incredible future God has in store for you as His child? Say, "No, I do not." That is correct. No matter what we imagine, it's going to be far better.

But the Holy Spirit's job is to let you know that you are an heir of God and joint-heir with Christ so that no matter how bad this week is going, you're like, "I know who I am! I know where I'm going." The Spirit is constantly riveting that message to our hearts.

LET'S GET DRUNK!

I thought that heading would get your attention! Isn't it amazing that the most common biblical illustration for the filling of the Holy Spirit is drunkenness?

When someone is drunk, they don't act like themselves anymore. Drunk people say things that amuse or amaze or anger others because they have no control of their tongue. And they have little control of their actions. If the police pull them over and tell them to walk a yellow line, they can't do it because they have no control over their bodies. Ask a drunkard a simple question, and you will not get a clear answer because they have no control of their mind. They also can lose control of their emotions. Drunk people become fearful and paranoid and angry and silly.

Three separate times in the Bible drunkenness is associated with being filled with the Spirit. (Besides Ephesians 5:18, see Luke 1:15 and Acts 2:4, 13–17.) It indicates a yielding of control. The point of Ephesians 5:18 is *don't be controlled by wine* because wine can be excessive. Instead, be controlled by the Spirit, because you can't get too much of that. You can't be too filled with the Spirit.

You may be wondering, "I am in Christ. I know that I know Christ. Why am I not being filled with the Spirit? Why am I not experiencing all the strength for change that the filling of the Holy Spirit can bring?"

HINDRANCES TO THE FILLING OF THE HOLY SPIRIT

While, of course, God is not human, He nevertheless is a person. He has genuine feelings about what we do and how we relate to Him. The Holy Spirit is not a force or an influence but a coequal person in the triune God. As such, the Holy Spirit is influenced by our actions. Specifically, when our actions are not pleasing to the Holy Spirit, they greatly limit His work in our lives. This is the great malady of the church in our day.

I want so much for you to experience the transforming power of the Holy Spirit in your life. Without His power, you will never realize the change you have been striving for. So let's take a moment and survey the biblical teaching on what we do that forfeits the filling of the Spirit in our lives.

1. Grieving the Holy Spirit

"Do not grieve the Holy Spirit of God, by whom you were sealed for the day of redemption," Paul warned (Ephesians 4:30). What does it mean to grieve the Spirit? The Greek *lupeo* means to cause pain or sorrow; to grieve. Oswald Sanders has written that "grieve" is a love word. You can anger or frustrate enemies, but you can only grieve loved ones. The Lord Jesus Christ loves us so much. And when we do things that He does not want us to do, it grieves His Spirit within us. It makes Him sad.

It's as though the Holy Spirit is that internal voice asking, "Why are we going here? Why are we watching this? Why did you say that?" When we take control of our lives and break God's standard of holiness, we grieve the Holy Spirit and forfeit His transforming power. No wonder we remain so unchanged.

2. Quenching the Holy Spirit

"Quench not the Spirit," Paul also warned (1 Thessalonians 5:19 KJV). Grieving the Holy Spirit is doing things we should have left undone. Quenching the Spirit is refusing to do things that He does want us to do. Every time the Holy Spirit convicts us to pursue certain behavior and we say no, we forfeit the Spirit's filling, and transformation ceases.

I observe this so often as a pastor. After a service I hear things like, "Boy, God really convicted me this morning and I need to get baptized"; or, "The Lord spoke to me, and I know I need to make things right with my mom"; or, "God has convicted my heart that I need to stop watching certain kinds of movies. I know they are not pleasing to the Lord." The next time I see the person I will often bring the matter up and ask if he or she followed through on what God convicted the person about. Surprisingly, the answer is many times, "No." That's quenching the Spirit.

You say some words to somebody, words you never should have, but you say them. The Spirit of God convicts your heart and tells you, "Go tell her you are sorry. Go make it right. Humble yourself." But you think, "She's done that to me before. It's no different." And then you come up with all of the rationalizations for not making it right.

Then the Spirit of God continues, "Make it right. Humble yourself. Be the first person," but you respond, "I'm not doing that!" When you refuse, you are quenching the Spirit in your life and forfeiting the transforming power of almighty God.

HOW TO BE FILLED WITH THE SPIRIT

We begin our "Let's Get to Work" exercise early, as part of the conclusion to this chapter. For real power to change, we need the Spirit's filling. (And remember that we should come back for refilling regularly.) Here are three steps to being filled with the Holy Spirit.

1. Confess all known sin (1 John 1:9)

Get a piece of paper and pen ready and get on your knees in a quiet place, alone with the Lord. Begin by praying this simple prayer: "Lord, I know I have been grieving and quenching Your Spirit, and I want to deal with my sin right now. Please bring to my mind all things in my life that are grieving to Your Spirit. Please remind me about times I have quenched Your Spirit and not followed Your promptings." Have your pen ready because the Holy Spirit truly wants to fill you, and He will not until you remove the barriers. He will bring to your mind many things. Relationships that are not right. Sins you have made right with Him but not with the people you injured. Actions and attitudes you have chosen that were sinful. Righteous priorities that you have known, but neglected.

As they come to mind, write them down saying, "Yes, Lord; is there anything else?" When the list is complete, go back over it, repenting of each specific matter on the list. As you do, promise the Lord you will do the horizontal work of restitution, making it right with others.

2. Ask the Holy Spirit to fill you.

I love what Jesus said in Luke 11:9-10: **"Ask, and it will be given to you; seek, and you will find; knock, and it will be opened to you. For everyone who asks receives, and the one who seeks finds, and to the one who knocks it will be opened."** And then Jesus says, **"What father among you, if his son asks for a fish, will instead of a fish give him a serpent?"**

Do you have any kids? I'm sure you love them, don't you? I bet that if one of your sons came to you and said, "Dad, can I have some bread?" you wouldn't answer, "Oh, yeah. C'mon into the kitchen. I'll give you some," and when he got there, "Ha, ha, ha, ha. It's a stone."

You say, "That's sick. What kind of a father would do that?"

And that's Jesus' point: **"If you then, who are evil, know how to give good gifts to your children, how much more will the heavenly Father give the Holy Spirit to those who ask him!"** (Luke 11:13). Isn't that a great promise?

That's what God's like. If we know how to give good gifts to people we love, do you think our loving Father knows how to do that? Let me tell you, He does.

Confess all known sin and just ask Him. "Lord, fill me with Your Spirit today." Pray this every day. "Lord, fill me with Your Spirit today."

3. Believe you have received the Spirit's filling.

Believe you have received the filling of the Holy Spirit, and begin to **"walk in the Spirit"** (see Galatians 5:16) by submitting to His control moment by moment. Jesus said, **"Therefore I tell you, whatever you ask in prayer, believe that you have received it, and it will be yours"** (Mark 11:24). So, if as you pray, "Lord, fill me with Your Spirit," you're telling yourself, "This isn't going to work. This is just another . . . This is not . . ." God will not grant your request. You have to believe that God really wants to fill you with His Spirit.

Don't let your heart fill with unbelief. Believe that the power we have learned about in this chapter is really available to you.

So, loved one, (1) confess all known sin; (2) ask God to fill you with His Spirit; and (3) believe that you have received the Spirit's filling. And then . . . get ready to experience *God's* transforming power!

Teacher Questions

1. Why is it essential that we exchange our life for Christ's? Explain this from Galatians 2:20.
2. How often are we to be filled with the Spirit? What does this mean?
3. What are some of the obstacles that keep us from experiencing the Spirit's filling?

Prophet Questions

1. How do we know we are filled with the Holy Spirit, according to Romans 8:14–17? Which of these characteristics is most common for you (and which is most uncommon)?
2. In what ways have you hindered or grieved the Holy Spirit recently (during the past year)?
3. Which of the three aspects of preparation for the Spirit's filling do you find most difficult: (1) confess all known sin; (2) ask God to fill you with His Spirit; or (3) believe that you have received the Spirit's filling? Why?

Shepherd Questions

1. In what ways do you relate to the description of the exhausting Christian life described on page 156?

2. How does the promised power of the Holy Spirit encourage you to pursue personal change?

3. What does it mean to you to be able to say to God, "Abba, Father"?

LET'S GET TO WORK

The final section of this chapter, "How to Be Filled with the Spirit," was your "Let's Get to Work" exercise, so you should have already completed it. If you have not done the three things requested in this section, complete this project now.

LOOK UP!

Try kneeling down as you pray. Pray out loud. And you may want to open your hands in front of you as a symbol of your readiness to receive.

Dear heavenly Father:

I admit that I've been living the exhausted Christian life. Trying to keep the balls in the air. Feeling the pain of watching them crash to the ground. Lord, forgive me for that. Lord, forgive me for thinking that I need You to save me but I don't need You to change me, that I can change in my own strength. Lord Jesus, how wrong that is.

Today I am choosing for myself the exchanged life. "I am crucified with Christ; it is no longer I who live, but You live in me." I acknowledge those truths before You. I claim and accept Your forgiveness. And I ask You now to fill me with Your Holy Spirit.

Live Your life through me today. Make me the man [woman] that You would have me be for the fame and the glory of Your own name. I pray this now in Jesus' precious name. Amen.

NOTE

1. Charles Price, *Christ for Real* (Grand Rapids: Kregel, 1995).

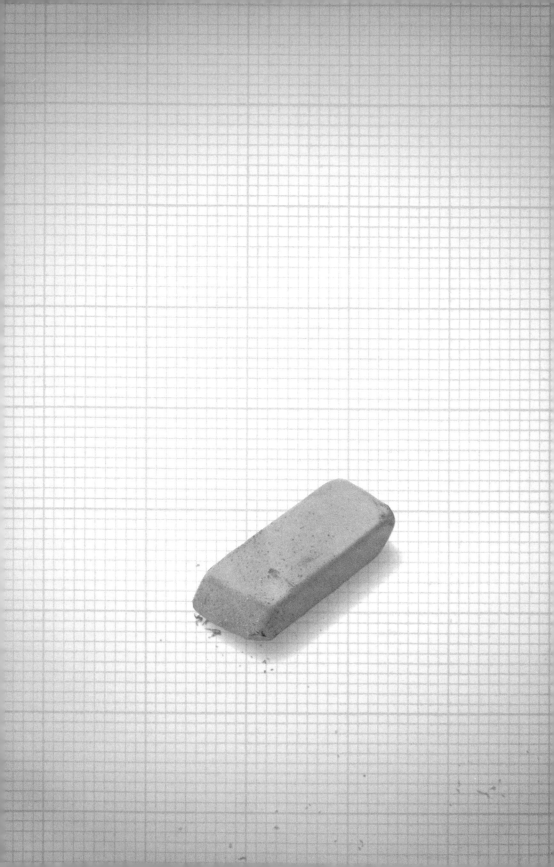

9

THE POWER OF **FAITH**

SAY IT IN A SENTENCE:

We experience change personally only when we exercise our faith in the truth of God's Word; knowledge of the Word by itself is not enough.

More than a century ago, Charles Blondin became famous as a resident of Niagara Falls, Ontario, in Canada. In the category of media figures with a daredevil reputation, Blondin was sort of a forerunner to Evel Kneivel or Alex Honnold. Instead of jumping motorcycles across amazing chasms or climbing daunting heights unroped, he would simply walk . . . on a tightrope. His favorite venue was very close to home. Week after week back in 1860, Blondin would show up down at the falls and amaze the citizens on both sides of the border by walking or hopping across the falls.

I suppose after a number of weeks the interest started to die down, so on a certain morning Blondin shocked the onlookers by declaring that the following Saturday morning he would take a man across the falls in a wheelbarrow. Now if you have never been to Niagara Falls, you will find this a little hard to appreciate. Niagara Falls is an awesome sight, with over 100,000 cubic feet of water tumbling over the falls every second. The Horseshoe Falls is 158 feet high and 2,600 feet wide, and the American Falls is 167 feet high and 1,000 feet wide. Though from a distance the falls are very beautiful, you are more awed by the sheer power and danger of the falls than you are enraptured by their appearance. Anyway, the town was buzzing all week with the news of what Blondin would attempt to do.

Finally, the morning came, and Blondin stopped by a local pub for some breakfast (or courage, ha!) on his way to the falls. As he entered, he overheard some men arguing and drew closer to investigate.

"I believe he can do it," yelled a man with his back to the door. "I guarantee he can. In fact, I will bet anyone here $100 that Blondin can cross the falls safely pushing a man in a wheelbarrow."

Imagine that man's surprise when Blondin tapped him on the shoulder and said, "I am so glad you have faith in me because I need someone to get in the wheelbarrow."

Do you think the man did? Of course he didn't, *yet he said he believed.*

That is the great problem in our day. So many people say they believe God's Word but when it gets right down to "getting in the wheelbarrow," they refuse; therefore they do not believe! Faith is getting in the wheelbarrow. Faith is staking your life and your happiness on God's truth. Anything less is mere sentiment. It does not save, and it most certainly does not transform.

Often people will come to me and say, "Oh, Pastor, I'm going through . . ." or "I'm really struggling with . . . ," and then they add something to the effect that, "The Christian life is so hard; it's so difficult." In recent years I always answer these kinds of inquiries with, "You're wrong; the Christian life is not difficult, *it's impossible.*" That's right,

LIVING LIKE CHRIST IS
NOT DIFFICULT, **IT'S IMPOSSIBLE!**

Day after day we face the bombardment of the Enemy and fail to recognize that, on our own, we have a snowball's chance in hell of experiencing victory. I repeat, living like Christ is not difficult—it's impossible.

That is why we are looking for power. **"Those who are in the flesh cannot please God,"** the apostle Paul declared (Romans 8:8). How could it be any clearer that in ourselves we have no resources to follow Christ? We have no strength to be like Christ. We have no energy to serve Christ or to lead our families as God would have us to. Surely your own experience verifies the fact that sheer will-power cannot conquer sin. I repeat, one more time: On our own, *living like Christ is not difficult—it's impossible.*

You say, "What does that phrase **"in the flesh"** mean, exactly?"

Well, strike the *h* from the word *flesh*. Now spell it backwards. What do you get? *Self.* That is the flesh: Myself; me; my fallen nature; my inclination to do wrong. That is the flesh. And in myself—in my own strength—there is no capacity to live a God-honoring life. Again, God has made no provision for you to live the Christian life—but only for God to live by His Spirit through you. That's the

Christian life—**"Christ in you, the hope of glory"** (Colossians 1:27b).

GREAT POWER AWAITS

But . . .

More and more as I study the Bible, I love the word "but." It's a strong contrast word and often comes after bad news in the Bible. But . . . the Bible is a book of good news, so the word "but" often forms a sort of bridge between the bad news and the good news. Sometime I'd love to share with you about the greatest "buts" in the Bible, but for now here's a strong one, from Romans 8:9.

The first word after Romans 8:8 is "but." **"Those who are in the flesh cannot please God. But you are not in the flesh but in the Spirit"** (verses 8–9 NKJV). The *English Standard Version* doesn't use "but," choosing the equally emphatic **"You, however"** to make sure we don't miss the contrast. God's Spirit is ready to give you the power to change! Romans 8:10 continues: **"But if Christ is in you, although the body is dead because of sin,"**—that means that your body has no capacity to fight sin—**"the Spirit is life because of righteousness."**

There's the power! The reason we have this life-giving Spirit in us is to power the righteousness God is trying to produce in us.

How Much Power?

Maybe you're thinking to yourself, "Exactly how much power are we talking about here?" Verse 11 gives the answer: **"If the Spirit of Him who raised Jesus from the dead dwells in you, He who raised Christ Jesus from the dead will also give life to your mortal bodies."** Paul's message was essentially this: "You wanna know how much power God has made available to change you? Go to Easter morning! The kind of power that lifted Jesus Christ from the grave—the greatest victory that was ever won—is the same power that lives in you."

Why is this the *greatest* power? It's the greatest because it was over the greatest Enemy—Satan. Because it dealt with the greatest problem—sin. Because it involved the greatest sacrifice—the death of God's own Son on a cross. And because the greatest price was paid—the precious blood of Christ.

Do you want to know what kind of power is available to help you change? It's the very power that brought our Savior back from the dead! You say, "Pastor James, do you really believe that the resurrection power of Jesus Christ is available to help me be the person that God wants me to be? . . . available for me right now—ready this moment—to turbo my victory?" Yes, I really believe that.

Look again at verse 11. **"If the Spirit of Him who raised Jesus from the dead dwells in you, He . . . will also give life to your mortal bodies."** Those bodies are yours and mine—bodies that can't get victory over anything. **"He who raised Christ Jesus from the dead will also give life to your mortal bodies through His Spirit who dwells in you."** What a great promise! The power to change comes to us from God's Spirit.

Who Turned the Lights Out?

Sadly, most Christians would agree that *understanding* the power of the Spirit is a million miles away from *experiencing* it personally. They say, "Knowing just isn't getting it done for me!" Maybe you're feeling as I used to. "Why do I always hear about the Holy Spirit's power but not experience it? Is there like a switch somewhere? Is there a room somewhere where I can go and turn this on?" Great question. Here's the answer:

FAITH IS THE SWITCH THAT TURNS
ON THE POWER OF THE HOLY SPIRIT.

The switch that turns on the Holy Spirit's power is faith (Hebrews 4:2). I love to go camping, and my favorite place is Algonquin Park in northern Ontario, Canada. There you have hundreds of square miles of wilderness without electricity or running water. You're not even allowed to take cans or bottles into the park. At night, the park gets so dark you can't even see your hand in front of your face, so we always take a really good flashlight.

Now imagine me stumbling down some wilderness trail in the night, looking for a place to do the kind of business you do down a dark trail in the middle of the night. Imagine I had my flashlight with me, but for some reason I refused to switch it on. And imagine that I stumbled around for hours looking for the right place, getting eaten by mosquitoes and scraping my legs.

"What a waste," you say. "All you had to do to spare yourself the frustration was turn on the flashlight; just flip the switch!" Right! And all we have to do to ignite the power of God's Spirit within us is to exercise our faith. Faith is the switch that turns on the power of the Holy Spirit.

Now there are some subjects in the Scripture—and faith is such a subject—that can be found on every page and in every paragraph. Faith is taught, encouraged, assumed, commanded, and illustrated everywhere in the Scriptures.

However, the most concentrated teaching in all of Scripture on faith is

Hebrews 11. I would encourage you to become familiar with the great survey of faithful people enshrined in that chapter.

In my mind, I add another name to that list of the faithful witnesses. My mom went to heaven just a couple of years ago. But before she died, she asked us to bring to her funeral the well-worn rocking chair in which she sat and prayed daily and put it next to her casket. She also asked to have her Bible placed open on the seat. I think of all of the years my mom spent in God's Word and the thousands of verses she studied and committed herself to. But she said while she could still speak, "Open my Bible so people can see the underlined passage, Hebrews 11:1."

In her heart and mind, this was the essence of all of it. It represented her own hope and the legacy she was leaving for the rest of us: **"Faith is the assurance of things hoped for, the conviction of things not seen."** That verse describes her life.

I can't help but think that you may be reading these words today and realizing that you know what God promises, but you don't experience it. You know what God says is in store for you, but you don't live like a person who has it.

"What's missing for me?" you ask.

This is it: Faith. **"Faith is the assurance of things hoped for . . . "** Faith is **". . . the evidence of things not seen."**

This truth applies to far more than just the gospel. You know that it is **"By grace you have been saved through faith"** (Ephesians 2:8). But that's only the amazing beginning! The way we *come* to Christ is also the way we *follow* Him: **"Therefore, as you received Christ Jesus the Lord, so walk in Him"** (Colossians 2:6). Every step with God is a step of faith.

This is the most important truth in the entire book, because if you don't combine all that you're learning with faith, it will make absolutely no difference in your life. *Unless you exercise your faith in regard to these truths, you will not be changed!* You may understand a lot about how to change according to God's plan, yet you will not change. We all know people who have a head full of Bible information, but aren't anything like Christ. It's not about knowing the truth; it starts with knowing, but it doesn't end there. You have to take what you know, and combine that truth with faith.

I like the NIV translation of Hebrews 4:2: **"The message they heard was of no value to them, because those who heard did not combine it with faith."** You are not different because you *know*; you're different because you choose to *do* by *faith*. Unless you add faith to the truths you're learning, this book will prove ultimately useless to you. Now I realize that is a very strong statement, so let me try to back it up from God's Word.

FAITH AND A KEY TRUTH

The Key Truth: Created to Honor the Creator

The foundational truth of the Bible is the glory of God. The Bible teaches that you and I exist and this solar system exists and this world exists to display the glory of God. We were created for Him. He is not *for* us; we are for *Him*. (See, for instance, Psalm 19:1; Isaiah 43:7.)

The central theme of the Bible is the redemptive work of Christ as the only hope for a fallen humanity. Genesis, the first book in the Bible, describes the problem. Christ came to redeem us from the problem of sin. The historical books of the Old Testament describe the futility of trying to keep God's law without the work of the Redeemer. The prophets foretell the coming of the Redeemer. The gospels record His sinless life and substitutionary death and resurrection. Acts and the Epistles detail the spread of the Redeemer's message, and the book of Revelation tells of the day when Christ returns to complete the process of redemption. Christ as Redeemer is the central theme of the Bible.

The Key Source: Faith

Therefore, *the urgent message of the Bible is that the benefits of the Redeemer are accessed only by faith.* Every good thing God wants to give to you comes through faith. Faith is the power switch. This is the urgent message of the whole Bible: God wants to give us so many good things, but none of it is available except through faith.

Again, Hebrews 11 contains the comprehensive treatment of this truth. **"Without faith it is impossible to please Him"** (verse 6). That's pretty straightforward. Do you want to be a godly husband? That would please God, but without faith, it's impossible. Do you want to be a hardworking employee? That would please God, but without faith, it's impossible. You want to be obedient to the Lord in your tithes and offerings? That would please Him, but without faith, it's impossible. You want to go as a missionary and serve Christ to the ends of the earth? That would please God, but without faith, it's impossible. You want God to change your character? You want to be more like Christ? You want Him to transform who you are? That would definitely please Him, but *without faith, it's impossible!*

Faith affects *everything*. In fact, we can say:

NOTHING HAS NOTHING TO DO WITH FAITH!

What does that mean? The whole point of Hebrews 11 is to teach us the universal necessity of faith. You must not have a separate drawer for the not-to-do-with-God things. *Nothing* has nothing to do with faith. Faith is about *everything* you're facing. You couldn't possibly have a burden that doesn't require faith in order to resource your victory! *Nothing has nothing to do with faith.*

FAITH IN THE OLD TESTAMENT
Faith of the Patriarchs

Hebrews 11 is the *Reader's Digest* story of faith in the Old Testament. The writers of Scripture keep pounding the same nail over and over, and I like that—because my head's a little thick. See if you can pick up on the repetition. Verse 4 tells us that **"Abel offered to God a more acceptable sacrifice than Cain."** How did he do that? **By faith.** Notice in verse 5, **"Enoch was taken up so that he should not see death."** Wow! What a phenomenal spiritual experience! How did that happen? **"By faith."** Look at verse 7: **"Noah, being warned by God concerning events as yet seen, in reverent fear, constructed an ark for the saving of his household."** "Great move, Noah! How did you do that?" **"By faith,"** the Scripture says.

"Abraham obeyed when he was called to go out to a place that he was to receive as an inheritance," verse 8 tells us. **"And he went out, not knowing where he was going."**

"That must have taken a lot of courage. How did you do that, Abraham?" **"By faith,"** the Scripture says.

In verse 11, **"Sarah herself"**—struggling with infertility as so many couples today seem to—**"received power to conceive, even when she was past the age."**

"How did you do that, Sarah?" **"By faith."**

Now begin to say it aloud. It goes on and on and on. And then Abraham and Isaac and Jacob (verses 17–21). **"By faith . . . By faith . . . By faith."** Faith is the greatest legacy you can give to your family. Nothing is better than teaching your children and your grandchildren to trust God; to believe what He has said; to live by faith.

The Faith of Moses

And when Moses was born, he **"was hidden for three months by his parents"** (verse 23, one of my favorite stories in the Bible, found at the beginning of Exodus). That was also done **"by faith."** Then Moses copied his parents' example: **"By faith, Moses . . . refused to be called the son of Pharaoh's daughter"** (verse 24, italics added). How many parents wonder, "Will my kid be in the world or will my kid be in the church following Christ?"

The text goes on to say that Moses **"[chose] rather to be mistreated with the people of God than to enjoy the fleeting pleasures of sin. He considered the reproach of Christ greater wealth than the treasures in Egypt, for he was looking to the reward. *By faith* he left Egypt . . . *By faith* he kept the Passover . . . *By faith* the people crossed the Red Sea as on dry land . . ."** (verses 25–29, italics added).

These victories by faith continued in the Promised Land. **"*By faith* the walls of Jericho fell down after they were encircled for seven days. *By faith* the prostitute Rahab did not perish with those who were disobedient"** (verses 30–31, italics added).

Abounding Faith

The text then just goes off on the faith theme in rapid-fire succession:

And what more shall I say? For time would fail me to tell of Gideon, Barak, Samson, Jephthah, of David and Samuel and the prophets— who *through faith* conquered kingdoms, enforced justice, obtained promises, stopped the mouths of lions, quenched the power of fire, escaped the edge of the sword, were made strong out of weakness, became mighty in war, put foreign armies to flight.

Women received back their dead by resurrection. Some were tortured, refusing to accept release, so that they might rise again to a better life. Others suffered mocking and flogging, and even chains and imprisonment. They were stoned, they were sawn in two, they were killed with the sword. They went about in skins of sheep and goats, destitute, afflicted, mistreated—of whom the world was not worthy—wandering about in deserts and mountains, and in dens and caves of the earth.

And all these, though commended *through their faith* (verses 32–39a, italics added).

Don't you see that faith is not a *part* of the Christian life; it's the *whole* thing. Faith is not, "Yeah, there's another thing you need in your spiritual arsenal. Have faith available when you need to pull it out. It's important." Wrong! Faith is not a *part* of the Christian life. It's the whole thing—faith! It's essential for everyone serious about change.

FAITH IN THE NEW TESTAMENT
Faith in the gospels

Check out some of the following verses in the gospels. **"Then He touched their eyes, saying, 'According to your faith be it done to you'"** (Matthew 9:29). The idea that where we are at in our lives and what we are experiencing—either joy and victory or sadness and defeat—is all about the measure of our faith. This particular verse is one of those truths that are so riveted in my mind that I can remember the first time God tackled me with it. I was in New York City preaching at Brooklyn Tabernacle. Kathy and I had gone out to dinner and an evening of stimulating interaction with Pastor Jim Cymbala.

I've read the gospels. But somehow it had never really caught my attention what Jesus says in Matthew 9:29. But in the context of the conversation—the subject's not important now—Jim Cymbala said to me, **"According to your faith, so be it done to you."** In a gentle way he was calling me out and pointing me to the crucial and central necessity of faith in my own life.

I mean, can that be said of your life today? Could that be said of your marriage?

"Yeah, well, we're kind of aimlessly drifting along . . ."

"According to your faith, so be it done to you."

Could that be said of your ministry?

"Well, we're not seeing God do so much as what maybe others are seeing."

"According to your faith, so be it done to you."

How many of our daily experiences are seriously out of sync because we are not living by faith?

The principle above was not an isolated case with Jesus. **"Then Jesus answered her, 'O woman, great is your faith! Be it done to you as you desire.' And her daughter was healed instantly"** (Matthew 15:28). Do you need some healing in your life? Faith!

God still heals people today, yet two extremes need to be avoided here. A part of the church runs off half-cocked and thinks that everybody gets healed—even though the apostle Paul himself was never healed (see 2 Corinthians 12:8–10). The other half collapses into the unbelief of "God doesn't heal anymore; that was an apostolic thing." Both of those are errors. God does not promise healing for everyone in all circumstances, and yet often we are impoverished in our bodies because we have no faith in the God who does heal!

Jesus also discussed the consequences of lacking faith: **"O you of little faith, why are you discussing among yourselves the fact that you have no bread?'"** (Matthew 16:8). His followers were upset because they didn't have lunch, even though prior to this Jesus had already fed five thousand people (Matthew 14:14–21). And He was like, "Guys, you don't get it. Where's your faith?" In Matthew 17:20, Jesus said to them, **"Because of your little faith. For truly, I say to you, if you have faith like a grain of mustard seed, you will say to this mountain, 'Move from here to there,' and it will move; and nothing will be impossible for you."**

Darlene Zschech, from Australia, sings a wonderful song on one of her worship CDs called "All Things Are Possible." I had a man come to me over a year ago and say, "You know that 'All Things Are Possible' song? When we sing that song, it's too rocky and too rowdy and if you don't stop singing that song, I'm going to have to leave the church." I was sorry to see him go, but, you know, we will never be too fired up about the promises of God as they relate to faith. I don't think God's looking down at us and saying, "Hey! You guys are just a little too excited about My promise that all things are possible. You need to just calm down." No! I believe we have let the "faith teachers" and all of their extreme unbiblical prosperity teaching cheat us out of the power of biblical faith. I challenge you right now to lay hold of the biblical teaching about faith and begin to really trust God for your transformation. Do so, and you will experience a power to be Christlike that you have never known before.

That's what the Word of God teaches, and I will not relegate the gospels to some other age and those promises as not available in our day as the followers of Jesus Christ. Mark 2:5 says, **"When Jesus saw their faith, He said to the paralytic, 'Son, your sins are forgiven.'"** Do you need your sins forgiven? Do you need to be free from the burden of guilt? Just trust Him and believe Him. He's promised that He will do that for you. So often we ask for His forgiveness but then we continue to carry the burden, not believing that God really has forgiven us. Hear these words of Christ about faith. From Mark 4:40: **"He said to them, 'Why are you so afraid? Have you still no faith?'"** From Mark 11:22: **"And**

Jesus answered them, 'Have faith in God.'" I love that. The disciples were asking Him some questions, and He answered, "Hey, have faith in God. Trust Him. Believe His promises."

How important was faith to the disciples? Look at two other verses in the gospel according to Luke: **"The apostles said to the Lord, 'Increase our faith'"** (17:5). They were starting to get it, and they came to Jesus and said, "Hey Jesus, we're starting to figure it out. It's faith, isn't it?" and Jesus replied, in effect, "Yes." And so they said, "Increase our faith." Later He asked, **"When the Son of Man comes, will He find faith on earth?"** (18:8b). The question in Luke 18 was not, "Does God answer prayer?" The question was—and is—"When the Son of Man returns, will He even find faith on the earth?" Will He even find a person who is willing to lay hold of Him by faith for His promises? I am determined to be that man, and I challenge you to do the same.

Faith in the Epistles

So much could be said here about faith. I typed the word "faith" into my computer search program, asking for references from Romans to Jude—all the letters (epistles) written by the apostles. I got 180 references, to say nothing of the synonyms: *believing God; trusting God; resting; and abiding in Him*—all of which contain a significant element of faith. The apostle John said that faith is the victory that overcomes the world (1 John 5:4).

Mark it down: Faith is essential. If you need a reference for that . . . just jot down: "the whole Bible."

FAITH IS PRACTICAL

Faith is as practical as you can get. I want you to go with me to the life of Jesus and see how Christ Himself used faith at the point of temptation to get victory.

I realize that some people believe that Jesus was not truly tempted by sin and that as God He could not experience true temptation, but the Bible teaches otherwise. Hebrews 4:15 tells us that He was One **"who *in every respect has been tempted as we are,* yet without sin"** (italics added).

Now some people will insist, "Well, if He never failed, how could He feel the weight of the temptation? I mean, if He never failed! The weight of temptation is the failure, isn't it?"

Actually, no; the weight *isn't* the failure. Think about this: who feels the weight more—the person who fails or the person who doesn't?

Perhaps a weight lifting analogy will help. When I was a kid, I used to like to watch weight lifting events on *The Wide World of Sports.* Most of us can bring to mind images of men lifting massive weights over their heads.

So out comes this weight lifter. When you hear the amount of weight on the bar you think of what you can lift and conclude, "That's not coming up." One of the classic weight lifting moves is called the "clean and jerk." It involves a violent pull upward on the bar and almost simultaneous crouch under it. Now the lifter is beneath the bar. He must then straighten his legs, using their strength to lift the weight. Once standing, the upward push and downward crouch is repeated to get the bar from chest height to the overhead position. Each round, more weight is added to the bar. By the end of the competition, only one athlete lifts the entire weight.

Question: Who feels the weight more—the one who finally lifts it all or the ones who fail and let it fall? Do you get it? Failure means you buckled before the full weight was on. Jesus Christ is the Great Victor because He felt the full weight of temptation and conquered it. So He knows the weight of temptation *more* than we do—not less for our failure.

But that's not all. Jesus did not use His divine powers to get victory over temptation; He was victorious by faith within the confines of His humanity. In fact, using His deity to get victory is exactly what Satan was tempting Him to do! **"If You are the Son of God, command these stones to become loaves of bread,"** the Evil One said (Matthew 4:3). Jesus answered, **"Man shall not live by bread alone"** (verse 4). He exercised faith in the Word of God to repel the attacks of the Evil One.

Think how vulnerable Jesus was at that point. He had been in the wilderness for forty days and forty nights. He had been fasting. He was hungry and tired and exhausted and lonely. He was facing Satan in His humanity. Notice the three temptations: make stone bread, throw Yourself down from the temple, and receive from me the kingdoms of the world if You worship me.

That last temptation was a really dumb one, when we inspect it. Yet in it lies a lesson for us: In the heat of temptation the offer is so attractive, but when you stand back from it, it really is ridiculous. Satan was getting desperate and said in effect, "Hey, you know what? I'll give You everything You made, and already own, if You worship me." *Such a deal!* In His humanity, Jesus was susceptible to the temptation; yet He readily realized it was neither appealing nor part of His Father's plan.

As you study the temptations in Matthew 4, you can't help but notice that

Jesus used faith in the Word of God as His only basis for victory. When tempted to "turn stones into bread," Jesus said, **"Man shall not live by bread alone, but by every word that comes from the mouth of God"** (verse 4), quoting Deuteronomy 8:3. When temptation came again—**"Throw Yourself down"** (verses 6–7)—Jesus answered, **"Again it is written, 'You shall not put the Lord your God to the test,'"** quoting Deuteronomy 6:16. Finally, when Satan offered **"all the kingdoms of the world . . . if You will . . . worship me"** (verses 8–9), Jesus said, **"Be gone, Satan! For it is written, 'You shall worship the Lord your God, and Him only shall you serve,'"** this time quoting Deuteronomy 10:20.

Three temptations. Three biblical answers. What a perfect example of the power of faith in God's Word.

PLACING OUR FAITH IN
SOMETHING POWERFUL: GOD'S WORD

Please understand, I am not teaching faith in faith—that cultic message of faith in the power of faith itself. That deceptive message is all over the modern church, and it's on television every day too! We are not talking about faith in faith. The Bible doesn't teach that there is any power in your faith or in what you say simply because you say it with confidence. There is no power in what *we* say.

The power of faith is in what God says. If what we say is God's Word, and we believe what we are confessing in the depth of our being, there we will find incredible power.

It's not our faith itself where the power resides. It's the *object* of our faith. A lot of people are trusting their good works to get them to heaven. Many people have great *faith* in good works to get them to heaven. They are not going to make it. It is what you have faith in that makes the difference. Have faith in the promises of God's Word. A grain of faith anchored to Almighty God will set mountains in motion.

OKAY, LET'S PUT YOUR FAITH TO WORK.

Here's a practical, personal definition of faith. Faith is:

(1) believing the Word of God and
(2) acting upon it,
(3) no matter how I feel,
(4) because God promises a good result.

Every one of those statements is so important. As we consider each, we'll learn how to empower faith in our lives.

FAITH IS . . .
Believing the Word of God

When you pick up the Book, you don't say, "Well, that may be true," or "I'll think about it," or "Well, I guess that is worthy of consideration." Let's bag that once and for all! Faith is *believing the Word of God*. Instead, when we read the Bible, we should say, "God said it, I believe it, and that settles it for me!"

God's commands are good. Every time God says "Don't," what He means is, "Don't hurt yourself." God loves you. God didn't sit up in heaven in eternity past saying, "Okay, what's next? Okay, adultery—will we make that a sin or a righteous act? Someone flip a coin." Not! All of God's rules are based upon His love for us. Everything He commends brings joy, and everything He forbids avoids pain.

Acting upon the Word of God

Faith involves believing the Word of God and then *acting upon the Word*. That's where faith gets feet and makes a choice. So much of the biblical teaching on change can be reduced to that word "choice." In our honest moments, we know that we are who we are because we choose. Right now as I write I am sitting inside on a beautiful sunny day by Lake Michigan, and I could be swimming or playing volleyball on the beach. I choose instead to do this work because I believe God has called me to serve others, and I want to be obedient. Over and over I have learned the hard way that I must act on what God calls me to do, that His joy and peace belong only to those who obey His will.

John 14:21 has been a very influential verse in my life. It records the words of Christ: **"He who has My commandments and keeps them, it is he who loves Me. And he who loves Me will be loved by My Father, and I will love him and manifest Myself to him"** (NKJV). All the intimacy and joy that Christ offers is tied directly to not only believing the Word, but *acting on it*.

Acting . . . No Matter How I Feel

Here's the third part: "Acting upon God's Word *no matter how I feel*." We must choose to obey God even during the times when we don't feel like obeying. Do you ever have times when you don't feel like obeying God's Word? Unless we want to be like roller coaster Christians for the rest of our lives, we have to get that third part in place: believing the Word of God and acting on it *no matter how I feel*.

Emotions are wonderful things. In their rightful place, they bring color and fulfillment to our lives. As our servants, emotions can do much good in our lives, but when they become "master" and start dictating our actions, we are headed for disaster. Think of your life as a train. Emotions make a lousy engine but a wonderful caboose. Learning this truth has been a real point of victory for me. When I feel frustrated, it doesn't matter how I feel. If I feel anxiety, it doesn't matter how I feel. If I feel like indulging myself, or avoiding a problem, or nursing a personal slight, I must choose to ignore how I feel. I must "believe the Word of God and act upon it no matter how I feel." That's faith!

Maybe you're saying to yourself, "That's my problem; I can't ignore how I feel. I am going in a good direction, obeying the Lord and doing so well, and *Woooshhhh!!* in comes a powerful rush of emotion. Before I know it, I have fallen into my old sinful pattern again."

How can we learn self-control? How can we train ourselves to look past the emotion of the moment and obey God consistently "no matter how we feel"?

. . . Because God promises a good result.

The answer is found in the last part of our definition. Believing the Word of God and acting upon it, no matter how I feel, *because God promises a good result*. Every command of God's Word brings blessing, joy, and fulfillment when obeyed, but brings pain and hardship when disobeyed. Or, as someone has put it, "Choose to sin, choose to suffer."

Hebrews 11:25 says that the pleasures of sin are just **"for a season"** (KJV). From experience we know that when we falter in faith and choose to disobey, we experience painful consequences. An unbeliever may be able to disobey God's law without experiencing guilt, shame, and consequences, but we cannot. On the other hand, joy, peace, contentment, and fulfillment are exclusively Christian experiences. Only a true follower of Jesus can enjoy the blessings that follow the choice to obey God. Even Christ used the future blessings God promised Him as a way to motivate His obedience in the present. **"For the joy that was set before Him [Jesus] endured the cross"** (Hebrews 12:2).

God promises a good result to every act of obedience and a painful consequence to every act of sin. Surely we needn't spend our entire lives wondering which path to choose. Choose to sin, and you choose to suffer; choose to obey, and you choose to be blessed.

PRACTICING FAITH

Okay, we've defined faith this way: Faith is "believing the Word of God and acting upon it no matter how I feel, because God promises a good result." Let's practice! Let's see how such a faith works in our lives.

A man walks into his pastor's office and says, "You know, I don't love my wife anymore. I just don't have those feelings anymore, so I am going to find somebody new and start again."

"That is a very, very bad decision," the pastor tells him.

"But I don't feel like—"

"Forget about what you feel!" the pastor interrupts. "Do what is right and trust God. God says that if you walk to the front of a church and stand before a group of people and vow a vow, 'do not delay paying it for He has no pleasure in fools' (Ecclesiastes 5:4). If you make this choice, you are going to put yourself into a world of hurt!"

"It just looks like it will be easier if I go this way . . ."

"No! Believe me; it won't be. Work things out with your wife! God's family is tragically littered with the broken families carelessly discarded by those who thought they could avoid the pain of unbelief and disobedience. You can't! No matter how tough it seems, **'Do not be deceived: God is not mocked, for whatever one sows, that will he also reap'** (Galatians 6:7)."

Here's another example of this faith principle at work. Becky, single and thirty-four years old, is not dating anyone, and she lies in bed every night hearing her biological clock ticking down. That's a very real thing for people. "I want to be a mother. I want to be a wife," Becky tells her close friend. "I met this guy . . ."

"Is he a Christian?" her friend asks.

"Well, I think—"

"Is he?" her friend persists.

"Well, he's really nice. I've been sharing with him and I think he's—" And then Becky's friend reminds her of 2 Corinthians 6:14: **"Do not be unequally yoked with unbelievers."**

Becky has a good and wise friend, one who loves her enough to confront her with the true meaning of faith. Believe the Word of God and act upon it no matter how you feel. Do so because God promises a good result. Do not compromise the Word. Do not think you have found a better way. You haven't! When you appear before the Lord one day and tell Him, "Well, I just thought this was a better plan," God will look you right in the eye and say, "I wrote the plan down." *Believe the Word of God and act upon it no matter how I feel, because God promises a good result.*

PRACTICING FAITH IN FORGIVENESS

"Well, someone hurt me deeply," you say. "And it wasn't any accidental thing. He did it on purpose. I am devastated. I hate him for it. I know God's Word says forgive, but I can't." Yes, the Word of God says forgive. It also teaches that the pathway of joy and peace for you is through forgiveness. You need to forgive.

"*Forgive?*! I want to *kill him*!" you reply. Once again, you must act on God's Word no matter how you feel. God promises a good result.

Perhaps you still feel, "No! I'm going to get even. I'm going to make him pay. I'm going to have him feel what I've felt." I urge you: Don't do that. Exercise your faith. And God will bless your obedience; He will give you a good result.

THE "SECRET" IS OUT!

Remember back in chapter 3? You allowed the Holy Spirit to get specific with you about one or two things that God wants to change in you next. And then as a result of chapter 4 you did the hard work of repentance. You really do want to change! You continued through chapters 4–7 and understood the process of change, but you knew you didn't have the power within you to work the process successfully.

So you kept reading, looking for the power to change. In chapter 8, I wrote about the power of the Holy Spirit being available to turbo your victory, but you want to know how to ignite that power, how to "turn the switch on." Now you know. Faith ignites the power of the Holy Spirit. Believe the Word of God and act upon it no matter how you feel, because God promises a good result!

HOW TO INCREASE YOUR FAITH

You say, "Well, I want to do that, but I don't have the faith that you have. My faith is so small." Okay! Here are two steps you can take that will immediately begin to grow your faith.

1. Expose your mind to God's Word.

You say, "I want that faith." Well, first, expose your mind to God's Word.

"Faith comes from hearing, and hearing through the word of Christ," Paul wrote (Romans 10:17). My favorite verse in the Bible is Jeremiah 15:16, where the prophet said, **"Your words were found, and I ate them, and Your words**

became to me a joy and the delight of my heart." Have you learned to love the Word of God? An increasing faith feeds upon a mind steeped in God's Word. Have you gotten past the discipline stage of reading it to the place where it becomes your desire and your delight?

I love the truth that's in the Bible. It's God's heart for us, and when we wash our minds with it daily and continuously, it produces faith within us. When we fill our minds with our car radio preset FM worldly music station, or the latest filthy television programming and other pagan entertainment, no wonder we struggle with faith. We fill our days and our ears with everything but the Word of God, and so we lack the faith to obey. Romans 12:2 teaches that our transformation comes by the **"renewal of your mind."** And that means immersing ourselves in God's Word.

We must read the Word; study it; memorize it; meditate on it. You may have wondered why most pages in this book have Scripture on them. What else is there? My words do not build faith. **"So faith comes from hearing, and hearing through the word of Christ"** (Romans 10:17).

Jesus was able to overcome the temptation recorded in Matthew 4 because He knew the lie, and He knew the truth that could replace it.

2. Practice Genuine Prayer

Faith comes through *genuine* prayer. I'm not talking about "Our Father who art in heaven . . ." or "Hail, Mary, full of grace . . . ." I'm not talking about ritualistic prayer—not pagan repetition. I'm talking about genuine, on-your-knees-before-God heartfelt prayer, laying hold of God by faith. You say, "I'm not very good at that. Where's the seminar on that?" The seminar on that is conducted in your home daily in a private place where you can kneel down. It's a seminar given by the Holy Spirit and available to you twenty-four hours a day, seven days a week. The way to learn how to pray is to get on your knees, open your mouth, and say, "Lord, teach me to pray. God, I come before You genuinely today."

I love what Jesus told Peter in Luke 22:32, **"I have prayed for you that your faith may not fail."** You say, "I don't want my faith to fail." Then pray. Jesus is praying for you.

The power of prayer to build faith is a phenomenal thing. I have experienced this many times in my life. I'm filled with anxiety or I'm filled with concerns and burdens. Then I remember, "Pray!" So I get by myself and kneel down in humility before God, and in the simplest language I know I begin to talk to my Father about it. Every time I do, it isn't very long at all that my genuine heartfelt prayer leads to getting up off my knees, feeling those burdens lifted, and knowing that my anxiety has been replaced by faith.

If you want the power to change, it can only come through the Holy Spirit. And the Holy Spirit pours on the power in response to your faith! You might begin by asking as the apostles did, "Lord, increase our faith."

Teacher Questions

1. Read Romans 8:1–11. Why is living the Christian life impossible? Can you show it in the Scripture passage? What do verses 9–11 say is our only source of power?
2. Read Hebrews 4:2 and explain why the Word must be connected with faith in our lives.
3. Which of the people mentioned in Hebrews 11 as examples of faith do you find most encouraging to your faith? Why?

Prophet Questions

1. What two methods were given for increasing our faith? Read the verses that correspond to each point. Which is the greatest need in your life now?
2. How can the power of faith be made more effective in your life as you seek to change to the person God wants you to be?
3. In what specific areas of your life do you now know you need to apply faith more consistently?

Shepherd Questions

1. We find comfort in the practicality of trusting God's Word. Read Matthew 4:1–11; what does Jesus' encounter with Satan tell you about having faith in God's Word?
2. Why is God's Word powerful in resisting the Enemy, when our words are not? Can you give a personal example?
3. What is it about Jesus Himself that invites you to trust Him more?

LET'S GET TO WORK

Take a moment to think about the next three days. Jot down the major challenge you will face each day, using a notebook or journal; then a verse reference to show how faith in God's Word will intersect that challenge and help you to experience victory. Day one is shown below as an example:

Day 1 Challenge: _____

God's Word says: Philippians 4:19—**"And my God will supply every need of yours according to His riches in glory in Christ Jesus."**

For days two and three, jot down a challenge and then meditate on the following verses. For day two, Psalm 84:11—**"For the Lord God is a sun and shield; the Lord bestows favor and honor; No good thing does He withhold from those who walk uprightly."** For day three, Joshua 1:8—**"This Book of the Law shall not depart from your mouth, but you shall meditate on it day and night, so that you may be careful to do according to all that is written in it. For then you will make your way prosperous, and then you will have good success."**

LOOK UP!

Dear heavenly Father,

Thank You for Your Word. Forgive me for sitting here and thinking that hearing the truth equals transformation. Lord, help me to understand that the power of Your Spirit to bring transformation is ignited within by my own faith. Remind me that's the part I can choose. I can't change myself, but I can choose to believe You and to trust Your promises and to live out what You say. Remind me that You will give victory if I believe Your Word and act upon it no matter how I feel.

Lord, thanks for those who have a history of Your faithfulness and I can draw down upon that to know that You bring good results. But I pray especially that You would help me to remember that You are good and faithful, and that You never fail Your children when we obey You by faith. Help me to step out and just trust You and see You work in my life.

Lord, even now let me anticipate the victory that You will bring as I trust You and act upon what I am learning. I pray this in Jesus' name. Amen.

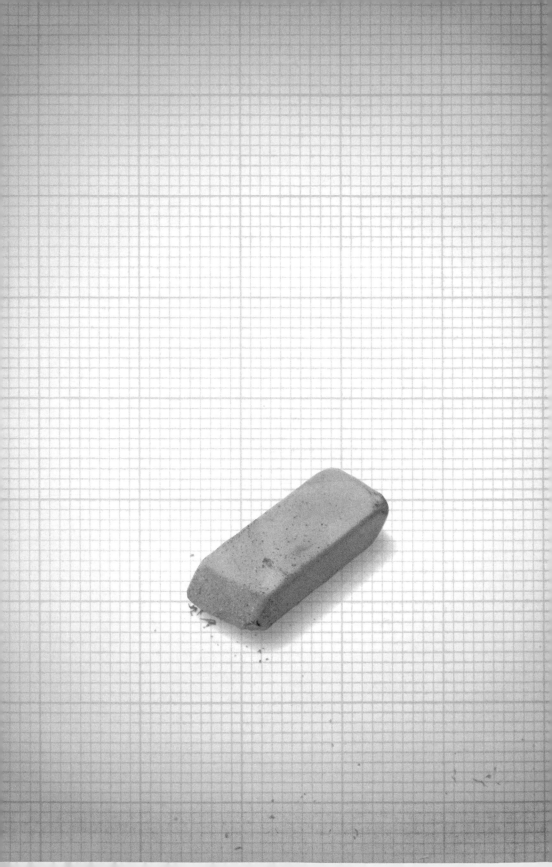

10

THE POWER OF BIBLICAL FRIENDSHIPS

SAY IT IN A SENTENCE:
*If you want to experience lasting change, you must
understand and access the power of biblical friendship.*

S tatistics indicate that people normally read only the first two chapters of a book. They get bored or distracted or find it too hard, so they drop the book and pick up something else. Most people are looking for the "easy fix." Well, this is chapter 10, so I know something about you:

1. You start reading books at the end (that's weird); or

2. you're looking for help in the matter of friendships and picked this chapter out of the table of contents (you're lonely); or

3. you have read the first nine chapters and are now beginning the final one (you're diligent!).

I hope you fit into category 3. If you have read the first nine chapters, then you know by now that I am only joking about items 1 and 2. More importantly, if you've read this far, God has been doing a lot in your life. When I present these truths in a church or a Bible conference setting, the response is overwhelming. There are letters and testimonies and conversations with people who are experiencing the transforming power of God as they never have before. Praise the Lord!

KEEP THE FIRE GOING

Perhaps you have experienced some victory in the past, yet you would admit that you found victory only for a time and then fell back into a pattern of defeat.

Maybe you got fired up at a youth retreat or a special conference or during a difficult time, and for once you were really walking in the joy of the Lord, but then it all fell apart. You are not alone! Most Christians today are not living at the peak of their spiritual experience. They know how to fire it up, but they don't know how to keep it going.

This chapter is about how to keep it going. The Christian life is not a solo thing. It requires teamwork. This chapter is about how to download the incredible resource God has given us in our brothers and sisters in Christ. We desperately need each other so that when we want to quit we can't because our friends "won't allow it!"

Let's begin with this thought:

LASTING CHANGE

REQUIRES BIBLICAL FRIENDSHIP.

The key word in this statement is *biblical*, because not all friendships are biblical. In fact, some are very *un*biblical. They not only do not help us, they impede our progress on the pathway toward transformation. Instead we need biblical friendships. After twenty-five years as a pastor, I can tell you that people who change—people who develop a life pattern of change, becoming more and more mature as followers of Christ—are surrounded by biblical friendships. Without those kind of friendships, they *cannot* flourish spiritually. Neither can you.

Change does not happen in a silo. For nine chapters I have been talking to you about change as though you could get it done standing inside a big cement cylinder. I may have given you the picture that transformation was just you and God. Maybe you have been seeing yourself with Bible open, eyes turned upward, and the Spirit of God filling you—just you and God, and change happens. That is *not* a complete picture! We cannot flourish spiritually in the long-term without each other.

It's time to knock the silo down and begin to pay attention to the people that God has placed around you as resources for change. That is why God has called together this thing called *the local church*.

FRIENDSHIPS IN THE SCRIPTURES

"One who is righteous is a guide to his neighbor, but the way of the wicked leads them astray," Solomon wrote (Proverbs 12:26). As you read God's Word, you cannot help but notice that great men and great women of faith always had supportive friends around them. Always!

Think of Abraham, who had Sarah, his loving wife and good friend. Yes, she made some mistakes, but Hebrews 11 tells us that she was a woman of faith. She stuck with Abraham through thick and thin. Without the loving, supportive co-operation of Sarah, Abe would have had a much harder time following God's call.

Think of Moses, whose life cannot be understood apart from the role of supportive relationships. Moses had Aaron, his brother, to speak for him, and his father-in-law, Jethro, to provide leadership consultation on the proper way to delegate authority. He had Miriam, his sister, to stand with him when the people rebelled.

Moses's friendships extended beyond his family. He also had Joshua and Caleb. When everyone else doubted, these partners in faith supported Moses's claim that the children of Israel could conquer the land. (See Numbers 13:1–3; 23–14:9.) Moses experienced firsthand the prosperity of biblical friendship.

The list could go on and on. Ruth and Naomi gave sacrificially of themselves to one another. Esther, alone and tempted so far from her natural surroundings, flourished in faith because she had this solid, caring friend, Mordecai. David and Jonathan became soul brothers. Elijah and Elisha, two prophets under attack, lifted each other up.

In the New Testament, Paul had Barnabas, who supported him when everyone else feared the former persecutor of Christians (Acts 9:27–28; 11:25–26). He also had Silas, who joined him in song, even though they were in prison (Acts 16:22–25); and Timothy, who would give comfort when Paul was again imprisoned near the end of his ministry (2 Timothy 4:13, 21). Peter had John; John had Peter. And, of course, Jesus had twelve close companions and when He sent them out to do ministry, He sent them "two by two." When He sent out seventy ministers (Luke 10), again He sent them two by two. Why? Because of the power of biblical friendship.

Some of the greatest disasters in all of God's Word came because people had the wrong (unbiblical) friends, or no friends at all. Eve's biggest problem was Adam. Adam's biggest problem was Eve. They didn't help each other. One of them should have said to the other one, "What are you thinking?!? Put that *down! Don't bite that!*"

King Saul had Samuel sent by God to help him be all God wanted him to be. Saul's problem was that he didn't listen. He had a biblical friend but refused to listen to him and, as a result, his life ended in tragedy. David's downfall was directly related to the lack of biblical counsel he received from his military leader and friend, Joab. The general refused to challenge David after the king gave orders to cause Uriah's death in battle (2 Samuel 11:14–15). Instead of warning the king against being an accessory to murder, Joab stayed silent.

No friends can be as damaging upon our thoughts and actions as unbiblical friends. Think of Jacob and the incredible potential of his life. In almost every instance Jacob was alone when he did some very foolish things. He deceived his brother; he lied to his father, and he ran from his problems. And how about Samson? You want to talk potential: Handsome and strong, he had a full understanding of the power of God. The Spirit of God was resting upon him (Judges 13:24–25; 14:6, 19). But his life was foolish and ultimately tragic, and in every passage we learn about him, he is alone.

We are just like the men and women in God's Word. We have abilities and a desire for God and great potential, but without biblical, truth-telling friends, our lives will flop just like theirs.

TWO KEYS TO BIBLICAL FRIENDSHIPS

You have been working so hard. Praying and studying and working toward the personal transformation that God wants to give you. As you move toward the end of this book, you must be wondering, "What will happen when I am done? Will I keep it going or will I fall flat on my face?" The key in all of this is your friendships. With functioning biblical friendships you can keep it going. I want to take you to a favorite passage of Scripture and share with you the two key ingredients of biblical friendship. That way you can evaluate whether you are such a friend, and whether you have the kind of friends you need to experience lasting change.

David was the second king of Israel, but the story of his friendship began before he became king. Saul was the first king of Israel, and David became a close friend of Saul's son, Jonathan. David and Jonathan are a picture of phenomenal, transforming biblical friendship.

If ever there was a friendship with the cards stacked against it, this was the one. Jonathan came from a textbook "dysfunctional" home. His mother was passive and his father was a tyrant, whose actions at times bordered on insanity. (See 1 Samuel 16:14–15; 18:10– 11; 19:9–10.) Saul had initially made David his own son, but now David was living on the run and hiding in terror because Saul had gone crazy and was trying to kill him. Beyond that bizarre development, Jonathan and David both had king plans. Jonathan was first in line to the throne under his father Saul, and David had been anointed king by Samuel according to God's direction.

You'd never think two people who wanted the same throne could become friends, but they did, and out of their adversity came a powerful picture of friendship. From the pain that brought them together we learn:

A BIBLICAL FRIEND

HOLDS YOU UP WHEN YOU STUMBLE.

Sometimes the pressure of life—stress at work, pressure at home, a health problem, a financial crisis—sometimes in all of our lives, we stumble. Sometimes things weigh so heavy upon us we can't help but collapse. Contrary to popular opinion, these difficult times are not random happenings. They are allowed by the loving hand of God to draw us to Himself and to conform our characters to the life of Jesus Christ. Like David, we must learn to submit ourselves to God during these times and let Him accomplish His good and perfect will (Romans 12:2), so God **"may exalt you in due time"** (1 Peter 5:6 NKJV).

I am sure there were many long nights during David's flight from King Saul when he wanted to give up or strike back or rebel against the Lord. I have never gone through something as tough as David did, but I am convinced that the key to his success was the nourishment and strength he gleaned from his friendship with Jonathan.

Do you have a friend or two like David did? A friend who can come to you in times when God is using some circumstance in a focused way to change you? Biblical friends provide the power to keep on changing in two essential ways: They hold us up and, on occasion, they hold us down. Let's examine these two keys to biblical friendship—and to lasting change.

HOW FRIENDS CAN HOLD US UP

How do friends hold us up? Let's consider the support Jonathan gave David during a crisis in David's life. **"Then Jonathan, Saul's son, arose and went to David in the woods"** (1 Samuel 23:16 NKJV). Jonathan was taking his life into his hands even to go and speak to his friend, but it says, He **"arose and went to David in the woods and strengthened his hand in God."** Notice what happened next:

And he said to him, "Do not fear, for the hand of Saul my father shall not find you. You shall be king over Israel, and I shall be next to you. Saul my father also knows this." And the two of them made a covenant before the LORD. David remained at Horesh, and Jonathan went home. (verses 17–18)

Notice five ways that Jonathan supported David. These are ways we can support our friends—and receive their support. As you read these five ways, ask yourself: "Am I that kind of friend?" and "Do I have a friend like that?"

1. Their Presence

First, a biblical friend holds you up when you stumble because *they are there for you.* **"And Jonathan, Saul's son, rose and went to David."** Jonathan had many reasons for staying away. He had everything to lose and nothing to gain personally. He was risking his father's wrath. When he got up to leave the table in the palace, his father grabbed his spear and threw it at his own son to try to kill him (1 Samuel 20:30–33). That's how crazy Saul was. In siding with David, Jonathan was risking his own position. After all, if Jonathan let King Saul kill David, Jonathan would inherit the throne. David was alone, and he was afraid. And Jonathan said to himself, "There is no way that I am going to let him down." He went to David.

Many true stories of sacrificial friendship arose from the ashes of World War II. I read one such story of two inseparable friends, Jack and Jim, who enlisted together. They went to boot camp together and saw their first combat together. Eventually they fought many battles side by side in trenches filled with the stench of war. During one attack, Jack was critically wounded in a field crisscrossed by barbed wire. Mines and obstacles also littered the area, and he couldn't get back to his foxhole. The entire position was under a withering enemy gunfire and mortar rounds, and it would be suicidal to attempt a rescue. Yet Jim decided to try.

Before Jim could get out of the trench, however, the sergeant yanked him back, ordering him not to go. "It's too late! You can't do him any good. You're only going to get yourself killed!" Jim waited a few minutes, but when the sergeant turned his back, Jim jumped out of the trench, consumed with loyalty toward his friend.

A few minutes later, Jim was back in the foxhole, mortally wounded and with his now-dead friend in his arms. The angry sergeant cried out, "What a waste! He's dead and you're dying. It wasn't worth it."

With almost his last breath, the soldier replied, "Oh, yes it was, Sarge. When I got to him, he said just five words, 'I knew you'd come, Jim.'" Now that's friendship. And you are not a friend unless you are present for your friend during hardship. That's the first thing Jonathan did; he went to David. Presence! But here's a second thing:

2. Their Prayers

A biblical friend holds you up when you stumble *by praying with you.* Samuel reported that Jonathan not only went to David but **"strengthened his hand in God"** (1 Samuel 23:16). This was not some Rotary or Lions Club, a mutual-admiration-society-facilitating friendship. Jonathan did not present himself as the answer to David's problems. The NASB translates it, **"He . . . encouraged him."** The Hebrew text is *much* more specific than that. It says literally **"and strengthened his hand in God."** Wow! David was a great man of God, author of most of the Psalms, a man after God's own heart (Acts 13:22), and a giant killer. David was a mighty man of faith. Notice that even great men and women of faith have times when their faith struggles.

David was hurting and disillusioned. Jonathan didn't show up with some stupid comments or fleshly counsel. He helped David take his problems to the Lord. He didn't say, "Well, Dad's going to come around soon, Dave." Or, "Don't worry about it; it's not as bad as it seems. Let's look on the positive as you sit here in this dark, damp forest with no food or hope in sight."

Often when we go to minister to people there is nothing to say. The burden is too big; the hurt is too great. It's about presence and it's about prayer. We need friends who will take us to God, and we need to be that kind of friend to others who are struggling to change. Often when we stumble under the "mighty hand," we need someone else to kind of give us a leg up in prayer toward the Lord. Can't you just hear Jonathan saying, "Hey, David, I can't solve this. But I know who can." He probably put his arm around him and said, "We need to pray about this. We need to take this before the Lord."

Do you have a friend like that? Do you have a friend who supports God's process of change in you by insisting that you take the struggle before the Lord in prayer? I am not asking if you know someone who *could do it*; I am asking if you have a friend right now in your life who says to you, "You know what? We need to get on our knees right now and take this thing to the Lord." How sad when so-called Christian friends never pray together. They don't have anything spiritual in common other than putting themselves in the same seats in church on a weekend. They don't discuss the things of God together. Hebrews 10:24 (NIV) says that we should **"spur one another on toward love and good deeds."**

The result of your being in contact with a biblical friend in prayer should be a closer walk with and a greater passion for Jesus Christ. The friendship should lead to a renewed commitment to submit to God's molding influence in your life.

3. Their Protection

A biblical friend holds you up when you stumble *by protecting you*. Jonathan gave his friend assurance: **"Do not fear, for the hand of Saul my father shall not find you"** (verse 17). He was saying, "Don't be afraid. My father will not find you." Now David was an emotional guy. You have to be an emotional guy to write the kind of poetry that he wrote in the book of Psalms. It's not hard to imagine that as he saw Jonathan approaching, David might have wondered if his friend was still loyal. Well, he didn't have to wait long to find out. Apparently Jonathan was able to discern that Dave's anxiety meter was redlining a little bit; he quickly said to him, "Hey! Hang on! Don't be afraid, okay? My dad's not going to find you. I'm not going to tell him; just chill! It's okay."

When David heard those words of support, he gained strength. There is nothing worse than a so-called friend who comes along when you are in crisis and says, "Hey, I can *see* why you're upset. Yeah, she drives me crazy, too!" Or, "You have every *right* to feel that way." When our heart is a tornado, the last thing we need is for somebody to show up with a fan. That's not friendship. Biblical friendship provides words that protect and support our troubled emotional state during hardship.

4. Their Personal Loyalty

A biblical friend holds you up when you stumble *by confirming their personal loyalty*. Jonathan said, **"You shall be king over Israel, and I shall be next to you"** (verse 17). As if to say, "Hey Dave, let me paint a picture of our future. I already figured it out; you're going to be king—not me! And don't even worry about whether that's going to sever our relationship. I'm fine with being number two as long as you're number one." No wonder David loved him.

When we stumble, we need friends who protect us with fierce loyalty. When you are struggling to change, the last thing you need is someone who turns against you when you stumble. Instead, we need loyal friends who will come to our aid and lift us up with life-giving loyalty.

I'm not sure who wrote this truth, which I found one day in an article, but it's an important truth about being a loyal friend:

> What is your response when your friend is criticized? Now there may be truth in the criticism, but it is nearly always one-sided and unfair. Do you spring to his defense with a concern that others focus on his weaknesses and not his strengths? It's not enough to later say, "Hey. So-and-so said this about you, but I didn't believe him." The real question is, *Did you challenge it?* Did you shift the focus to your friend's strengths?

That's loyalty. That's protection. As a biblical friend, you hold another up— and he holds you up when you stumble.

You say, "I want to change so much." Listen. You need to get these kinds of friends.

5. Their Promise

A biblical friend holds you up when you stumble *by confirming the friendship with a promise.* **"And the two of them made a covenant before the Lord"** (verse 18). I know some men who would say, "Oh, that sounds so girly, doesn't it? Two men making a covenant? Isn't that weak?" That's not weak at all! It's strong! Two men standing together and one admits, "I can't be what God wants me to be without you." And the other replies, "Well, hey, you know what? I can't be what God wants me to be without you, either. I really need you! Let's stand together in this. Let's make a commitment to each other that together we're going to be the men that God wants us to be."

That's commitment, and it's that kind of committed friendship that brings power to the process of change.

Years ago I read the following. I've tried to be this kind of friend and I have sought out these kinds of friends—a friend who can say with all honesty:

> Brother, I want you to know that I am committed to you. You will never knowingly suffer at my hands. I'll never say or do anything knowingly to hurt you. I will always in every circumstance seek to help you and support you. If you're down and I can lift you up, I'll do it. Anything I have that you need, I'll share it with you. And if I have to, I'll give it to you. No matter what I find out about you and no matter what happens in the future—either good or

bad—my commitment to you will never change. There is nothing you can do about it and you don't have to respond. I love you and that's what it means. [source unknown]

The key word in all of this is in the final sentence: "love." Change is not easy, and when we want to quit or slow down or get off the track or focus on others, Proverbs 17:17 says, **"A friend loves at all times, and a brother is born for adversity."** Do you have that kind of loving friend to keep you on the pathway of change when you get discouraged and want to quit? I pray that you do, and if you don't, that you will find someone, and be that kind of friend for others.

Now here's the second part of biblical friendship:

A BIBLICAL FRIEND
HOLDS YOU DOWN WHEN YOU STRAY.

We don't think of this often—and we may not want to. But it is true: A genuine friend will restrain at times. He will rebuke you if necessary. She will correct you. Not only does a biblical friend hold you up when you stumble, *that friend will also hold you down when you stray.* We stumble from the pressures of life, but when we stray it is through our own wicked, rebellious heart.

Second Samuel 11 and 12 describe the darkest days of David's life, when he strayed from the Lord. David had been following the Lord faithfully for a long time, but he saw a married woman, Bathsheba, and lusted after her. He compounded his mistake by taking her—he was king, after all—and sleeping with her. She conceived a child. He covered it up. He murdered her husband and hid his treachery for over a year.

When you read the story, you can't help but wonder, "Where were David's friends?" Jonathan had been killed in battle. Where were the truth-tellers who step up and say, "What are you *doing*? What are you *thinking*? Why are you destroying your life?"

Apparently David's so-called friends were like, "Wait! I'm not going to tell him. You tell him." "No way, man; you tell him." Very sad. It went on for a whole year. Things went on for so long that God actually had to get somebody and send him to David. A new friend. A prophet who would tell it like it is—Nathan.

How tragic that David didn't have any old friends who could have seen his decline and got to him before he crashed and burned. Instead, **"And the LORD sent Nathan to David. He came to him and said to him . . ."** (2 Samuel 12:1). There was some stuff that needed to get said, and Nathan was willing to say it.

HOW FRIENDS CAN HOLD US DOWN:
SPEAKING THE TRUTH IN LOVE

A Brutal Story Told in Love

Nathan made his point in the form of a story. You can read it yourself in 2 Samuel 12, but let me try to summarize. Nathan stood in front of King David and said, "Hey David. Let me tell you a story. There was this guy, and he had sheep and more sheep and more sheep and herds of sheep and barns full of sheep and sheep stacked upon sheep. And there was this other guy who had one little lamb. And the guy who had all the sheep was out cruising one day and he saw the little lamb and thought, 'I want that one, too.' So instead of being satisfied with what he had, he went and took the little lamb from the poor guy who treated his lamb like a pet and fed it from his own table. He just ripped the lamb away from that poor guy and took that one for himself, too. (Here's the setup:) Hey, David, what do you think of a guy like that?"

And as we often are when we are covering our own sin, David got self-righteous and said (I'm paraphrasing now): "I'll kill that guy! Get that guy over here to the palace right now! I'll wipe him from the earth!"

And Nathan looked him right in the eye and said, "You are the man."

I bet you could have heard a pin drop in the palace then. All the people who had winked at David's sin for a whole year were standing there. This was in the public court of the palace. And they all whispered, "I can't believe he said that. I can't believe he said that. It's going to hit the fan now. Watch out! Watch out!"

Well, he didn't stop there. Nathan went on to pronounce a pretty heavy judgment on David for his wickedness. He detailed all of the consequences David should expect, starting with the death of the boy born from adultery. (See verses 10–12, 14 for the pronouncement.)

Everyone waited to see how David would respond. Second Samuel 12:13–15a reports what happened next:

David said to Nathan, "I have sinned against the LORD." And Nathan said to David, "The LORD also has put away your sin; you shall not die. Nevertheless, because by this deed you have utterly scorned the LORD, the child who is born to you shall die." Then Nathan went to his house.

Loved one, that is biblical friendship. It's having a friend who tells you the truth for your own good. The sad fact is that most of the people who will read this book do not presently have a friend like that. There are far more people who have the kind of friend who holds you up when you stumble but lack a friend who holds you down when you stray.

Excuses We Make for Not Speaking the Truth in Love

Often we create a variety of excuses in order not to speak the truth. Think of all the reasons Nathan could have given for not speaking truth to David.

- "Well, there's somebody closer."
- "I'll lose my position or maybe my life."
- "Let God tell him."
- "I'm afraid."
- "I'll do it later; we're just getting acquainted."

Instead of making excuses, Nathan cared enough to take hold of David and make him listen.

I respect that so much. I hope and pray that I am being that kind of friend to you in this book. Nathan was willing to put the whole relationship at risk to get David to a better place with others and with God. He said in effect, "This may be the last conversation we ever have, but it's going to be one that has truth in it." That's the key word: truth. Love is what we need in friendship when we stumble, and truth is what we need when we stray.

It was Howard Hendricks I first heard say, during a 1983 pastors and wives conference in Huntsville, Ontario (Canada), "Every man needs someone who can look him in the eye and say, 'You're neglecting your wife.'" To which men so often reply, "Well, my wife will straighten me out." News flash: When a man makes a decision to flush his life, his wife has a very difficult time getting his hand off the lever. A man needs someone very strong—another man—to come alongside and say, "Nope, no way! You are *not* doing that with your life." Women also need friends who can be honest with them.

The Bible says that we all fall in many ways. Sometimes we stumble through the weight of life and need a supporting friend to love us; others times we stray through our own rebellion and need truth-telling friends to confront us and get us back on God's program.

My Testimony Regarding Truth-telling Friends

Each of us has a need for a biblical friend. You do. I do. As of this writing, I'm fifty-one years old and, in my life, I have done a lot of things I regret—many of them even since I became an adult. In spite of that, God has blessed me immensely and sometimes I wonder why. One common thread I see is this: I have always been blessed with friends who could say, "Hold on for a minute. We're not going there. Stop; I don't care what you say; you're wrong."

Such biblical friends keep us steady, keep us accountable. Let me tell you about a few of those friends. During high school I was like, "Clue Phone: It's for James." I was so far off track. But I did have a youth pastor, Marvin Brubacher, who spoke truth to me. He took an interest in me when it was 100 percent by faith. He took me aside and was not impressed with me at all and simply said, "It goes like this."

During college, I had a dean named Doug Schmidt who "stood on my chest" when I was hard to hold down, and held out for God's highest and best in me. He believed in me when others didn't—that's "holding you up"—but he also spoke truth.

As I look back through my walk with Christ, at every point of change there have been these truth-telling friends. When we moved to Chicago for seminary, a family of three alone in that big city, my wife was at several key points that person for me. Kathy said, "No, I don't think that's what we should do. I don't think that could possibly be God's will for us."

Now the key ingredient in this, of course, is love. Change is not easy. Sometimes you want to quit. Sometimes you want to slow down, get off the track, to focus on others. But Proverbs 17:17 says, **"A friend loves at all times. And a brother is born for adversity."** You see, you find out where your real friendships are when the tough times come, when the challenges come; when you've got egg on your face, when you've made a bad decision, when it is not convenient to be your friend, when it is not helpful to be your friend, and when it is not profitable to be your friend. Now look around and see who remains. Those are your friends. Okay? And **a friend loves at all times.** Proverbs 17:17 goes on to say, **"And a brother is born for adversity."** Now Kathy and I have met a lot of great friends through the years at Harvest: Bill Ciofani, Perry Wilcox, Larry Talshub, to name just a few, have all been great friends to me. But as I was preparing this updated chapter, the person I thought of honestly again was Rick Donald. I mean, that guy, by God's grace, is an awesome friend. I can think of so many times in my life when he called me, "Can I just pray for you right now?" I tell people Rick Donald is my pastor. Every pastor needs a pastor, and I'm blessed to serve in the same church with my pastor. Most senior pastors don't have a pastor, but I have one. Rick Donald loves me and he cares for me. If God took me out of the world today, my family wouldn't have to figure out who would speak at my funeral. It would be Pastor Rick. I wish I could walk you down the hallway and take you into all the rooms of the crisis times in my life over the last twenty-five-plus years where Rick Donald has been that faithful friend who sticks closer than a brother. God has enabled him to do that, and I just covet for each of you the experience of the power of a true friend.

The power of having a biblical friend in one's life makes me ask you the question directly:

DO YOU HAVE A BIBLICAL FRIEND?

As I am writing this page, I am praying that God will show you where to start. Maybe you have biblical friends already or maybe they are around you, but you need to cultivate this kind of understanding with them. Maybe you need to verbalize your friendship and what it means, even as David and Jonathan did. You have been working so hard at the matter of change, but you won't be able to sustain that without the power of biblical friendship.

Kathy and I have been trying to teach this to our kids. When our little girl, Abby, was eight years old, she had a problem with one of her friends at school who was too possessive of her. Abby was very upset about it, so I gave her some counsel and sent her off to school. Later in the week she came home so excited and said, "Dad! Dad! I have to tell you what happened." Apparently she had a little confrontation with her friend, who became angry because Abby was talking to another girl. She said, "Dad, I did it! I took her aside and I said, 'I can't have you as my only friend. I have to expand my friendships. I'll give you the whole day to think about it.'" I thought that was so great! It was the power of biblical friendship to confront and help a friend.

CHANGE THAT LASTS

We have focused throughout the book not just on change, but *change that lasts*. That begins, first and foremost, with God's help. But friends—true, biblical friends—are instruments God will use in your life. Do you want change that lasts? Then do these three things:

1. *Choose a friend who is committed to change.* You cannot go where God wants you to go unless you hook up with somebody who also wants to be what God wants him or her to be. It's a two-way thing. Change flourishes when it's a partnership. So choose a friend who's committed to change. Make an appointment with them and share your vision with them. Ask them if they are in it for the long haul and want to be all that God wants them to be.

2. *Review the biblical pattern for change.* Use the summary sheet in "Let's Get to Work" at the end of this chapter to review the biblical pattern for personal change with your partner.

3. *Commit to ongoing accountability for change.* Share your goal. Share your observations about how your friend is doing and hold each other accountable. I'm in a number of accountable, biblical friendships. If you're not in a small group, if you don't have these kinds of biblical friendships, you might be able to talk a better game after this book but you won't keep changing. Get connected to some people who can help you keep it going.

Thanks for reading to the end of this book. I pray that you have found in its pages a life-changing message. I believe a joyful life of transformation is possible, because the Bible says it is. I covet for you that personal relationship with Jesus Christ that leads not only to the forgiveness of sins, but, as a new creation in Him, a life of victory and ongoing change in which you become more like Jesus. If you follow the process of change and access the power to change as taught in these pages, you will experience the abundant life that Jesus promised: **"I came that they may have life and have it abundantly"** (John 10:10).

Teacher Questions

1. Why is it important to have a friend who will tell you the truth? How is truth-telling a sign of love?
2. Why does it often take one person to fill the role of Jonathan in your life (to hold you up in support) and another to fill the role of Nathan (to hold you down in accountability)?
3. What was the most valuable lesson you learned in this chapter about *being* a friend?

Prophet Questions

1. Which is harder for you to do: love your friends or tell the truth to your friends (which is a loving action)? Why?
2. What cost must we be prepared to pay if we choose to be messengers of truth in our relationships? Why is truth so often neglected in relationships?
3. What is the hardest thing you ever had to tell a friend?

Shepherd Questions

1. How has God used this book in your life?
2. What have you learned that will help you maintain the progress that has been achieved thus far?
3. In what ways have you found in Christ a friend who sticks closer than a brother?

LET'S GET TO WORK

Within the next ten days, pray and think about someone you want to have as a biblical friend, someone who can "hold you up" and also may "hold you down." You may seek two or more friends, as some are better able to hold us up in support and some are able to hold us down in accountability. (See the second teacher question above.)

Then meet with your partner to review "The Biblical Pattern for Change" beginning on the next page.

THE BIBLICAL PATTERN FOR CHANGE

Part 1: The Preparation for change

1. "Take Out the Garbage"

    Summary: *True life change comes only through partnership with God and begins by rejecting all self-centered change methods.*

    Faulty Method #1: Environmental change (Luke 15:11–19)

    Faulty Method #2: Change by digging up my past (Genesis 45:8; 50:20)

    Faulty Method #3: Change through self-discovery (Jeremiah 17:9–10)

    Faulty Method #4: Legalistic change (Romans 7:7–9)

    Faulty Method #5: Monastic change (Romans 7:15–19)

    Faulty Method #6: Intellectual change (Romans 7:20–23, 25b)

    Biblical Change: Admit—I am the problem (Romans 7:24).

    Turn—Only God can change my heart (Romans 7:25a).

2. "Sign Me Up"

    Summary: *For life change to happen, we must cooperate fully with God's desire to transform us.*

    God has a great résumé on change.

    God's plan for change begins with conversion (Matthew 18:3).

    God's plan for change continues through sanctification
    (1 Thessalonians 4:1–3a).

3. "Let's Get Specific"

    Summary: *For life change to begin, I must identify one or two specific things God wants to change in me next.*

    Ask in faith for God's wisdom (James 1:2–7).

    He's trying to change me (verses 2–4).

    He offers wisdom about the specifics (verse 5).

    He will only show us if we ask in faith (verses 6–7).

    Review biblical lists for specific things to put off and on
    (Colossians 3:5–15; Galatians 5:16–23).

    Isolate your own areas of need (Romans 14:10–12).

    Confess your sin to a friend (James 5:16).

    Express to the Lord your willingness to change
    (1 John 5:14–15).

Part 2: The Process of Change

4. "Step One: Repentance"

Summary: *True repentance is the first step in all change, but it is not easy.*

Repentance is not easy (2 Corinthians 7:9–10).

Repentance is sometimes impossible (Hebrews 12:16–17).

How do I repent? (Luke 15:17–21).

What are the fruits/results of repentance? (Luke 3:8; Acts 26:20).

5. "Step Two: Now I Can Choose"

Summary: *I can never be different unless I believe with all my heart that the power of sin has been broken in my life—that I am dead to the power of sin because of my relationship with Christ.*

Know that in Christ I am dead to sin (Romans 6:1–7).

I am dead to sin: God's grace demands it (verses 1–2).

I am dead to sin: Christ's victory assures it (verses 3–5).

I am dead to sin: My experience confirms it (verses 6–7).

6. "I'm Dead to That"

Summary: *For life change to happen, we must apply the power of our identification to Christ at the specific point of temptation.*

The power of sin is broken, once for all. Believe it (Romans 6:8–10).

Living for God is day by day. Choose it (verses 10–12).

Victory over sin is moment by moment. Reckon it (verse 11).

7. "Lord, I'm Yours"

Summary: *Victory is accomplished when we offer ourselves alive to God moment by moment.*

You are always a slave to someone (Romans 6:15–16).

It feels like victory, not slavery (verses 17–19).

It requires a choice.

It happens moment by moment.

Part 3: The Power to Change

8. "The Power Source"

Summary: *For life change to happen, we must access the power of God for change, admitting that we do not have the strength within us.*

The exhausting life (Romans 7:15–19)

The exchanged life (Romans 7:24–25)

The empowered life (Romans 8:1–13)

Powered by the Holy Spirit (Romans 8:2–5, 8–11, 13)

Being filled by the Spirit is being controlled (Ephesians 5:18).

Hindrances to Spirit filling

1. Grieving the Holy Spirit (Ephesians 4:30)

2. Quenching the Holy Spirit (1 Thessalonians 5:19)

How to be filled with the Spirit

1. Confess all known sin (1 John 1:9).

2. Ask (Luke 11:9–13).

3. Believe (Mark 11:24).

9. "The Power of Faith"

Summary: *We experience change personally only when we exercise our faith in the truth of God's Word; knowledge of the Word by itself is not enough.*

Living like Christ is not difficult—it's impossible (Romans 8:8).

God's Spirit is our only power source (Romans 8:9–11).

Our faith is the power switch (Hebrews 4:2).

Faith is essential (Old and New Testaments).

Faith is practical (Matthew 4:1–11).

How to increase your faith

Expose your mind to the Word of God (Romans 10:17).

Practice genuine prayer (Luke 22:32).

10. "The Power of Biblical Friendships"

Summary: *If you want to experience lasting change, you must understand and access the power of biblical friendship.*

A biblical friend holds you up when you stumble (1 Samuel 23:16–18).

A biblical friend holds you down when you stray (2 Samuel 12:1–15).

Change that lasts comes by doing three things.

Choose a friend committed to change.

Review the biblical pattern for change.

Commit to ongoing accountability for change.

LOOK UP!

Dear heavenly Father:

Thanks for the things that You've been teaching me. And thank You for the ways that You have been changing me. I desire Your deepest work of transformation within me. As I continue to change and am gradually conformed to the likeness of Christ, don't let me give up.

I ask that Your transforming power be at work in my heart and mind to make me more like Jesus as long as I live on earth. Please help me to be real and honest and transparent with others. Cause me to seek and maintain friends, so we might sharpen one another and make each other strong in You. Give me courage and faith as I live these truths out and share them with those I love.

I pray this in Jesus' precious name. Amen.

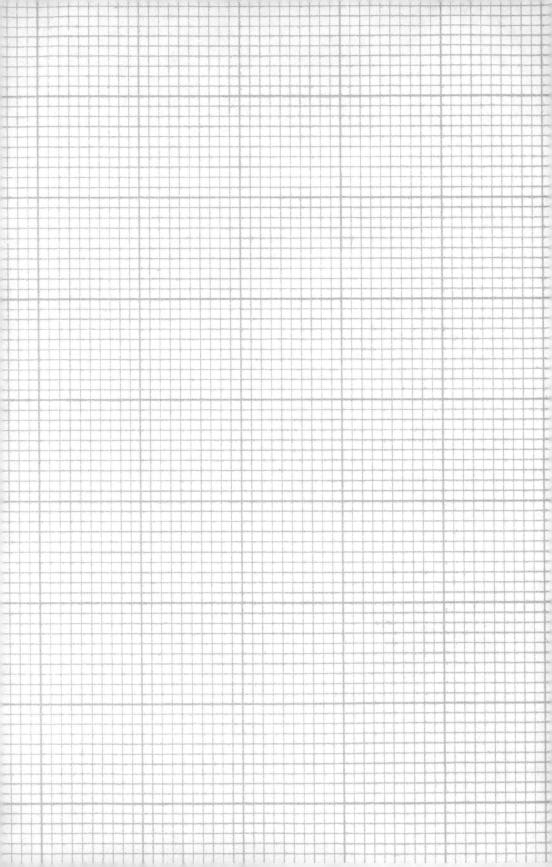

ACKNOWLEDGMENTS

Proverbs 3:27 says, **"Do not *withhold good* from those to whom it is due, when it is in your power to do it"** (italics added). I love that verse. It continues to express so well what is on my heart as I bring the updated message of this book to a conclusion.

I am thankful to my wife, to whom this book is dedicated. I am thankful for my three children, Luke, Landon, and Abby, who are so fresh and enthusiastic in the way they approach life that they constantly energize my desire to be changed. In the past decade it has been a joy to watch my own children come into adulthood, marriage, and parenthood. God has been faithful on His part in all the changes that have taken place.

I am thankful for my mom and dad and the foundation of loving support and commitment to Christ that they have hung over my life like a banner of encouragement. The absence of my mom, now in heaven, has highlighted the eternal value of the changes that only God can bring about in someone's life.

I am thankful for the all staff of our teaching ministry Walk in the Word, who under the leadership of Janine Nelson, have broadened the reach of God's message of transformation through radio, print, video, and beyond. Thanks to Neil Wilson, who joined our staff this year to help with writing projects like this one.

My gratitude to the elders at Harvest Bible Chapel, whose partnership in ministry continues to bring God's wisdom and direction. And my thanks to the people of Harvest Bible Chapel, my partners in change for more than twenty years. Your unfolding stories of transformation highlight the truth of God's Word.

Thanks also to the amazing team at Moody Publishers under the leadership of Greg Thornton, who have shown patience, perseverance, and guidance in our ongoing projects together. And to Dr. Paul Nyquist, president of Moody Bible Institute, for friendship and counsel.

Most of all, I am thankful for the persistent, loving, sanctifying ministry of God's Holy Spirit. There have been many times since I came to Christ when personal change was the farthest thing from my mind. Times when the idea of my writing a book on how God changes people would have made me laugh out loud, because I was struggling to get victory in my own life. A decade later, ongoing personal transformation continues to be God's work in my life.

Yet in all of that, the Lord has faithfully pursued me through times of failure and discouragement and through times of rebellion and disillusionment. I have now been a follower of Christ for more than forty years. I'm grateful in this update to be able to add some insights from experience, sharpen the illustrations, and refresh what continues to be at the center of everything I see in ministry: that Almighty God is in the change business and He knows what He's doing.

And more than ever I can say from experience: **"Being confident of this very thing, that He who has begun a good work in you will complete it until the day of Jesus Christ"** (Philippians 1:6 NKJV). May this book be used by God to accelerate His agenda for transformation in you.

JAMES MACDONALD

2012

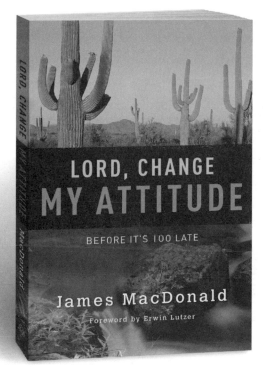

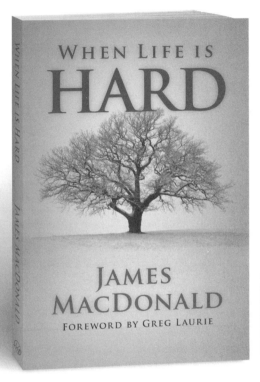